Contents

iv

Preface

The world of education has undergone quite considerable change in the last decade. During a time of such rapid changes, the in-service education of teachers is of central importance in ensuring that any changes introduced prove of benefit to learners and that schools are able to face uncertainty with confidence.

The contributors to this volume are all involved in the in-service education of teachers. The various cameos that follow illustrate ways in which higher education, local education authorities, schools and teachers have been able to work together on activities that have contributed to both teacher development and school development. The contributions demonstrate ways in which it is possible to take control of uncertainty and develop a positive response to change.

Five inter-related themes emerge throughout this book which are seen as influencing the effectiveness of in-service activities. The context in which in-service initiatives take place and the existing climate for in-service education is the first theme. Is there a culture for in-service education which ensures that experiences are acted upon? This is strongly related to the second theme, which concerns the appropriateness of the in-service strategy adopted to suit a particular context. A great deal of recent in-service work has relied on short, sharp *training* experiences aimed at delivering large amounts of information or developing specific skills in the most cost-effective way. How do these compare with more sustained experience, where the focus is on *education* of participants and where the opportunity for reflection and debate are regarded as essential? The third theme addresses the important concepts of quality, effectiveness and efficiency. Finally, and probably most importantly, the concluding themes of the book argue for the development of teachers as lifelong learners and reflective practitioners, learning from their experience and that of their colleagues and thereby contributing collectively to improving the effectiveness of their school and their practice.

Cambridge, April 1994

Aknowledgements

Our thanks are due to all the teachers with whom we have worked over recent years and especially to those who have contributed directly to this book. Many of the school-based studies in this volume would not have been conducted or made public without their co-operation and participation.

We also want to thank our secretaries at the University of Cambridge Institute of Education for their patience and help in typing our drafts. We are indebted to them for their painstaking work and tolerance.

Finally we want to thank especially Barbara Shannon for co-ordinating the final version of the manuscript and for ensuring consistency amongst the contributors. Without her substantial contribution this collection would not have been possible.

Introduction

The in-service education of teachers is of considerable importance at a time of substantial change in schools. It is widely recognised that school development does not take place without teacher development. The question is, what forms should teacher development take if it is to play a part in school development?

Teacher development can occur in many ways. For example professional learning can arise at the individual level as a result of everyday experience in the classroom. For others it takes place through interaction with colleagues in planning together, teaching together and researching and evaluating their work together. On other occasions, specific arrangements are made that involve teachers in their own and the school's development. Here we have in mind professional development days, participation in school and departmental working groups and links with colleagues in other schools. Alongside these opportunities is involvement in a range of school-focused, externally supported activities. Traditionally, only this latter group of opportunities has been described as in-service education (INSET).

At the University of Cambridge Institute of Education (UCIE) we concentrate entirely on in-service education and research and are dedicated to collaboration with schools, colleges and local education authorities (LEAs). We aim to contribute to the development of the educational service as a whole, to school improvement and to the development of individual teachers through our teaching and our research.

This book arises from the recent teaching, consultancy and research undertaken by the team of tutors at UCIE. In the following chapters, we have tried to illustrate that in-service activities take various forms, and that our work in this field is constantly developing to improve our capacity to support teacher and school development in a changing environment.

The first chapter, by Gillian Morley, provides a review of the recent historical context of INSET which has been characterised by frequent changes in structure and funding and increasing political intervention. She draws attention to the shift that has taken place away from a concern with individual needs and interests towards those of the institution and a closer connection with central government's educational policy.

Michael Fielding focuses critical attention on the language of in-service situations and asks some searching questions of the relevance of much of it to the reality of schools and teachers' development. He reminds us that language opens up or closes possibilities that are available to us. In the context of the in-service education of teachers, he suggests teaching and learning are now dominated by the metaphors of the market and are seen as serving almost exclusively utilitarian purposes. This he believes is superficial and deprofessionalising, leaving insufficient room for engagement, dialogue and the necessary uncertainty of exploration.

Factors associated with learning are also addressed in the chapter by Mary Jane Drummond and Colleen McLaughlin. They stress the importance of approaching learning as an affective experience as well as a cognitive one. In order to be effective, in-service experiences have to take account of the emotional capacities of the learner. Emotional and professional development, they believe, cannot be separated.

The contribution by Colin Conner assesses the benefits of participation in courses leading to a higher degree. He explores the extent to which developmental priorities in schools can be pursued in parallel with those of the individual. Drawing upon responses from past Masters' degree students, he discusses the factors which contribute to making the course a successful experience for them and the pertinence of courses of this kind in the current economic climate. The evidence which emerges strongly suggests that the experience of participating in a higher degree course has a significant effect on teachers' thinking and practice that is sustained well beyond the end of the course. It is also evident that there are benefits to the institution as well as the individual. This conclusion is also supported by Marion Dadds.

Using case studies, she illustrates the effects of in-service experiences on teachers' classroom practice. In particular, she considers the ways in which in-service course assignments have fostered change in the school context. By listening to teachers and trying to understand their experience of setting up and managing a school-based investigation, she has attempted to reconstruct 'the conception, life and development' of such projects. What the case studies do is to remind us that managing change through the INSET project is a complex and demanding task which requires a broad ranging set of interpersonal and investigational skills.

Mary James illustrates how the complementary qualities and skills of educators in LEAs and institutions of higher education can combine to provide support to meet the development needs of teachers and schools. Through the PIER Project (Partnership in Educational Research), opportunities were provided to undertake research-based projects on assessment issues identified by the schools. The investigations which emerged centred on the integration of assessment into day-to-day classroom practice to enhance effective learning. Ideas were developed and refined in consultation with senior colleagues in school, with the LEA project management team and with external consultants whose role was to assist with planning, to act as a 'critical friend' to the project team, and also to provide input at training sessions on methods of classroom research.

Continuing with the theme of external support for schools, Tony Bowers describes the uncertainty created by recent Government legislation concerning special schools which has created problems for those working in special education. It is at such times of uncertainty that he argues for the importance of careful reappraisal and planning. He illustrates ways in which an external consultant can create an environment for such reappraisal and identifies seven important factors which he believes will help special schools to prepare themselves for the future. A central feature of his proposals is the importance of the involvement of the whole staff and recognising the contribution that each teacher can make to the growth and development of the school.

Martyn Rouse discusses the lessons that have been learned from a series of staff development initiatives jointly carried out between the Institute of Education and a number of LEAs. Schools taking part in this initiative were attempting to develop whole school responses to meeting special educational needs in the primary school (SNIPS). In a number of the schools participating in the project, school improvement became closely linked to staff development. Martyn Rouse identifies the kinds of conditions that contributed to successful implementation of initiatives. In particular, he emphasises the importance of identifying a clearly negotiated focus which is integral to current developments in the school. The active involvement of participants is also stressed, as is the importance of the support provided by a local network of colleagues engaged in a similar venture and the advice and guidance of tutors.

Judy Sebba's contribution offers further illustration of the ways in which colleagues at the University of Cambridge Institute of Education have worked with teachers who support children with special educational needs. Her chapter stresses the importance in staff development of helping teachers to develop the skills of reflective practice, by analysis of their experience in order to make better sense of the teaching and learning that takes place in their classrooms. Through a series of examples, she identifies a number of common features which contribute to effective practice. It is important, she suggests, that in any staff development initiative, schools are supported in the identification of their specific needs, that existing expertise and experience is recognised and used, and that appropriate attention is given to the existing culture of the school.

David Hopkins and Mel West contribute chapters relating to the 'Improving the Quality of Education for All' (IQEA) Project, which seeks to bring about school development and staff development simultaneously. David Hopkins describes the principles and the procedures on which the project is founded, leading up to the seven elements which best represent the strategy of the external provider, UCIE in this case, summed up in the phrase 'Working with, rather than on'. He makes the important point that change is a journey, not a single event. Mel West explores another precept of the IQEA Project, that school improvement works best when a clear and practical focus for development is linked to simultaneous work on the internal conditions within the school. He illustrates the application of this principle in an upper school, demonstrating the practical ways in which it was put into practice.

Howard Bradley's chapter is concerned with the implementation of a national initiative, teacher appraisal, which could if successful form the bridge between the meeting of individuals' professional needs and those of the school. However, few school staffs welcomed appraisal or felt they had ownership of it and this chapter follows the development of a programme which was successful in circumstances which past experience has shown to be more conducive to failure. He shows that it is possible to help schools across the threshold of change, even if the staff has no initial ownership of it, but that for maximum benefit to the school the internal conditions must still be right.

The chapter by Geoff Southworth examines the part headteacher mentoring plays in the development of headteachers. Drawing upon the year-long experience of a new head and his mentor, a number of points are explored. Mentoring is seen as offering benefits to both participants because it provides professional support and challenge to them. The preparation programme is recognised as playing a part in assisting mentors to focus on their role and to rehearse their approach. The major conclusion about mentoring is that it facilitates a critically reflective approach to headship.

Rex Gibson writes about the 'Shakespeare and Schools' Project he has co-ordinated in recent years. He describes how this INSET project has directly and positively influenced teachers' classroom practice. Moreover, he identifies a number of principles which underpin the approach to teaching Shakespeare in schools and which characterise effective INSET. Together these principles suggest that there is no one way to teach Shakespeare, just as there is no single approach to INSET. He supports a belief which underscores this book, namely that there are many ways of providing INSET and that there needs to be such variety.

Mel Ainscow's chapter describes an international project which he is currently directing and from which he draws a number of re-commendations as to the types of strategy that need to be adopted if developments are to be successful. The chapter also shows how those working with an international perspective gain from, and contribute to, the work of colleagues in other contexts and environ-ments. As Ainscow says, one of the significant outcomes of the project is the conviction that improvements in teacher education are most likely to occur when colleagues collaborate in order to explore their experiences and understandings.

Each of these chapters tells its own story and, like every collec-tion of short stories, each reaches its own conclusion. Nevertheless, the whole book is pervaded by a number of themes which are central to the development of INSET in the future. These themes are signposts along the route to increasing our understanding of the principles and the mechanisms of improving the quality of teaching and learning in schools.

The first theme concerns the relationship between in-service education and change. It explores the contextual factors which influence our ability to establish a causal relationship between the two as well as the methodologies through which that relationship might be best developed in given circumstances. The second theme is related to the first. It involves the great debate about education and training and which is the more appropriate to professional development and school improvement. It calls upon our knowledge of adult learning as well as that of organisational development. The third theme grows out of the first two. In individual learning and institutional development it asks whether we are seeking efficiency or effectiveness. It seeks a definition of quality and it poses the question whether through INSET we are aiming to raise the level of average competence or to support and liberate the most creative. The fourth theme concerns the importance of developing, and using, the reflective practitioner in our schools. It considers how INSET can contribute not only to the reflective practitioner's individual development but also to the way in which school-focused in-service activities can use the reflective practitioner's skills and continue to enhance them. Finally, and linked with the fourth, the fifth theme considers continuing professional development in the context of lifelong learning in a continually changing world.

These themes are taken up in the final chapter in which Howard Bradley, Colin Conner and Geoff Southworth seek the lessons in their colleagues' experiences and show how INSET itself has developed.

CHAPTER 1

RECENT DEVELOPMENTS IN IN-SERVICE EDUCATION AND TRAINING FOR TEACHERS: Where have we been and where are we going?

Gillian Morley

Fifteen years ago a short discussion paper entitled 'Making INSET Work' was circulated to schools by the Department of Education and Science. This asserted that in-service education for teachers was 'at a take-off point in this country' and 'if it is to achieve its full potential then every teacher in every school needs to be involved in an ongoing discussion about it' (ACSTT, 1978, p.16). Since then radical changes in government policies have forced schools to think of INSET not only in terms of 'individual teachers attending courses which are designed and provided by outside agencies' but 'in the context of a wider approach in which teachers and schools also plan their own INSET programmes in the light of needs which they have identified' (*ibid.*, p.3). In a climate of rapid educational change, requiring new knowledge and skills to implement centrally directed curriculum intiatives and education reforms, the importance of having a teaching force committed to personal and professional development has been inescapable. With the emphasis placed on raising standards and greater public accountability, the call for making in-service education for teachers more effective has inevitably remained high on the agenda.

In reflecting on the changes that I have witnessed since joining the Cambridge Institute in 1979, I was reminded of an experience which stands in stark contrast to today's world of 'client-led INSET' and devolved budgets. The recollection of attending a rather formal meeting of one LEA's INSET Advisory Committee served as a reminder of how far the locus of control and decision-making has shifted to schools. The Committee's membership included teacher representatives, teachers' centre leaders, LEA advisers and officers, and higher education. Meetings were usually held in a Council Chamber, and the forum provided a means for reporting on INSET matters and receiving information rather than a mechanism for shaping INSET activity. When teachers' perceptions of the Committee were sought in 1987, with a view to creating a more responsive group that could steer the Authority through the uncharted waters of new arrangements for funding INSET, the comments, perhaps not surprisingly, ranged from 'pompous and bewildering' to 'bureaucratic and inaccessible'. The Government's new framework, Grant Related In-Service Training, required more active involvement of teachers and schools in shaping INSET as a recent experience of a similar county forum, now titled INSET Strategy Group, demonstrates. At this meeting, held in the more relaxed atmosphere of a Professional Development Centre, the main topic for debate was 'providing for quality INSET'. Discussion was informed by findings from recent studies of in-service provision and concentrated on structures and processes rather than content.

The new grants system, however, has changed more than LEA consultative mechanisms. Along with other developments, such as LMS and self-managing schools, the devolution of INSET monies to individual schools has forced LEAs into a 'service' culture and an 'agency-based' approach to providing INSET. The emphasis of the LEA's role is now on the management and administration of the programme and not the delivery of training through a team of advisers, advisory teachers and teachers' centres, and decisions about INSET priorities are now defined by the annual DFE Circular.

This chapter attempts to identify some of the cumulative effects of the move towards placing greater responsibility for managing INSET at the school level. Has this 'new INSET' world lessened bureaucracy and increased accessibility? Is there really more choice and diversity? What have been the gains so far of the shift to greater school autonomy for in-service education? Perspectives from headteachers and INSET co-ordinators gathered in my own study (Morley, 1991) and research by others on the impact of the effects of devolved staff development budgets (Day, 1993; Galloway, 1993; Glover and Law, 1993; Harland *et al.*, 1993) demonstrate some of the factors which have contributed to what has generally been seen as a positive transition to more local control of in-service education. These are worthy of more detailed analysis than is permitted here but they indicate aspects which need to be borne in mind if there is to be genuine professional development in the future.

It will be assumed that readers will be reasonably familiar with the structures that have been available to support the in-service education of teachers in the past and the annual cycle of DES/DFE circulars that have, since 1983, set the Government's national priorities for training. The substance of the respective documents issued between 1944-1993 is available from a number of sources, e.g. Williams, 1991; GTC, 1993. As they provide an essential backcloth to today's context, specific reference has to be made to some documents but to cover these fully would occupy more space than is available here.

The case for radical change

Despite the significant growth and diversity of INSET provision during the 1970s, the opportunities available to teachers were seen as predominantly meeting the needs of enthusiastic individuals and peripheral to the school. As a study of LEA short courses in 1979-80 concluded 'there would seem to be a need to move forward from benevolent opportunism – where some teachers attend some courses of interest to them – towards a more systematic attendance pattern at courses designed to fit a policy for rational curriculum development which has the support of the school' (Rudduck, 1981, p.176). Too often in the past teachers had been expected to take on board new initiatives and curriculum developments with little understanding or ownership of them and without due regard to the available knowledge, experience or resources to support their implementation in schools. The growing awareness of the value of school-based curriculum development (Stenhouse, 1975) and school-centred in-service education (Bolam, 1982; Chambers, 1982; Elliott, 1983) reinforced the need to put teacher development more explicitly into the context of the school and to acknowledge the weaknesses of the centre-periphery (top-down) model.

A major review of INSET, undertaken by the Advisory Committee on the Supply and Education of Teachers (ACSET) in 1984, put forward a number of closely interrelated and carefully balanced recommendations to the Secretary of State. To effect educational change at the speed required, schools would not only need all teachers from time to time to avail themselves of in-service training (DES, 1983) but a staff committed to agreed goals developed through professional interaction, ownership of the decision-making processes, and adequate financial resources. A radical change in the funding and organisation of in-service education was required, and the legislation to implement some of the ACSET recommendations through a new central policy for resourcing INSET, was signalled in the 1985 White Paper 'Better Schools'. Improving 'the professional effectiveness of teachers and the management of the teacher force' (DES, 1985) was one of the four key areas identified for action. The three other priorities focused on the curriculum, the examination system and assessment, and school government which the 1988 Education Reform Act addressed. DES Circular 6/86: Local Education Authority Training Grants Scheme (LEATGS) provided the structure through which annual grants would be allocated to LEAs for in-service training related to the national agenda for action.

The LEA Training Grants Scheme (LEATGS) came into effect from April 1987 and was designed to encourage the effective management of the teaching force and the provision of training to meet selected needs accorded national priority. To promote the professional development of teachers all schools and LEAs were required to develop clear and coherent policies for in-service training which should be monitored and evaluated to ensure that needs were being matched to purposeful provision. Potentially this offered great challenge and opportunity to teachers and INSET providers. Over time we have seen a transition from a scenario which was largely 'provider led' with central funding for long courses to a 'client-led' approach meeting short-term objectives. There has also been evidence of some frustration and disappointment as all parties have learned to cope with an 'INSET revolution' which on the one hand devolved more INSET resources and choice to schools, and on the other increased central control over the agenda by the Government.

Developing a sense of ownership

Two years before LEATGS was put into place, an interim scheme was launched by the Manpower Services Commission. This provided new and additional funding to support TVEI Related In-Service Training (TRIST) for secondary schools faced with a plethora of curriculum initiatives requiring new approaches to teaching and learning. Schools identified their training needs within the eligible categories related to the TVEI-curriculum and bid for funding through their LEA manager. TRIST was complementary to the other in-service opportunities still available to schools, but the experience gained paved the way for how schools would respond when LEATGS arrived.

TRIST did not lend itself to the 'expert' provider dictating the menu. Instead more flexible 'custom-built' services were demanded by schools, with external providers taking a role which was open to negotiation. Teachers with appropriate expertise were encouraged to become recognised and valued internal providers. Advisory teachers became vital elements and established themselves as support agents, yet LEA advisers became marginalised and boundary figures (Holly, 1987). If higher education played a role it was more likely to be in terms of evaluation, or supporting innovative approaches through joint HE/LEA projects (e.g. Cambridge Institute, 1989). When TRIST ended in 1987, GRIST/LEATGS came into place for *all* schools. This time the funding on which it was based absorbed *all* the forms of in-service education that had hitherto been available to meet short-term and long-term needs for teachers' professional development through the 'traditional providers' of higher education and local education authorities.

For the first three years LEAs submitted an annual bid to the DES for funds to support training within designated national priorities (70% grant) and for locally determined priorities (50% grant). LEAs had to meet the remaining percentage of the costs to secure the central funding. Bids for a separate Education Support Grant (ESG) enabled a substantial number of advisory teachers to be appointed by LEAs to give teachers professional support in their own classrooms in specific areas of the curriculum. Following a scrutiny of LEATGS (Glickman and Dale, 1990) under the auspices of the Government's Efficiency Unit, it was felt that a unitary grant mechanism – Grants for Education Support and Training

(GEST) – should be introduced to bring these two elements together for administrative purposes from April 1991. This reduced the rate of grant to 60% and funding was fully assigned to national priority activities – predominantly related to the implementation of the 1988 Education Reform Act. The intention of the new mechanism, GEST, was to improve co-ordination between the grants and reduce the burden of administration, offering a broader view of activities, greater efficiency and economy of operation. The removal of the Education Support Grants and the central contribution to locally assessed needs, which had enabled LEAs to support a wide variety of activities including the infrastructure for managing INSET, teachers' centres and curriculum centres, had far-reaching consequences for LEA provision.

The objective of ensuring that LEAs managed in-service training and established systems to determine needs and to meet them, were considered in the scrutiny report to have been largely achieved. The needs of individual teachers were being set within the context of institutional needs. Impressed with the energy and creativity which had been focused on INSET, some disappointment, on the part of teachers and others, was also noted with LEATGS seemingly not fulfilling its promise of promoting the professional development of teachers. Concern was also expressed that the management systems were not able to harness to best effect the particular expertise of higher education institutions. A report by HMI on the first year of the scheme claimed substantial evidence of a strong sense of ownership of the INSET by teachers (DES, 1989) but in their report on the second year of the scheme HMI noted many instances of individuals continuing to feel their own needs had been overlooked or marginalized, even though these had been communicated to senior staff or to the LEA, or to both (DES, 1991).

Adapting to the challenge

The more systematic approach to INSET planning set the challenge to find new ways of harnessing the professional development needs of individual teachers with whole school development needs, to reduce the disparity in training opportunities, to make INSET more purposeful, more effective, and more responsive. With the central push on economy and efficiency it is perhaps not surprising that 'value for money' quickly came to the forefront of decision-making in schools and LEAs, and with it the new INSET vocabulary of market forces, cost-effectiveness, finance-led, tendering, consultants, clients. It is these values that have led to provision being dominated by 'short-burst learning opportunities' (Day, 1993) rather than the notion of sustained development opportunities for the extended professional and reflective teacher. While teachers and schools learned to adapt to the overwhelming pressure to do more INSET and take on more school-led activity, higher education had to learn to survive by remaining proactive in creating course programmes that would be marketed in attractively designed, glossy packages, yet retaining flexibility to be responsive in a climate demanding custom-built services tailored to meet identified needs.

LEAs understandably became caught up in the annual bidding cycle and were soon to be faced with managing further devolution of INSET funds to schools which the DFE began to require as a condition of grant for some categories of training, and encouraged wherever possible for other grants. Higher education sought new ways of meeting professional development needs. With seemingly little recognition centrally of the need to take a less piecemeal approach to funding and therefore programme planning, ad hoc and short-term arrangements were bound to become the norm.

In the introduction of the LEA Training Grants Scheme the DES had emphasised the importance of collaboration between LEAs and higher education but did not impose a judgement on how far this expertise should be tapped. Whilst in the 1980s considerable energy had been put into developing joint LEA/HE regional programmes in a variety of areas designated as national priority, the 'market place' approach which laid emphasis on the need for a cost-effective system had arrived. The requirement for courses below 60 hours provided by higher education institutions (HEIs) to become self-financing, making no call on the HEI's funds from the Government, put a new complexion on the feasibility of earlier, low-cost collaborative models. The apparent failure of LEAs to harness the expertise of HE, as suggested in the 1990 scrutiny report, was fairly predictable. LEAs, previously dependent on using HE courses to access central funding for longer courses and secondments, now had direct access to this money. The high costs of releasing teachers to participate in award-bearing courses which were perceived to meet individual rather than institutional needs, was a major factor to be considered in spreading the LEA budget.

Actively or passively LEAs restricted the access of schools to HE provision (Glover and Law, 1993), HE became marginalised (Day, 1989) and collaboration between the two was now more likely to be driven by the LEA's desire to gain course accreditation from HE. Long-term strategies by which HEIs' contribution might be enhanced and purposefully developed were stifled by the uncertainties surrounding levels of support from one year to the next.

The insecurity caused by the short lifespan of the grants system in terms of forward planning was highlighted as a particular problem for LEAs and HE in Harland and Kinder's (1992) evaluation of 20-day designated courses for primary teachers, which the DFE required to be developed by HE in collaboration with LEAs. From the outset of the training grants scheme, a longer-term view with regard to funding was urged. The annual cycle, compounded by the variation between financial and academic years and loss of local priorities funding, not only inhibited commitments to longer courses but also left advisory teachers on vulnerable short-term contracts. In the draft circular announcing the reform of the grants programme in 1990, acknowledgement was made of the scrutiny report's recommendation that the combined GEST programme should give LEAs greater assurance about the prospects for future funding. Accordingly for selected national priorities, and new grants, indications as to whether DFE funding may be available for a further year (or two) began to be included in the indicative allocations. In formulating their bids for 1994-95, however, LEAs were advised to assume some further scaling back of GEST to reflect the continued growth of the grant maintained schools sector, and not to make assumptions that similar support would be made available in later years.

In the face of declining support for the long courses on which its own funding is dependent, HE had to learn to re-package its award-bearing provision. Courses are now set more firmly in the whole school context and on a modular basis to enable teachers to accumulate credits over an extended period. The HMI report on the implementation of LEATGS in 1989-90 (DES, 1991) noted that HEIs were becoming more responsive to the training needs of schools. The recent OFSTED report on GEST 1991-92 similarly noted the improved access and increasing flexibility of HE award-bearing provision. The report comments on the way HE providers are becoming more skilled at tailoring courses or designing them from scratch to meet the requirements of specific clients, as well as the care taken to maintain academic standards (DFE, 1993). Despite the ever-changing ground rules it has been possible to develop some imaginative and successful models using the complementary expertise of higher education, LEA advisory staff and staff in schools willing to adapt to the challenge.

Other chapters in this book serve to demonstrate some of the innovative approaches that have been adopted and how, through partnerships with schools and LEAs, it is possible to negotiate jointly taught programmes that meet local needs and, where appropriate, build in opportunities for accreditation within a modular award-bearing structure. Now that LEAs are being forced to set up self-funding agencies to provide INSET, and some have already experienced the harsh realities of 'INSET in the market place' (Harland *et al.*, 1993), it will be increasingly important to hold on to a spirit of collaboration rather than competition, and put longer-term educational outcomes above economic expediencies. A 15% reduction in the total GEST funding available for 1994-95 and the emphasis on training related to National Curriculum and school management may reflect today's economic and political climate. It cannot increase confidence in a model that urged teachers and schools to be more systematic and purposeful in their INSET planning in order to ensure that informed choices about priorities are matched, within the resources available, to appropriate provision. Schools can only exercise choice in selecting training if genuine alternatives are available and affordable.

Creating an environment for professional development in schools

The need to take a more holistic approach to school improvement and teacher development is clearly demonstrated in much of the current literature, and a great deal of energy has been put in to getting teachers in and across schools to work together and to generate a commitment to INSET. But innovations, including a more democratic model for INSET, should be seen as the starting point and catalyst for change and not something that can be implemented overnight. Account has to be taken of other pressures and initiatives, and there needs to be a regular review of direction to adjust to externally-led changes and the externally imposed priorities. In contrast to the speed with which so many initiatives have been thrust on schools, the involvement of colleagues who may in the past have been somewhat isolated in their practice and perhaps resistant to change, has required time to build up trust and a non-threatening atmosphere for participation. Through increased opportunities for teachers to work alongside colleagues in the classroom, sharing ideas at a professional level on 'non-contact' (closure) days, and opportunities to visit other schools, as well as the more traditional course-based approaches, wider acceptance of the need for some form of involvement and a feeling of ownership has been fostered.

The shift towards in-service education being seen as integral to, not, as in the past, outside, the concern of the school has been accompanied by the view that INSET is done *with* not *to* teachers and school-staff-individual development should be seen as complementary strands. With greater emphasis being placed on professional development as a process not an event and set in the context of institutional development, the broader concept of staff development has had to shift from 'bolt on' and 'ad hoc' to a task which is as essential for the school as the education of children. Like children, teachers have individual needs and will be influenced by the climate and conditions in which they work. The marriage of these assorted needs presents a huge challenge to achieve a programme that benefits the staff as a group as well as individuals.

Most schools now have a designated INSET/Professional Development Co-ordinator, but their individual energy and enthusiasm will not in itself sustain progress unless their strengths are co-ordinated and supported within the culture of the school (Fullan *et al.*, 1990; Stenhouse, 1975). While a lot of attention has been focussed on needs identification and the administration of school-managed INSET, the effectiveness of schools' needs identification systems and the capacity to meet needs is open to question (Harland *et al.*, 1993). Greater sophistication may be evident in the processes schools have used to identify needs, but the delegation of financial resources alone will not empower teachers to achieve a more satisfactory level of professional development. This has to be matched by a more sophisticated learning agenda set in a culture of professional collaboration and an understanding of how individuals learn and respond to the complex process of change.

Although there may be 'consensus' within a staff group about the school's INSET priorities, collaborative processes do not develop automatically and inherently generate conflicts and compromises. As with any whole school policy, there needs to be a shared understanding of what is to be achieved, by whom, the underlying principles, and the criteria for judging success. This is more likely to be achieved through active participation in the decision-making but another important dimension is the attitudes, skills and knowledge of INSET. What is the conceptual understanding of those charged with managing the programme, what values and principles do they hold about effective staff development processes, what is the nature of their information or resource bank? What role do school governors play?

Great variation exists in the interpretation given to the role and the status accorded to INSET co-ordinators in schools (DFE, 1993) and it is likely that there may also be a number of interpretations of what it is the programme is trying to achieve. To gain most success not only do the responsibilities need to be clearly defined for the co-ordinator and any other colleagues who have a staff development role (e.g. where does appraisal sit?), but participation by staff needs to lead to a common understanding of the aims and priorities and ways in which these might be achieved. No staff development programme can be a panacea for all problems but unless the values that underpin it are shared publicly, there may be unrealistic expectations and disappointments.

If professional development activities are to be valued by everyone involved, those charged with the responsibility for their planning and co-ordination need a personal belief in their worth, good interpersonal skills, trust and enthusiasm. Equally important are the skills and time to use resources creatively. This requires a sound knowledge of internal and external resources, an understanding of adult learning, and a mind which is open to new possibilities. Given the emphasis on negotiation, client-centredness, and value for money, it is disappointing that relatively little attention has been paid to the importance of understanding the nature of learning opportunities that will best serve different needs.

Matching need with provision

Tensions will inevitably arise in setting priorities against limited resources but in selecting appropriate means of meeting the needs, distinctions between the criteria used to judge efficiency, economy and effectiveness often get blurred. The respective weighting given to these will vary according to individual agendas, conceptual frameworks and contexts. Finance and minimising pupil disruption are important factors but whether one is looking at expensive external provision or at a low-cost in-house day, the essential features lie in the matching of need with style of provision.

There are still many sources which support teacher development – teachers, schools, LEAs, HE, professional associations, private consultants – each has its place and contribution. It is important to respect and celebrate the difference between different types of support. It is also important that choices are made on the basis of valid information, rather than historical or taken for granted assumptions. They should involve those who have most at stake in the process, and the decisions should be linked to a sense of responsibility for implementation, monitoring, and possible revision.

A school's context (the size and stability of its staffing, the head's leadership style, the school ethos and culture, and the availability of resources) contributes to determining the shape and success of the staff development programme, quite apart from any external influences. The staffing profile affects the ability to draw on in-house expertise and the need to access external support. Age, gender, career cycles, ambitions and staff morale all play their part, as does the nature of prior INSET experience. For example, if support on an externally-led course carries with it the expectation that information will be shared back in school with colleagues, someone who is lacking in confidence or insecure with the staff group is unlikely to be the best candidate. They may first need to gain confidence by participating in school-based activities led by those who have strengths to share and can demonstrate by example in a safe environment. A confident member of staff may need a more critical external perspective to enable them to stand back and reflect on their practice, to challenge their beliefs and assumptions with teachers from other schools.

Where in-house expertise is available and used well, school-based INSET can be a cost-effective and less disruptive form of provision, as well as being tailored to specific needs. However, most schools recognise that there are dangers of looking only at the price-tag and being too school-centred. Whilst it is important to have in-house opportunities for staff to share and learn from each other and to take responsibility for improving their practice, a diet which is only teacher-led can reinforce rather than challenge current practice, may lead to insularity and complacency, and may overlook an individual's need to 'step outside'.

Given the wealth of course information schools receive, it may not be difficult to identify common topics, but matching a need and determining the nature of the experience that will lead to the desired change or improvement requires more than a coincidence of agendas. The most likely influences will be prior knowledge, reputation for quality, and a degree of subjectivity. In common with a recent survey of INSET perceptions in secondary schools (Glover and Law, 1993), my own study of perceptions in primary, secondary and special schools (Morley, 1991) found that familiarity, credibility, and known expertise (usually through first-hand knowledge, or personal recommendation) had significant influence. Ease of access and timing are considered, as well as finance, but the greatest weighting appears to be given to (perceived) relevance to the school and practical application. Courses had to 'fit our thinking', 'match our priorities', 'be helpful for individuals wishing to improve their own skills'.

Until recently schools have had access to a wide range of LEA support through adviser-led courses, advisory teachers, teachers' centres and curriculum development centres, but as funds devolved to schools have increased the breadth of provision has declined. The INSET support that LEAs do provide will more often than not have to be purchased, as with HE or independent consultants, and credibility and perceived value for money become new factors in the selection of such provision. Whether as a provider of the activity or potential participant it is important to consider:

—What type and length of experience will be appropriate in order to achieve the defined need?
—How does this relate to the prior experience and expertise of the individual or the group?
—How will the learning be applied, and how does this relate to other developments and innovations being undertaken?
—How will the experience be evaluated and against what criteria?

The recent OFSTED report on GEST 1991-92 considered the quality of training days organised and delivered by schools to be 'variable but generally satisfactory and occasionally of a very high standard' (DFE, 1993). A review by NFER (Harland, Kinder and Keys, 1993) of the same period, however, found contrasts between primary and secondary teachers' views of school-initiated INSET.

Their study found that primary teachers were generally satisfied that school-led training was relevant to and matched their needs (with external providers to extend their own understanding) – although 'on our own we can waste a lot of time – get bogged down'. Secondary teachers made a distinction between the value of department-based INSET and discussion of whole school policy issues but the comments reported generally indicated some dissatisfaction. This might be explained in part by factors of size, it might be related to lack of ownership, i.e. a topic imposed by senior management and not seen as a real problem of great significance or meaning to the individual, and also the extent to which in-house strengths have already been exploited. It may also signal a plea for finding a balance between meeting immediate practical concerns and deeper levels of professional development.

Whilst the value of extended opportunities to reflect on practice is recognised by most schools, higher education courses require a significant financial and personal commitment. Those whose past experience of award-bearing INSET has left them viewing HE as 'remote' and 'theoretical' (Glover and Law, 1993), may make different judgements about 'value and effectiveness' from those whose course experiences had enabled them to stand back and reflect on their practice, and to gain a wider, more critical perspective, underpinned by theory and informed by current research. The recent OFSTED report noted that many students on Diploma and Masters' courses talked of the impact on their department or school of the work they had been doing (DFE, 1993). Recognition that such courses are not just for the individual's benefit but can, under the right conditions, be an important driving force for whole school development (Dadds, 1993) is essential if we are to hold on to a concept of genuine professional development rather than technical competency.

Taking control of the professional development agenda

Professionalism is a form of liberty that is not simply conferred; it is earned. Teachers themselves must not only be enabled; they must be convinced that the tasks in their work can be accomplished only under professional standards, norms and conditions. Then teachers themselves must set about achieving these. (Lieberman, 1988, p.4)

'Professionalism' means more than coping with what has been described as the 'innovation overload' on a day-to-day basis. It is not about the receipt or delivery of subject-based knowledge. It requires an understanding of the processes of learning, the enthusiasm and motivation to grow, and a shared commitment to finding ways of doing things better. However, collaboration at any level takes time and the development of trust. It requires dialogue, openness, and a mutual feeling of ownership. Understanding and respect for the other parties' needs and expertise have to be reached, and there may need to be compromise to resolve conflicts. Parameters and principles have to be agreed and above all there has to be a commitment to a common purpose. It is most likely to succeed where there is some prior knowledge, understanding and respect for the ethos and culture of the respective partners.

A culture of professional collaboration has begun to develop at a number of levels and there is evidence of a move towards a more coherent approach to planning for school and staff development which actively involves teachers. We have witnessed an increase in the number of teachers involved in INSET activities but the pressure for quick-fix, short-term training focussed on technical skills and practical knowledge may in fact endanger the move towards a more professional teaching force, unless a balance can be struck with the development of more rigorous and challenging opportunities. Awareness alone is not enough, and wherever training is located, it must be backed up by an understanding of principles and the ability to apply the skills and knowledge, if it is to change practice.

Making schools responsible for determining priorities may have helped to break down some of the institutional barriers which previously frustrated teachers in applying their learning from INSET considered to be outside of the school's concern. Responsible schools will have seized the opportunity of giving this high priority and developed an integrated and coherent plan of action based on long-term vision and consolidation, rather than short-term immediacy and fragmentation.

Whatever choices are made in deciding how to meet identified needs, the importance of balancing school and individual needs must not be forgotten. Time for critical reflection on practice in a supportive learning environment is not an optional luxury, it is a vital ingredient of professional development. Carr and Kemmis (1986) suggest if teaching is to become a more 'genuinely professional activity', three sorts of development are needed:

—the attitudes and practices of teachers must become firmly grounded in educational theory and research;

—teachers' professional autonomy must be regarded as collective as well as an individual matter and include participation in the decisions about the broader educational context in which they operate;

—professional responsibilities must include a professional obligation to interested parties in the community at large.

There are tremendous possibilities for genuine professional development if we acknowledge a community of people who work for common aims, respecting and supporting each others' contributions and expertise, with agreed goals and strategies. It is unlikely that we will turn our back on the energy that has been put thus far into creating firmer foundations on which teachers' professional growth can be fostered. We now need to redefine our agendas and make explicit the criteria by which successful educational outcomes will be judged. If we continue to be led by a purely market economy approach which uses business concepts of efficiency, we will be in danger of encouraging a teaching profession made up of educational technicians who 'do' rather than visionaries who constantly search to understand 'why' they do and 'how' they can do it better.

References

ACSET (1984) *The In-Service Education, Training and Professional Development of School Teachers,* Report of the Advisory Committee on the Supply and Education of Teachers (London: DES).

ASCTT (1974) *In-Service Education and Training: some considerations,* Report of the Advisory Committee on the Supply and Training of Teachers (London: DES).

Bolam, R. (Ed.) (1982) *School-Focused In-Service Training* (London: Heinemann).

Cambridge Institute of Education (1989) *Thinking Schools: Support for Innovation Project* (Cambridge: Cambridge Institute of Education).

Carr, W. and Kemmis, S. (1986) *Becoming Critical* (London: Falmer Press).

Chambers, P. (Ed.) (1982) *Making INSET Work – Myth or Reality?* The Work of the CUED-IN Group (Bradford College).

Dadds, M. (1993) Thinking and being in teacher action research, in Elliott, J. (Ed.) *Reconstructing Teacher Development* (London: Falmer Press).

Day, C. (1989) 'INSET: The marginalising of higher education', *British Journal of In-Service Education,* **15**, pp.195-6.

Day, C. (1993) The development of teachers' thinking and practice: does choice lead to empowerment?, in Elliott, J. (Ed.) *Reconstructing Teacher Development* (London: Falmer Press).

DES (1983) *Teaching Quality* (London: HMSO).

DES (1985) *Better Schools* (London: HMSO).

DES (1986) *Circular 6/86: Local Education Authority Training Grants Scheme: financial year 1987-88* (London: DES).

DES (1989) *The Implementation of the Local Education Authority Training Grants Scheme: report on the first year of the scheme 1987-88*, Report by HM Inspectors (London: HMSO).

DES (1991) *The Implementation of the Local Education Authority Training Grants Scheme*, Report by HM Inspectors (London: HMSO).

DFE (1993) *The Management and Provision of In-Service Training Funded by the Grants for Education Support and Training (GEST)* HM Chief Inspector of Schools, Office for Standards in Education (London: HMSO).

Elliott, J. (1983) 'School-focused INSET and research into teacher education', *Cambridge Journal of Education*, **13**(2), pp.19-31.

Fullan, M., Bennett, B. and Rolheiser-Bennett, C. (1990) 'Linking classroom and school improvement', *Educational Leadership*, **47**(3), pp.13-19.

Galloway, S. (1993) Identifying INSET needs, in Burgess R.G., Connor, J., Galloway, S., Morrison, M. and Newton, M. (Eds.) *Implementing In-Service Education and Training* (London: Falmer Press).

Glickman, B. and Dale, H. (1990) *A Scrutiny of Education Support Grants and Local Education Authority Training Grants Scheme* (London: DES).

GTC (1993) *The Continuing Professional Development of Teachers:* papers presented by Williams, M. and Bolam, R. for the General Teaching Council (London: GTC (England and Wales)).

Glover, D. and Law, S. (1993) *Changing Partners: professional development in transition* (Keele University).

Harland, J. and Kinder, K. (1992) *Mathematics and Science Courses for Primary Teachers: lessons for the future* (Slough: NFER).

Harland, J., Kinder, K. and Keys, W. (1993) *Restructuring INSET: privatisation and its alternatives* (Slough: NFER).

Holly, P., James, T. and Young, J. (1987) *The Experience of TRIST: The DELTA Project* (Cambridge: Cambridge Institute of Education).

Lieberman, A. (Ed.) (1988) *Building a Professional Culture in Schools* (New York: Teachers' College Press).

Morley, G. (1991) *Adapting to the INSET Revolution: a case for responsible autonomy*, unpublished MA dissertation (Norwich: Centre for Applied Research in Education, University of East Anglia).

Rudduck, J. (1981) *Making the Most of the Short In-Service Course*, Schools Council Working Paper 71 (London: Methuen Educational).

Stenhouse, L. (1975) *An Introduction to Curriculum Research and Development* (London: Heinemann).

Williams, M. (1991) *In-Service Education and Training* (London: Cassell).

CHAPTER 2

DELIVERY, PACKAGES AND THE DENIAL OF LEARNING: Reversing the Language and Practice of Contemporary INSET

Michael Fielding

Linguistic robbery and the manipulation of change

The language we use to describe our work is not an issue which is peripheral to what we do, how we do it, or, indeed, our personal identity. Most teachers reading this chapter would be unhappy to be called instructors rather than teachers and, although many work in schools, would be equally uncomfortable about their commitments being described as schooling rather than education. We choose with some care the language we use to describe to others what we do. However, our choice is not unfettered. The language which is imposed on us by the professional, social and political contexts in which we work is significant. Whilst for many people the linguistic clothing of their job is sufficiently comfortable within appropriate contexts not to be a problem, there are times when it becomes an issue, not just of fashion or convenience, but one which has significance for individuals committed to certain values and certain views of the nature of their job. Language constrains as much as it enables, and those restrictions and possibilities circumscribe not only our actions but our sense of who we are and who we might become.

The 1980s saw some devastating examples of personal distress and disorientation caused by the emergence and domination of Thatcherism which transformed many aspects of personal and professional life into extensions of or participants in the market place. Casualties were as numerous in the world of business as anywhere else. In his compelling study of the experience of people who suffered from the 1980s 'business culture', David Smail makes a number of acute observations on the role of language in the process of disorientation. Particularly striking is the way he portrays experiences of what might appropriately be described as linguistic assault which leave the recipients bruised and bewildered:

> The sublime confidence with which the managerial mediocrity imposed its debased language of 'performance indicators', 'Total Quality', and so on, on people who had all their lives spoken, albeit uncritically, a far more ethically nuanced language left them conceptually completely off-balance.

Smail goes on to highlight the importance of language as a conceptual safeguard against simplistic distortions which betray our capacity to question, discriminate or oppose. A revealing passage instances people who:

> struggled...to force the previously unarticulated complexity of their experience into the linguistic moulds imposed by the hyped-up banalities of Businessese

and that rather than

> being offered a 'whole new way' of 'developing their management skills', or whatever, they were in fact being robbed of the linguistic tools to express the violence being done to their understanding. (Smail, 1993)

The notion of linguistic robbery is important. Not only does it deprive the individual of a means of expression, it diminishes the possibility of understanding, and by implication, critiquing the world in a particular way. It is very much more serious than being robbed of a car or an article of clothing, either of which is to a significant degree replaceable. If pursued systematically and in conjunction with an aggressively promoted alternative vocabulary which suggests a different view of the world, linguistic robbery can begin to undermine the credibility of the conceptual story which the stolen language strove to give voice. This kind of seman-

tic violence condemns the victims to silence with regard to important aspects of the world they have hitherto experienced. If the
robbery involves the diminution of an 'ethically nuanced language' in favour of one which has little moral resonance then in
some contexts – for example, education, in which the presence of
morality and the notion of the good life is fundamental – the consequences will be very serious indeed. One of the concerns of this
chapter is to explore ways in which educational discourse has been
subject to a degree of heuristic and moral lobotomy which is both
reflected in and sustained by INSET. So much of the INSET work
which is characteristic of the mid-1990s has difficulty finding professional space which can legitimately be exploratory, questioning
or to any significant degree disruptive of imposed frameworks.

It is important not to push this metaphor too far; it is, of course,
possible to reaffirm certain kinds of language, but the difficulties of
doing so should not be underestimated. Language is not just
powerful, it is a means of exerting power. Dominant forms of
discourse are as much mechanisms of control as they are of communication. Consider, for example, Stuart Hall's disturbing
reflections on the almost subliminal effect of the market on his colleagues at the Open University, people whom in many respects one
would least expect to succumb. The Open University, he says,

> is filled with good social democrats. Everybody there believes in the
> redistribution of educational opportunities and seeks to remedy the
> exclusiveness of British education. And yet, in the past ten years,
> these good social-democratic souls, without changing for a minute
> what is in their hearts and minds, have learned to speak a brand of
> metallic new entrepreneurialism, a new managerialism of a
> horrendously closed nature. They believe what they have always
> believed, but what they do, how they write their mission statements,
> how they do appraisal forms, how they talk about students, how
> they calculate the cost – that's what they are really interested in now.
> The result is that the institution has been transformed. (Hall, 1993)

In citing Hall's example I am not suggesting that colleagues at the
Open University no longer have available an ethically nuanced language with which to critique the current hegemony of market forces or
that they are any less committed to the social democratic project of the
university itself. But, according to Hall, the dominant language, which
he describes as 'metallic' and at one with 'a new managerialism of a
horrendously closed nature', has resulted in, at the very least, a redirec-
tion and refocussing of effort which has 'transformed' the institution.

Why language matters

The Smail and the Hall examples underscore the importance of the language we use and the language to which we are subjected. Language opens up and closes down possibilities that are available to us; the language we use speaks through us as much as it speaks for us. The words we use and the way we use them help us to discover, explore and make meaning as much as they help us to express what is already familiar, known, or straightforwardly clear.

The contexts and purposes of our conversations and encounters prompt us to mix and match the language of possibility and uncertainty with the language of what exists and what is expected. That process of mixing and matching is not, however, unconstrained. Public education is under siege from a reductionist populism which deploys a false clarity under the rallying cry of a manufactured, mistrusting common sense. The persistence and strength of such cries reflect the degree to which the version of common sense implied is no longer sensible or commonly held. This false consensus conspires to produce what Henry Giroux so tellingly calls the 'politics of erasure' (Giroux, 1992) in which oppositional or even mildly interrogative voices are not heard beneath incessant government edict and media barrage amounting to a civilian equivalent of the now familiar military use of sound as an offensive weapon. The sound bite is, perhaps, its everyday equivalent; though the decibels differ, the intention and the effect is the same - discussion of the complex and contested nature of reality is deafened by solutions to questions that have not been asked and by silence for those that have. The discourse of possibility is denied or distorted by the insistent drum of certainty.

A current difficulty for many people in education is that, having been subjected to an unremitting barrage of government edict and counter-edict for such a prolonged period, they have lost the confidence and, if only partially and temporarily, the capacity to articulate understandings and aspirations which require different expression linked to different frames of reference.

In this situation three sorts of difficulties often arise. Sometimes an exhausted resignation sets in and we begin to talk, think and act in ways which mirror what the new language requires of us; at others any antagonism we feel leads to frustration and resentment because the dominance of the discourse is so widespread or so deep-rooted. A third possibility is that the discomfort we feel will be only fitful or fleeting, often because of the pressure of our jobs.

The last of these difficulties is the most worrying, the most common and the one I recognise most reluctantly, but most readily, in myself. Unwittingly we find ourselves not only using the language but seeing the world through a semantic lens we regard as distorting and dangerous and subsequently behaving in ways which surprise us unpleasantly. Just as it is all too common to find a gap between the aspirations our cherished words point to and the imperfect reality of our actions, so it is equally, if not more, disturbing to find that words we abhor and use despite ourselves lead us to act in ways we regret or find disconcerting.

The language and the discourses to which the words contribute vary considerably: sometimes they are political, as, for example, the current obsession with the market as supreme arbiter in human affairs; sometimes they are psychological, as with the companion obsession with measurement and the necrophilia of numbers; sometimes the discourses overlap or complement each other creating a particularly powerful alliance, as in national league tables of exam results. Our view of the attractiveness and legitimacy of the discourse will vary and we will, of course, be party to different discourses operating simultaneously despite the tensions and contradictions that may inhere in them. What is important to recognise in all this is the inevitability of our entanglement in the personal, social and political web of language in action, and the action of language in shaping the world as it is and as it might be.

'Delivery', 'packages' and the denial of learning

The possibility of professional learning is too often prevented by the poverty of the language we use to describe it. It is frequently a language whose images and interconnections point to the denial of learning and the structures of control. 'Delivery', 'packages', and the injunction to 'take on board' what has been made and approved of by others reduces teachers to the role of curriculum courier anxiously awaiting the unpredictable imperatives of the next promotion. Teaching and curriculum are dominated by the metaphors of the warehouse and the operative, and the wider context of education itself is conceived of and driven by the mechanics of the market. Learning begins to resemble the apprehensive opening of unwanted presents; having, with appropriate prompting, recognised what they are, we are then faced with the subsequent dilemma of what to do with them.

In such a context the learning of pupils and students and the processes of teaching are couched in terms which leave no room for the grip of engagement, the demands of dialogue, and the necessary uncertainty of exploration. Small wonder that professional learning is too often, despite our best intentions and considerable efforts, mechanistic, unremittingly and almost exclusively utilitarian, demeaning of teachers, superficial, anti-life and anti-learning. Too often sterility of form matches stultifying content, or polished presentation excludes the possibility of doubt or disagreement. Handouts and ring binders too often provide the end rather than the starting point of discussion and bullet-points too frequently deny the untidiness and contested nature of dialogue. Too often the mantra of group work is invoked without understanding, variety or appropriate judgement. More importantly, the parameters of professional development in general and INSET in particular are constrained so often and with such effectiveness that much of the learning that takes place is monochrome, narrow and only incidentally or briefly satisfying. The impoverishment of the language we speak betrays our deeper purposes for objectives whose clarity blinds us to their inadequacy. The consequences and enactment of that betrayal find expression in INSET which may, to varying degrees, be efficient and may, to varying degrees, be effective. However, too often it is likely to mask the surrender of effectiveness to efficiency and, more seriously, the capitulation of effectiveness to a view of education whose characteristic form is the slogan and the sound bite and whose vision of the future is shackled to a chimerical golden past and the sacrifice of social justice on the altar of unfettered individual enterprise.

Language and deception and the deception of language

There are three ways in which language is frequently used to hamper the possibility of learning, particularly within the context of INSET. These are, firstly, the use of language which denies the voice of the learner; language which redescribes learning as a mechanistic process which is clear, safe from controversy and secured by authority. The dominant image is the teacher as haulier. The second use of language is more subtle. Here the instrument of control is deception rather than denial. The dominant image is one of personal engagement and consensual commitment; in reality those merits are manufactured and mask a state of affairs in which the priorities of managers lie barely concealed beneath the surface of managed opinion. Finally, language is used in a way which has much in common with a colonial past: a dominant usage is established and its predecessor or rival banned, denied or obliterated. Language is as much a means of repression as expression. This third use of language as the site of ideologically contested views of the nature of education will only be touched on briefly. It is pursued in more detail elsewhere in connection with the notion of 'empowerment' (Fielding, forthcoming) which is now beginning to challenge 'ownership' as the kitemark of managerial competence.

(i) Teacher as haulier: learning and the mechanics of silence

What is particularly worrying about the language of 'packages', 'delivery' and 'taking things on board' is that its strongly mechanistic feel reinforces a view of learning as a transaction located within a dominantly commercial world in which something made by someone else is, by virtue of being delivered, assumed to result in learning. The authentic voices of the teacher and the pupil are entirely absent from the process. The injunction to take something on board comfortably incorporates the imagery of packages being delivered; in all three cases it is not just that there is no apparent place for engagement or critical encounter; their very possibility is excluded by the occupational imperatives of the haulier on which the metaphor rests.

In INSET evidence of the brown parcel view of teaching and learning is not difficult to find. Teachers are not only swamped by actual packages of information which they are required to 'take on board', they are also discouraged from asking questions which go beneath the surface of the glossy exterior. Few have the presence of mind, pent up exasperation, or tenacity in the face of overwhelming odds to raise fundamental issues to do with whether or not the brown parcels ought to be returned to the sender and professional dialogue replace the monologue of prescription. Those who do are often marginalised, dismissed as sixties eccentrics, or frowned on for rocking the already unsteady boat.

Even the language of some contemporary educational research on effective INSET can be fitted too readily into a mechanistic paradigm (e.g. Kinder, 1993). Kinder's talk of 'first, second and third order outcomes' is in danger of accruing an unwanted and unwarranted authority through an appeal to an apparent hierarchy and a doubtful specificity. The overarching imagery of 'inputs' and 'outcomes' and the complementary 'providers' and 'consumers' not only reinforces the tyrany of technocratic views of learning, it dulls the imagination, prohibits initiative and treats the learner as an inert object whose journey along the conveyor belt of someone else's process results in a new product suitably designed for the current consumption imperatives of the market. Here the language and structures of evaluation begin to reproduce the machinery of silence which does so much to reinforce the notion of teacher-as-haulage-contractor.

Finally, it is worth noting that in the context of INSET the mechanics of silence is indiscriminately overwhelming: the prescriptive logic of delivering packages carries with it the likelihood that those who lead the INSET are constrained in much the same way as those who participate. Learning is not just about cognitive structures and systematic approaches: it is about human beings creating, exploring and puzzling over meaning together. In helping young people and ourselves to learn joyfully as well as effectively we must remember that the enabling devices of systems and procedures are just that – they are means which are to be ultimately judged by the quality of human flourishing that they promote. An authentic personal response – a shared look of satisfaction, an honest show of disappointment, a hand on the shoulder, the dance of delight in the eyes, the laughter of shared error, the passion of interest or commitment – is, on occasions more powerful and more important than the rigours of the most refined of systems. INSET in delivery mode frequently denies the excitement of exploration: not only is none required; often none is acceptable. Small wonder that it has about it the frenzy of indecent haste ('There is a huge amount to get through today, colleagues') or the dullness of duty – unwrapping packages too often takes more time than getting to grips with contents that are unwanted, unrecognised and only partially understood by those who have had to deliver them.

(ii) The discomfort of premature intimacy and the dishonesty of false consensus

There are, of course, more subtle ways of denying voice than silencing it. The most frequent and most effective is linguistic sleight of hand, sometimes used unintentionally but more often than not with a significant degree of awareness.

Of the numerous examples to hand two that have particular resonance for me are the injuction to 'share' experience, expertise, uncertainty or whatever and the holy grail of 'ownership'. I have used both frequently, but now do my best to avoid the second and use the first with care.

Sharing and the politics of persuasion

I became particularly sensitive to the ubiquitous use of 'share' when a headteacher whom I know quite well laughingly told me that I had won an unofficial award for transgressing on clichéd ground by using the word 'share' in a session I ran at the conference she was jointly responsible for organising. We laughed it off, but the conversation remained with me and it later occurred to me that what I thought was an innocuous, gently mutual verbal punctuation mark in the normal narrative of in-service work was for some colleagues becoming a linguistic alarm bell. What was the warning pointing to? In puzzling that through I have come to think that the adverse reaction many teachers now have to 'share' – either in the form of speakers saying they are going to 'share' something with conference members or teachers themselves being asked to 'share' their experience with someone they have never set eyes on before – is partly due to overuse and partly due to not wishing to be privy to what is being shared. More than either of these is the sense that sharing carries with it not only a sense of something significant or important but something which both parties are likely to value. Sharing has an air of mutuality about it; even though it is not always reciprocal the sharing of something valued with another person carries with it a faint trace of intimacy or vulnerability. It is this susurrus of value and intimacy which in part accounts for the rejection of too swift, too presumptuous or too frequent invitations to share experience and, more than any of these, the imposition of consensus and common values through an enforced 'sharing' of an often unwanted information or alien perspective with a captive audience.

I am emphatically not suggesting that the word 'share' should never be used nor am I suggesting that people should not share things or views with each other. What I am suggesting is that we need to be sensitive to its appropriateness and be aware that the discomfort that may greet too careless a use is quite proper. Indeed, I would also want to take the point a step further and urge that the discomfort take the form of rejection in cases where the element of intimacy and mutuality is false, forced or in any way symptomatic of deception or manipulation. In instances where speakers bring unwelcome news this will not, of course, stop the bad news coming. But at least participants will recognise it as bad news, greet it with appropriate hostility and give the messenger a hard time. They will understand that they are being 'told' about something. To willingly allow this process to be redescribed as 'sharing' is, at least in some circumstances, to begin to collude in a manipulative exercise which has nothing to do with mutuality or common values, still less with the exploration and creation of new meanings and understandings.

Ownership: talisman or trick?

I have never been comfortable with the notion of 'ownership', still less with its frequent elevation to a kind of managerial talisman. As with 'sharing', its use is not necessarily objectionable; it is, however, a word which should set a number of questions running in the minds of those whom it is thought should 'own' the initiative, change or development. First, who thinks I should own this? Secondly, why? Thirdly, who else is being invited to 'own' it? Fourthly, whose idea was it in the first place? Or, alternatively, if I don't own it, who will? Too often the answers to these questions point eventually to ownership as a process in which a particular group or individual (more often than not senior managers or other committed interest groups) attempt to get those with whom they work to agree with their views or strategies with a significant degree of conviction. Ownership in these instances is about getting your ideas accepted by others to such a degree that they think the ideas are, if not theirs in origin, then theirs by commitment.

Whilst this may be either innocuous or justifiable it is often neither. There are a number of objections to ownership as a dominant and too often manipulative and misleading metaphor in educational discourse. One way of gaining access to the first objection is by exploring the distinction between 'ownership' and 'authorship'. In many instances those who are being invited to 'own' someone else's idea or strategy would much prefer to 'author' them than 'own' them, and for a number of reasons. To begin with, the substitution of a creative metaphor for a commercial one runs deep in much the same way as Erich Fromm's distinction between 'being' and 'having' as fundamental, contrasting human dispositions. The dominant context of the metaphor of ownership and the metaphor itself are deeply at odds with what many teachers feel they are about as people and as professionals. Allied to the inappropriateness, even offensiveness, of the notion of ownership to some colleagues there is the enormous gap which separates ownership from authorship in terms of the voices of those involved. Authorship by definition involves the exploration and articulation of meaning; ownership has no such internal imperative and too often mistakes the flowchart of team, department, or whole staff discussion for the messiness, contradiction and conflict of the creative process.

The second objection suggests that ownership betrays other competing values and is a reminder not so much about ends but means linked to certain ends. Just as for some the prospect of a property owning society is unattractive because it violates a whole set of social and personal aspirations for the strengthening of mutuality and the development of alternatives to incessant consumption, so in school the context of ownership of a new strategy is also unattractive because the legitimation of senior management views by convincing others that the views are theirs is a denial of professional dignity and equality and a serious underestimation of teachers' capacity to spot what is really going on. The possibly deceitful nature of processes involved are at odds with what education aspires to be.

The overall objection to ownership as a managerial touchstone is that trying to get people to own ideas is a category mistake; ownership is most often and most fittingly applied to things and the attempt to transfer it to ideas and values is to be involved in an inappropriate undertaking. Things have no will, no agency, no voice; people should have. Ubiquitous talk about ownership puts these characteristics at risk. Small wonder that when the drum of ownership is banged too loudly and too often it becomes oppressive, and deafened teachers suspect a linguistic and real sleight of hand.

My concerns about the language of 'sharing' and 'ownership' do not amount to an embargo on either; both are pointing to important aspects of collaborative working practices which are central to the eventual development of creative learning communities in schools and colleges. My concern is that we should use both terms with care and be sensitive to the fact that these words are but two examples of contemporary uses of language in INSET and in the life of schools that frequently mask a reality which has more to do with containment and control than valuing and nurturing diversity. Invitations to share and own are too often premature, inappropriate or false. It is perhaps worth asking of any use of these words whether the processes which accompany the invitations are sufficiently reflexive, malleable and open to enable those involved to work through the contradictions and complexity of feelings as well as thoughts and for the locus of power to be clearly identified. The articulation and exploration of difference in pursuit of a vibrant and dynamic community is as difficult as it is necessary. But it is not well served by language which hides more than it reveals and by processes which seem to encourage but in reality silence voices which are seldom heard and invariably ignored.

(iii) Language as a repressive instrument

The third use of language as an obstruction rather than an aid to learning concerns the colonisation of certain key concepts in such a way that particular meanings are suppressed or marginalised by a dominant usage which sets the terms and conditions for debate. Here language is as much a means of repression as expression.

A current example of this is the notion of 'empowerment'. Much contemporary usage of the term in education suggests it is not problematic. Basically, what is being argued for in the push to empowerment is that people are given more responsibility and more control (power) to do their job in ways which are satisfying to them and which help them to combine efficiency with effectiveness. To empower someone on this account is to give them more professional space and appropriate means to use it creatively as well as responsibly; it is a value-free process which is at the heart of the 'quality' movement in management thinking and practice in education and the world of business.

In one sense there is nothing the matter with this. After all, it appears to be part of a concerted drive to acknowledge and enhance teachers' professionalism. There are, however, three major difficulties which are seldom recognised or acknowledged. Firstly, this neutral, process view of empowerment has supplanted an alternative view which is neither value-free nor confined to process. Secondly, what John Pilger has called 'the unremitting denial of context' (Pilger, 1993) seriously undermines most claims to the neutrality of empowerment. Thirdly, empowerment too readily falls prey to the manipulation of the less by the more powerful.

The alternative, emancipatory view of empowerment which has been superseded by the neutral view argues that empowerment cannot just be about processes. It must contain within it a firm commitment to a particular view of a better society. It takes as central the key question 'Empowerment for what?' and argues that these questions of values and purposes are not interesting after-thoughts but essential starting points. Since education is centrally concerned with particular views of the good life which amongst other things has a genuine commitment to think and act critically the purposes of empowerment are fundamentally important. To suggest it is just about a set of procedures or processes is to miss the point. As Roger Simon argues:

> Without a vision of the future a pedagogy of empowerment is reduced to a method of participation which takes democracy as an end and not a means!...It provides us with no guidance as to what forms of knowing and learning might help enhance our chances of developing a just and compassionate society when justice and compassion are so urgently required. (Simon, 1987)

The second difficulty the proceduralist view of empowerment faces is that its refusal to look at the context in which its advocacy is set results in its blindness to the political nature of its operation in real life. The current dominance of the self-managing school as a managerial icon of good practice is one example. In a devastating critique Stephen Ball admits to the temptation

> to see the devolution of budgets and self-management as ways of getting those being cut to cut themselves and to think that it is for the best because they control their own decline. There is a shift of institutional focus from the cuts themselves to ways of coping with the cuts....The ideological role of self-management in relation to the state is never more clearcut. (Ball, 1993)

What appears to be empowering turns out to have consequences which are quite opposite. Parallels within institutions abound.

Finally, the emancipatory critique reminds us that empowerment is inextricably linked to relations between those who have power and those who have less or none at all and empowerment is a process in which the transfer of power is firmly in the hands and at the discretion of those who have it already. This is often ducked, ignored or forgotten by advocates of the process view. Too often the language of empowerment raises expectations which are not and cannot be met and those who speak such language are frequently well aware of what is actually going on. The reality in many cases is that the arena of empowerment is relatively small and the boundaries firmly fixed, though often indistinctly drawn. Empowerment is a notion with a spring in its step; unhappily the step is more often than not constrained in ways which are not immediately apparent.

We need to take great care to look closely at the language we use to shape reality and the language that is used to shape it for us. INSET, like many other forms of professional development, is vulnerable to the controlling ambitions of those who have agendas that are often clearer and more concerted in the process of realisation than our own. That caution needs to be particularly well developed when we face the emergence of notions like empowerment which marginalise or erase the very promise they seem to offer; whilst it appears to encourage different voices, in fact it so often restricts what those voices are allowed to talk about. Yet what they do or do not talk about is precisely what determines whether or not the process is one of empowerment, one of control or one of enervation.

Reversing the language and practice of contemporary INSET

In looking for alternatives to the kind of technocratic, manipulative discourse which has affected education in general and INSET in particular it is helpful, not to go back to basics, but forward to fundamentals. Education is about human being and becoming; it is an exploratory process which we undertake together, one in which our humanity is developed and extended in and through our relations with others. The language of delivery, packages and the metaphors of the warehouse are diminishing rather than enriching of that humanity. We need instead to renew and develop a language of possibility, a language which celebrates difference, delights in and extends what we share, and understands that the creation of a vibrant, inclusive community lies in our capacity to do both together.

Such a language reflects and supports the development of emancipatory practice (Fielding, 1989). It acknowledges the centrality of authorship and the necessity of critique; it underscores the crucial dimension of professional equality; and, in encouraging both to condition each other, creates community. Instead of the closed imperatives of much contemporary INSET which silence the authentic voice of enquiry, deny professional equality, and prohibit the possibility of community, the language of possibility welcomes the vibrancy of challenge, affirms the centrality of mutual professional learning, and in doing so helps to give shape and life to a learning culture which celebrates and extends the simple complexities of wisdom.

We must refuse to let go of the ethically nuanced language of educational discourse which forces us to return to purposes and possibilities in a contemporary world which diminishes both into the barren lexicon of the operative and technician. We need to return again and again to the insights of people like John Macmurray (Macmurray, 1958) and Ben Morris (Morris, 1972, 1975) whose voices remind us insistently and elegantly of the human purposes of education in relation to which all our efforts and aspirations have significance and meaning. Writing in a superb unpublished essay 'Learning to be Human' in the late 1950s John Macmurray reminds us of the centrality of personal relations in the process of education and at the same time warns of the blind alley of overemphasis on technique and organisation.

> No technical training in educational methods can ever be a substitute for (certain human qualities), however unexceptionable the methods may be in themselves. Education is not and cannot ever be a technical activity. The attempt to turn would-be teachers into technicians by teaching them classroom tricks is as stupid as it is ineffective.... Here I believe is the greatest threat to education in our society. We are becoming more and more technically minded: gradually we are falling victims to the illusion that all problems can be solved by proper organisation: that when we fail it is because we are doing the job in the wrong way, and that all that is needed is 'know-how'. To think thus in education is to pervert education. It is not an engineering job. It is personal and human. (Macmurray, 1958)

In thinking about INSET and its contribution to individual and institutional learning it is time we listened more confidently, more attentively and more openly to the exploratory, interrogative voices of education before and beyond the confined certainties of training. Outside the context of that wider dialogue of human purposes and aspirations in-service training loses its irridescence, its inspiration and its conviction and becomes little more than a collection of free-wheeling tools and techniques with no intrinsic value or significance. That reclamation of the educational purposes of professional development has much to gain from the rejection of a discourse which has neither patience nor understanding of anything which lies outside the impoverishment of heightened self-interest and the penury of the market. The language we use to help us nurture what we believe, help us develop our understanding, and help us plan imaginatively and caringly for the future will significantly affect the integrity as well as the quality of what we do.

References

Ball, S. (1993) Culture, cost and control: self-management and entrepreneurial schooling in England and Wales, in Smyth, J. (Ed.) *A Socially Critical View of The Self-Managing School* (London: Falmer Press).

Fielding, M. (1989) The fraternal foundations of democracy: towards emancipatory practice in school-based INSET, in Harber, C. and Meighan, R. *The Democratic School: educational management and the practice of democracy* (Ticknell: Education Now).

Fielding, M. (forthcoming) 'Empowerment – Emancipation or Enervation?: Management, development planning and the delusions of the market'.

Giroux, H. (1992) *Border Crossings* (London: Routledge).

Hall, S. (1993) 'Thatcherism Today', *New Statesman & Society*, 26 November.

Kinder, K. (1993) Making INSET Count, *Topic (NFER)*, Issue 10 (Autumn).

Macmurray, J. (1958) Learning to be Human. Moray House Annual Public Lecture, 5 May (unpublished).

Morris, B. (1972) The personal foundations of education, in Morris, B. *Objectives and Perspectives in Education* (London: Routledge and Kegan Paul).

Morris, B. (1975) On discovering what it means to be human, in Niblett, W.R. (Ed.) *The Sciences, The Humanities & The Technological Threat* (London: University of London Press).

Pilger, J. (1993) 'When war is peace, and vice versa', *New Statesman & Society*, 12 November.

Simon, R. (1987) 'Empowerment as a Pedagogy of Possibility', *Language Arts* 64(4).

Smail, D. (1993) *The Origins of Unhappiness* (London: Harper Collins).

CHAPTER 3

TEACHING AND LEARNING – THE FOURTH DIMENSION

Mary Jane Drummond and Colleen McLaughlin

Introduction

In this chapter we will explore what we have called the fourth dimension of teaching and learning. The majority of courses that are offered at the Institute can be thought of as three-dimensional; first, they take place over time, sometimes over two years, rarely over less than a school term. Secondly, they are courses for groups of teachers, taking place in a particular kind of social space; and thirdly, they are courses relating to the practical, everyday world of schools and classrooms – the real-world dimension is inescapable. We have come to see that there is a fourth dimension, the emotional one, that pervades our work. We will argue that to be effective teachers, we have to take account of the emotional capacities of the learners on our courses. Emotional and professional development cannot, we believe, be separated.

Working with teachers – the background

The vast majority of the people who attend our courses, both full-time and part-time, are teachers (though some are educators in a wider sense); all of them are, of course, unique individuals of infinite variety, and yet all of them have characteristics in common that we need to consider in this account of their learning and our teaching. As they come in through the doors of the Institute, they cannot leave their past experience outside in the bicycle shed or car park; they do not stop being teachers simply because we now write to them as course members or pin up notices for them on the students' notice board. 'Once a teacher, always a teacher': what is it about the practice of teaching that might affect the practice of learning?

Philip Jackson's classic study 'Life in Classrooms' (1968), argues that for students 'the crucial facts of life' can be summed up in three key words: crowds, praise and power. Teachers' lives, too, are touched by these three facts of life.

However powerless an individual teacher may feel at a particular moment of crisis, or when faced with the intransigence of a superior authority (headteacher, inspector, official directives), in the school, in the classroom, in the corridor, even in the toilets and playground, all teachers have the power of authority on their side. Schools are, in a sense, predicated on obedience. Students, pupils, little children, are there to obey the teachers, who are there to give orders (however benevolently). Mary Willes' account of young children starting school, 'Children into Pupils' (1983), makes it acutely clear how quickly these children learn the rules: 'finding out what the teacher wants and doing it constitute the primary duty of the pupil' (p.138). Of course she exaggerates, but her central thesis stands: teachers, like the Roman centurion, are accustomed to having their words attended to. 'I say unto one, Go and he goeth, and to another, Come and he cometh' (Luke 7, viii).

Most of the time, most teachers are in control, not only of their own lives, but of the lives of others. And those others, more often than not, are in substantial numbers. Teachers, like the students Jackson observed, have learned to live in a crowd. The significance of this semi-permanent condition of crowdedness is that teachers, in their daily routines, have relatively little time left to be alone with themselves, with their private thoughts, anxieties, or aspirations. Living out in the open, as it were, surrounded by a group of students or by young children in large numbers, with other adults, teachers, assistants or parents never very far away, and usually within earshot, means that teachers are always aware of an audience. They can always feel other people's eyes upon them, and are always conscious of the effect – or lack of it – of their words and deeds. What is more, since the classroom world is a stage, the teacher players on it cannot help but know what sort of performance they are giving; just as pupils learn to live 'under the constant condition of having (their) words and deeds evaluated by others' (Jackson *op. cit.*, p.10), so do their teachers. The daily act of being a teacher includes, most of the time, looking and sounding like a teacher, in the eyes and ears of the beholders.

Observational studies of classrooms have been accumulating for several decades; there is an established body of knowledge about how effective and experienced teachers look and sound, about well-worn patterns of verbal and non-verbal interaction. Some of this knowledge is, naturally, self-knowledge: teachers do not always need an outside observer to show them their professional tricks and manners. Infant teachers laugh at Joyce Grenfell's monologues ('George! George!! No, George, a hippopotamus isn't a flower!') because they recognise themselves all too easily. A teacher's voice, a teacher's look, a teacher's question and answer routine: these are all part of the professional stock-in-trade that goes to make up the 'experience' of the experienced teacher.

Other studies have helped us understand more about the emotional experience of being a teacher. Holly and McLaughlin (1989) worked with a group of teachers who agreed to keep journals about their teaching lives. Over a year, one central theme emerged: the feeling of isolation. This feeling took a variety of forms; the teachers described physical, temporal, psychological, intellectual and social isolation. Perhaps most significantly, the teachers reported a sense of isolation from themselves.

But teachers are not born as teachers; we were all children once, and this experience, of having once been a child and a pupil, is one more common characteristic of our professional lives. As children and pupils, teachers have learned all about praise, criticism and feedback on the receiving end. 'I speak as an ex-child' said Iona Opie, in a recent lecture about her work on children's lore, language and imagination. If teachers do not often speak as ex-children, they still bring traces of that experience with them into the classroom – and into Institutes of Education.

These characteristics – the knowledge of crowds, of control, of power and authority, of isolation, of constant evaluation, of particular ways of speaking and doing – are, we believe, important starting points for beginning to think about teachers' learning.

Working with teachers – the context

The transition from the school, the familiar working environment, to the foreign ground of the Institute is, for some teachers, a difficult step in itself. Recently a teacher described her worries about finding the building, and how ashamed she felt of having asked her husband to drive her to the Institute on the first day of her part-time course. This teacher's anxiety about the possibility of getting physically lost is echoed in other discussions of the emotional dimension of in-service provision.

On a recent training day for a whole staff group, the first discussion was about 'hopes and fears'. There were fears expressed in plenty: a fear of saying the wrong thing, of making a fool of oneself; fears about power relations in the group, about not being treated with respect. There were fears about the Institute tutor too: would the group understand what she was saying? What sort of language would she use? Would her expertise be too powerful, too intimidating? Would her contributions unsettle people, undermine their confidence?

These anxieties, we believe, are both natural and inevitable. Fear of oneself and one's own inadequacies is, after all, an inescapable part of the human condition. As one key text puts it, very forcibly: 'no matter how mature and capable we are, we continue to harbour some dread of helplessness, of being lost, overcome with fear of disintegration' (Salzberger-Wittenberg *et al.*, 1983, p.8). The unfamiliar context of an Institute course may be enough to trigger some of these feelings; one course member wrote, looking back over her experiences: 'At the start, I was apprehensive – it was a *Cambridge* course after all – was I up to it?'

Fears of other people too are more than likely, given the exposed working conditions of the small discussion group or the plenary session, where everyone's contributions seem to be under scrutiny. One teacher wrote in her course evaluation: 'At the beginning of the course I was terrified of all those apparently efficient, effective, erudite teachers'. These feelings are expressed in a variety of ways: some course members fall silent, some become competitive and some cover up their achievements. Some chide their fellow course members for having completed required readings or other course tasks. There are many variations on what we may call 'flip-chart behaviour', when small groups of course members are asked to record their discussions on flip-chart sheets. There is often good-humoured but revealing debate about who is to take up the pen and write, about correct spelling and phrasing, about appropriate language, and about the contributions of other small groups. It is common to hear comments such as 'Oh, very impressive,' or 'That's the intellectual group,' or 'We said that, we just didn't write it down': these seem to indicate some of the course members' anxieties about one another.

Anxieties about the tutor's role are also common; these may not be made explicit till later but are, none the less, an important part of the course members' experience. A teacher once commented to one of us: 'I don't see you as a real person with a life, I see you as someone who parachutes into the course and is here solely for us.' The image of the parachute is a powerful one. The tutor, wearing the parachute, will land safely, exercising a degree of direction and control; for those without a parachute, there is a sense of danger, of free-fall. As one teacher asked at the final session of a two-year part-time Diploma: 'What happens when you wish you'd never started learning?'

Working with teachers – the process

> *A flashback*: an Institute tutor (one of us) was walking through the lobby, where people were chatting and drinking coffee. A teacher coming to the end of her year's full-time Diploma walked past the tutor, who had been her course co-ordinator during the year, and said 'F*** you!' After a moment's hesitation, the tutor and teacher sat down together to talk.

What was this teacher saying, in her sudden uncensored expletive? Talking to her tutor, she described how she had just realised that she had changed and been changed during the year. She had also realised that not all the changes she could identify were positive ones; some were painful.

This teacher's experience is not unique. We have both heard teachers talk about change and learning in one breath, and we have both listened to them describe how changes in themselves have been accompanied by a sense of pain or loss. The teacher who swore at her tutor was reacting to her sense of fundamental and deep-rooted change – changes in herself as a person and not just as a teacher, and changes she had not anticipated. In registering for an Advanced Diploma, she considered she had signed on for learning, but not for any kind of emotional disturbance; she expected cognitive but not affective challenge. She had not thought of her learning as potentially a deep emotional process, linked to her sense of purpose and meaning in life.

The courses we provide at UCIE are intended to help course members to look again at their established practices, to learn new ways of thinking, seeing and doing, to explore new attitudes and to ask new questions. For these intentions to be realised, tutors and course members need to share a model of adult learning, in which learning is more than an addition to an existing store of knowledge. Effective adult learners do not retain, intact, all their previous learning; changes have to be made.

One way of conceptualising the changes that take place in adult learning is offered to people undergoing counsellor training. A stage of *unconscious knowingness* gives way to *conscious unknowingness*, which in turn is replaced by *conscious knowingness*. We can recognise these three states both in ourselves and in those undertaking our courses. Coming to know what one does not know can be a painful experience, perhaps especially for teachers, who are practised in the art of knowing. One teacher on a short in-service course wrote: 'I frequently left the evening meetings feeling depressed and insecure about my teaching – this I viewed as the disturbance of some of the dead wood.' If the insecurity and depression that this teacher describes become too intense, however, little learning can take place. 'Real learning and discovery can only take place when a state of not knowing can be borne long enough to enable all the data gathered by the senses to be taken in and explored until some meaningful pattern emerges' (Saltzberger-Wittenberg *et al.*, 1983, p.58). The learner must be able to endure the painful state of 'not knowing', waiting while the dead wood is cleared, trusting that new insights, new patterns and new growth will eventually appear.

There are parallels here with an account of the creative process given by Marion Milner, a psycho-therapist, who learned in adulthood to paint (1971). She emphasises the need to be 'prepared for mental pain' as part of the experience, as she describes the counterpoint of action and inaction, consciousness and blankness. The process of creation can be thought of in four stages (Gordon, 1993). First there is an active period of *preparation*, when materials, talents, ideas and emotions are made ready. This is followed by a necessary stage of *incubation;* the artist, painter (or, we would argue, learner) endures a time of passivity, experiencing emptiness and loss of control. The main activity is that of letting go, surrendering control. Only if this emptiness can be tolerated, will the next stage, *inspiration,* follow. The final stage is one of *testing out* the idea or creation. If we think of learning as a form of creation, following this description, we can see how, sometimes, the pain of the 'incubation' period may be almost intolerable. To lose one's sense of control is, for some teachers, too high a price to pay for learning. One teacher, taking a year's course in counselling, reported a 'bad session' with one of her pupils. An experienced teacher, she had not known anything like it since her earliest days of teaching. She felt completely out of control; she felt a failure; she seriously considered giving up the course. She told her tutor that she had even thought of giving up teaching. To be able to continue with the course, as, in the end, she did, she had to learn to tolerate what she saw as 'failure'. Another teacher attending a shorter, part-time course, burst out in a large group discussion: 'Oh, it's all such a muddle now. Before I started, everything was so clear. Now it's all confused and I don't know where I am.' The sympathetic and supportive attention she immediately received from her fellow course members suggested that they too were experiencing some degree of uncertainty and confusion.

Deal (1990) vividly describes the changes taking place during learning, and indicates how extensive they may be in their effects. 'Change produces loss and loss creates wounds...change shatters reality, causing us to feel out of control, and undermining our sense of efficacy...change alters our relationships with objects, activities and symbols that give meaning to our lives and create a world that makes sense to us' (p.136). Deal's concept of change and loss can help to explain some of the ways in which our course members respond to the personal and emotional experience of learning.

Sometimes course members seem to want to preserve the past, to stick unchanged with the states of mind that are now threatened by new ideas or new questions. To this end they challenge us, or their fellow course members, by denying the feasibility of change. They use words like these: 'It won't work in my school/classroom with my headteacher/children/parents.' Or, instead, some course members seem to rush headlong into the future, embracing new thinking as a long sought for answer to all their problems and anxieties. Just as one can deny the possibility of a changed future, so one can deny the reality of the past and one's pain at its loss. The course members who try to avoid this pain sometimes blame the tutors as they come to face the emotional reality of their learning. 'Why didn't you warn me?' 'You never told me it would be like this!' In a sense, these teachers are saying to their tutors, with some justification: you got me into this. Now get me out. Save me. Tell me. Make it all right again.

Implications for teaching and learning

Everything we have said so far has implications for the work we do with teachers. If we choose to shut our eyes to the emotional dimension of teaching and learning, it will not go away. To disregard teachers' feelings in the face of all they have told us, and all we have seen for ourselves, will not help us to enhance their professional powers: their powers to think, to learn and to change. The ostrich position ('if I can't see it, it isn't there') is not an effective starting place for in-service education.

We have indicated a range of feelings that, we believe, needs thinking about: course members' feelings about themselves, about other teachers, about their course tutors and about their own learning. What can we, as tutors, do to recognise and accept these feelings, and then go on to turn them to good account?

Some of the practices, derived from what we know of course members' feelings about themselves, are obvious enough. If teachers feel isolated, and they do, we give them time and space to achieve a sense of community with other course members. Holly and McLaughlin (1989) reported that 'one of the most important aspects of journal sharing was to come into meaningful contact with other teachers' (p.277). If, on the other hand, teachers feel crowded and exposed, and they do, we give them time and support for individual and private reflection. If they feel powerless, or robbed of authority, and they often do, it is our responsibility to help them to admit to their powers and achievements. When they feel as if they were obliged to act as full-time experts, all-knowing, all-authoritative, all-competent, we try to create a climate of rational doubt, of safety in uncertainty; we try to establish a culture where asking questions is more highly valued than knowing all the answers. If they show their fears of negative feedback ('Look here,' said a teacher on the first day of a two year part-time Diploma, 'I can stand anything except criticism!') we try to show how some kinds of critical comment are both complimentary and constructive. We do this by carefully organising the process of giving and receiving feedback, so that course members can take part in these processes without disabling themselves or others. For example, on a counselling course, the tutor asks pairs of course members to work together, observed by a small group of others, who are later invited to give feedback to the pair. The form of this feedback is discussed in advance; clear criteria are put in place, and the feelings of course members about giving and receiving feedback are acknowledged and respected. Without agreed criteria, without a recognition of the feelings involved, it would be easy for the group to start to use the language of praise and blame, deeply affecting the course members' sense of themselves. If our courses are not to be ruled by the law of the jungle, where the only outcome will be the survival of the fittest, the course tutors have to accept their responsibility for managing the emotional agenda of the group.

Teachers' feelings about their fellow course members also deserve our attention and respect. The sense of community within a group that can be built up from the beginning of a course can be a powerful source of reassurance. Looking back, course members remember some of their illusions about one another. Three members of the same short course wrote, independently, 'I was surprised to find that I wasn't the only one who couldn't cope and that some days you wondered why were you ever a teacher.' 'I was surprised that everyone felt as threatened as I did.' 'I was surprised to find that most teachers feel they have shortcomings.' At the end of another course (two-year, part-time) a teacher remarked, reflecting on the goodwill in the group, 'We don't threaten each other in here.' She was reminded by another course member that 'We did, at first.' We have to acknowledge that course members' feelings about each other are sometimes so powerful that they can affect the ability of individuals to contribute to or profit from the work of the group. It is not enough for the tutor to sit back and wait for emotional disturbances to blow away; people's feelings can have quite damaging effects, and once the damage is done, it may be too late for the tutor to restore a temperate climate of care and consideration. Right from the beginning, ground rules can be established, setting down a 'code of conduct' in the emotional domain, ensuring that continuous attention is paid to the development of constructive group interactions.

The emotional relationship between course members and the tutor(s) is perhaps more problematic. The emotional demands of course members can, sometimes, pressure the tutor into responding inappropriately. There is a temptation, for example, to act over-protectively, to try to save teachers from the pain of 'not knowing', to provide them with the easy answers they seem to be asking for. It is tempting, too, seeing teachers hesitating in the face of uncertainty, to take over, seizing control in their place, denying them that temporary loss of control that we see as a crucial element in creative learning. One course member described this part of the process as 'free-fall'. He wrote: 'Till now, my habitual form of learning has been the standard lecture. I found that I relied on this less and less. I found the open sessions difficult at the beginning of the course; I wanted some reassurance that what I was actually doing with kids was OK.... Once I came to the conclusion that I was more or less OK, it became easier to enjoy the free-fall.'

Teachers' emotional reactions to the process of learning, however, are the most challenging that we face. When the teacher quoted earlier asked one of us, 'What happens when you wish you'd never started learning?', the tutor was, understandably, silent. It was noteworthy that other members of the group were not confounded by the question; they took it and elaborated on it, expressing their own versions of the same idea. 'Deep down, you know you'll never be satisfied again' said one, and another agreed with him: 'I know I'll never have peace of mind again.' What could there be, in any case, for a tutor to add to the thinking of these teachers, so resolutely committing themselves to a view of learning as change, to change of a kind that means both pain and opportunity. The moral of these exchanges is that regular opportunities for course members to talk about their feelings are invaluable, helping them, as these examples show, to develop some degree of tolerance of the pain of loss, change and learning. Sharing our common understanding of what we have called the fourth dimension of learning can help everyone·to feel less isolated and inadequate in their emotional responses.

The fourth dimension – principles of procedure

In this short exploration of the emotional dimension of adults' teaching and learning, we have identified some of the issues that may make the teaching less than effective, and the learning less than worthwhile. We have not tried to suggest a set of practices that must always be adopted in every set of circumstances; we are more interested in trying to establish some general principles that we can draw on in deriving, justifying and explaining our practices. We will end the chapter by outlining five principles that we see as fundamental to the practice of in-service education.

First, we are committed to establishing, with the teachers who attend our courses, a resolute sense of purpose. We do not refer, in this phrase, to a list of course aims and objectives; we are still talking about events in the emotional domain. We are concerned to foster a sense of determination and engagement. Without a fully felt purpose for learning, all those involved will be, in a sense, playacting. Without a passionate belief in the meaning and purpose of what is being undertaken, teachers and learners alike will emerge from the process unchanged and unsatisfied.

Secondly, we work to ensure that the teachers on our courses experience a personal sense of control, a sense that they are in charge of their learning and that no one else can or will do it for them. This sense of control is all the more important when it seems, as it sometimes will, to be at risk. Teachers will not learn effectively if they feel they have lost control of themselves as teachers. The difficulty is that this simple principle seems to be at odds with what we have earlier identified as a creative loss of control, a state that we see as a crucial component of learning. However, there is no real contradiction between the terms; both are necessary. Increasing one's control by losing it, temporarily, in the act of 'free-fall'; directing one's own learning by letting it run free; holding on and letting go: these are complementary parts of the effective learner's sense of control.

The next requirement is for a fully-developed sense of support for each individual's learning and for the work of the group as a whole. This sense of support is to be distinguished from a culture of cosiness, in which everyone always agrees with everyone else and in which many teachers fall, mentally, fast asleep. Supporting teachers' learning means finding ways to challenge, to encourage divergent thinking, to ask new questions, and stir up taken-for-granted assumptions, without damaging the teachers' commitment to what they are doing. The sense of support we are advocating will do much to make the course group feel like a safe place to do risky – even dangerous – things.

It is equally important to establish, for each individual, a sense of self. As one teacher put it, with some satisfaction, at the end of the first year of a two-year Diploma: 'On this course, you're a person first, and a teacher second.' The sense of being an unidentifiable pawn in the machine has no place in effective adult learning. Some teachers may come unprepared for the personal element in their learning; they may react unfavourably, taking their surprise out on their tutors (by verbal abuse, or other means) but the personal, not just the professional, is none the less essential. Teachers whose sense of self is, for whatever reason, under threat or temporarily damaged will need particularly caring attention if they are to learn effectively. Indeed, unless both tutors and course members are prepared to admit the centrality of this sense of self in their joint enterprise of teaching and learning, the outcomes will never be more than skin-deep. On the surface, in some groups of learners, all may seem to be sweetness and light; but unless deeper feelings are acknowledged, unless the personal sense of self, so often kept secret, is recognised as part of the professional curriculum, little learning of value will take place.

Finally we advocate the gradual development of a sense of success. We described earlier how course members often allude to their fears of failure; we have also seen signs, less obvious perhaps, of fear of success. It is as if one was saying to oneself: 'This is too difficult for me. I can't aspire to such achievements. It's safer not to learn successfully. I'd rather stay as I am.' Fear of success is only another form of fear of change. All will be well, our fearful selves tell us, as long as nothing changes. And if fear of success does win the day, nothing will change; the possibility of successful, worthwhile learning will be lost. On the other hand, if every step taken in the learning process seems to make things worse, if every experiment ends in failure, if every enquiry ends in a blank, few learners will persist. When there is not even a whisper of success to be heard, a sense of personal failure can seem overwhelming. Owning up to one's successes is admittedly difficult for some, brought up to be modest and self-deprecating as a way of life; but within a supportive group it is possible for teachers to learn to talk about what they do well, even about what they are learning to do better. And talking about one's successful teaching, has, we believe, an important part to play in teachers' purposeful, worthwhile learning. The fourth dimension of learning opens up for teachers what John Cowper Powys would call a 'multiverse' (not a universe) of feeling: pain and loss certainly; anger and resentment sometimes; but also joy, delight and pride in the present and hope for a better future.

References

Deal, T. (1990) 'Healing our schools: restoring the heart', in Lieberman, A. (1990) *Schools as Collaborative Cultures: creating the future now* (London: Falmer Press).

Gordon, R. (1993) Loss, Change and Creativity. Lecture to Society of Analytical Psychology in Cambridge (unpublished).

Holly, M.L. and McLaughlin, C.S. (Eds.) (1989) Professional development and journal writing, in Holly, M.L. and McLaughlin, C.S. *Perspectives on Teacher Professional Development* (London: Falmer Press).

Jackson, P.W. (1968) *Life in Classrooms* (New York: Holt, Rinehart and Winston).

Milner, M. (1971) *On Not Being Able to Paint* (London: Heinemann Educational Books).

Salzberger-Wittenberg, I., Henry, G. and Osborne, E. (1983) *The Emotional Experience of Learning and Teaching* (London: Routledge and Kegan Paul).

Willes, M. (1983) *Children into Pupils* (London: Routledge and Kegan Paul).

CHAPTER 4

HIGHER DEGREES THAT SERVE THE SCHOOL OR INSTITUTION: Is there still a justifiable place for study at Masters' degree level in the current in-service climate?

Colin Conner

In a recent telephone conversation, a local headteacher asked me to explain why he should support one of his staff on a part-time higher degree. With a very limited budget for in-service education, now that the budgets are largely devolved to school, the costs involved in allowing his colleague to join the MA course were considerable. This was particularly the case when compared with a lot of recent activity in the school that had been short-term and concerned with the immediate problems he and his colleagues faced. 'It is no longer possible for in-service training to be concerned with individual professional development,' he suggested. When I tried to explain that it is possible to link personal agendas with those of the school he didn't seem convinced.

This chapter is an attempt to reply to the concerns raised by the reaction of the headteacher described above. The opening section traces the recent history of changes in funding for in-service education (INSET), especially as it applies to advanced study. This is followed by an analysis of comments from teachers who have completed their studies for a higher degree and which provides evidence that individual and institutional interests can be satisfied in the context of further study.

During the last ten years there has been a major shift in the attitude towards further professional development opportunities for teachers. Prior to the 1980s, a complex funding structure operated which Harland, Kinder and Keys (1993) suggested:

> ...favoured the use of long-term award-bearing courses as the major form of professional development provision.

In this context, INSET tended to be experienced via full-time secondment, as a part-time experience, released for a day a week or part of a day, or through evening attendance at an institution of higher education. The major purpose of such attendance was usually the completion of a course of advanced study leading to some form of further qualification, often an Advanced Diploma or a Masters' degree. Participation in such courses tended to be a very individualistic experience, serving the interests of the individual teacher and rarely of benefit to the school. Dobbins (1989) comments that:

> In the main, INSET was led by the providing establishments and more often than not did not meet, in total, teacher requirements as they were expressed in a rapidly changing education system.

Jones, O'Sullivan and Reid (1987) argue that during the 1980s the Government sought to increase its influence on the overall management of the education system, including the in-service training of teachers, with the particular intention of making it more relevant to the needs of the school. Critics of the pool system for organising INSET had been vociferous during the 1970s and 1980s. Eraut (1972), for example, had advocated a need for INSET to be more responsive to the needs of the school as a result of his evaluations of in-service activities, especially in terms of their effects on practice in schools. Others were concerned that there was a need to move,

> ...beyond a view of INSET which too often placed the teacher in the role of passive recipient of menu led 'courses' to one which encouraged school-centred, collaborative and dynamic approaches to professional development. (Harland, Kinder and Keys, 1993)

A number of writers warned of the 'inherent limitations' of school-centred in-service activities, however. Rumble (1981) commented that if a school draws exclusively on its own resources 'there is a danger of parochialism and bias'. This was a point made in the recent 'Three Wise Men' report, 'Curriculum Organisation and Practice in the Primary School' (Alexander *et al.*, 1992) which suggested that organising INSET totally in the school context and drawing solely on existing expertise could lead to schools 'recycling their own inadequacies'. Whilst accepting the potential benefits of 'school-centred' innovation, Hargreaves (1987) claimed that 'hope, faith and optimism do not so much permeate the discussions and evaluations of school centred innovation as consume them'. School-focussed in-service education, in other words,

> ...is strong on rhetoric, but as yet still relatively weak in substantiating its claims to providing a full and comprehensive programme of staff development that might meet the intellectual and professional needs of all teachers across schools. (Nixon, 1989)

Henderson (1979) suggested that a possible answer to this dilemma was to develop in-service education that was school-focussed rather than school-based.

> If INSET activities are developed from a school's identified needs, the mismatch common with the course-based model is avoided and classroom implementation becomes much more probable since all the staff are engaged in planning from the start, and account can be taken of the constraints of human and physical resources available to the school.

Closely allied to this emphasis on school development and improvement was another important alternative to the traditional course model. Teachers' action research and self-evaluation as a form of INSET was advocated as a more appropriate means of developing both schools and teachers (Cooper and Ebbutt, 1974; Elliott, 1981; Holly, 1986). In Great Britain, many of the ideas for developing teachers' professional competence in this way are derived from the work of Lawrence Stenhouse. Hammersley (1993) describes the central features of Stenhouse's ideas as follows:

> At the core of Stenhouse's work is a view of the learner, whether child or adult, scholar or teacher, as producing knowledge which is always tentative, and open to debate...

and that,

> ...the teacher is (or ought to be) a skilled practitioner, continually reflecting on his or her practice in terms of ideals and knowledge of

local situations, and modifying practice in the light of these reflections, rather than a technician merely applying scientifically produced curriculum programmes.

The extent to which these claims have been realised through action research is questionable however, and the tendency has been for many action research projects to be based upon the interests of an individual teacher or a group of teachers and not to involve the school as a whole, with varying responses from those not involved (James and Ebbutt, 1981). There are, however, a number of interesting developments which are attempting to work with whole schools. The recent report of the National Commission on Education (1993) makes particular reference in this context to the benefits of linking with higher education and illustrates this through two examples. The 'Two Towns' project based at the Centre for Successful Schools at the University of Keele has targeted disadvantaged inner city schools and has sought over a four year period, to challenge low expectations, poor staying on rates and limited progression to higher education. The IQEA project (Improving the Quality of Education for All) based at the University of Cambridge Institute of Education and described in a later chapter by David Hopkins, was complimented in the National Commission report for its attempts at collaborating with schools in Yorkshire and the South East to develop a model of school development with a programme of support for the process.

The changes that have taken place in the organisation and funding of in-service education during the period described have had a particularly significant effect on the funding available to study for a higher degree and has resulted in a progressive reduction in the numbers of teachers supported by LEAs on a Masters' degree programme (Day, 1989; UCET, 1993a and 1993b). At the same time, there has been a progressive increase in the number of teachers who are prepared to fund themselves on a part-time basis (Triggs and Francis, 1990), but no clear strategy for using the skills of teachers following sustained in-service courses (Bradley and Howard, 1992). Some argue that the attitude of the Government towards higher degrees is an attempt at marginalising the contribution of higher education to the process of teacher professional development. Day (1989), for example, comments:

This is not to suggest that the traditional course no longer has relevance to teachers' development needs, but simply that those who fund in-service have effectively reorganised priorities so that immediate short term training needs are met or appear to be met by sharp, short in-service work.

It is interesting to note in the HMI review (OFSTED, 1993) of the management of in-service funded by GEST, the whole emphasis in the report is on describing the effects of such short, sharp experiences, which they describe as 'training' experiences. This seems a very narrow interpretation of professional development. The introduction to the report argues that:

> A highly skilled teaching force is essential if standards are to be raised in the nation's schools. The development and refinement of teachers' skills require effectively delivered and appropriately targeted training.

They describe five types of training that the Government clearly believes will fulfil these expectations:

1. *Training* designed to extend and supplement initial teacher training.
2. *Training* which responds to new initiatives, (for example, the introduction of the National Curriculum).
3. *Training* to extend a teacher's expertise to meet personal, school or regional needs.
4. Updating of professional development to meet *specific needs* identified by appraisal.
5. *Training* to provide post-initial qualifications in specialist areas, (for example, teaching the hearing or visually impaired).

All of these, except the last category, tend to be undertaken as short experiences with the emphasis on skill or knowledge acquisition where,

> ...the professional learning opportunities (are) curriculum led and based on implicit and problematic assumptions of economy and immediacy. They (are), in effect, exemplifying a view of teacher as technicist/employee. (Day, 1993)

It was this kind of view that led Goodyear (1992) to argue that:

> The meaning of 'professional' has slid away from the rich suggestiveness of, say, 'professional judgement' or 'professional integrity'

towards the narrower end of its continuum, where it is synonymous with 'proficient', as in, 'they made a professional job of it' ... 'professional development'...refers primarily to the acquisition and extension of skills needed to implement and assess the national curriculum ....

Many would argue however, that the most important factors which contribute to changes in practice and thinking and which have the potential to contribute to the development of teachers' expertise are those experiences which demand:

...reflection on and confrontation of past and current thinking and practice, a sharing of this with others and critical consideration of the views of others. (Day, 1993)

A similar viewpoint is reflected in an investigation into teachers developing understanding of their roles and responsibilities and the effects of participating in a higher degree programme on this process by Holt and Johnston (1989), who suggest that:

...in an area as complex as teaching, there are many ideas on which knowledgeable educators will disagree. Teachers, therefore, should become involved in an on-going conversation about which idea or practice is better. Allowing oneself to be challenged by positions different from one's own is part of the continuing process in which all teachers and researchers should participate.

Williams (1991) endorses this viewpoint and argues that current in-service provision is largely inadequate because of its 'lack of a reflective emphasis'.

It is concerned more with a basic level of coping than with a more mature, reflective stance. As such it is episodic in character, lacking any sequential structure or provision for incremental growth. It ignores arguments for progression, balance, depth, breadth and differentiation in the continuing professional development of teachers.... Teachers are having their needs defined for them, not by them. These needs are rarely located in any professional development structure that has been negotiated by teachers....

A variety of recent studies offer testimony to the claimed benefits of involving teachers in decision-making about their in-service needs and creating an opportunity for them to reflect upon and confront their existing practices with a view to improvement. A study by Dadds (1991), for example, illustrates how in-service experiences take time to be incorporated into classroom practice and that, if given time, they can begin to influence the thinking and practice of other colleagues. Evidence from the MA in Applied Educational Studies at the University of York (Lewis, 1988; Vulliamy and Webb, 1991) also illustrates that it is possible to link the work of Higher Education to schools in a positive way. In their evaluation of the Outstation MA programme at the University of York, Vulliamy and Webb have provided evidence that the two-year part-time experience on the MA has had a significant effect on the thinking and practice of their participants, particularly in terms of their ability to cope with the increasing demands placed upon them by Government legislation.

> ...our study points to the vital role that INSET can play in bolstering the confidence of a profession at a time when this seems most urgent.

One other major benefit identified by this study was the effect on practice of investigating the perceptions of pupils.

> Those teachers, who carried out research which involved collecting the views and experiences of pupils, claimed that this aspect of the research process had the greatest impact on their teaching. The data challenged their assumptions about the abilities of individuals, pro-vided explanations for seemingly inappropriate behaviour and revealed the value of pupil views as a source of critique and ideas.... The research gave many teachers added motivation, increased con-fidence, and an enhanced self image, together with the skills of collecting, analysing and evaluating information to inform decision-making and a recognition of the role of pupils, staff and institutional structures in the change process.

The importance of the skills listed here have been recognised by many authors as being of particular significance during a period of rapid and dramatic change and have influenced the construction of a number of MA courses. The MA in Applied Research in Education established under the direction of Lawrence Stenhouse at the Centre for Applied Research in Education (CARE) at the University of East Anglia is a notable example. Amongst the basic principles for the course is that of the 'teacher as researcher'. Walker (1985) argues that,

> ... research is an essential element in the teacher's role. As teaching has become increasingly professionalised and the management of

educational organisations more systematised, so 'research' has increasingly become something that teachers are expected to include in their repertoire of skills.

A parallel course to the one established at the University of East Anglia has been running at the Institute of Education for the last ten years. It has allowed us to explore the effects of participation in this course on the thinking and practice of some of those who have followed it. The course lasts for two years and is part-time. Students attend ten evening sessions per term and participate in a residential 'research weekend' each term, where course members focus upon an issue of current concern. During the course they produce the equivalent of four short assignments and an 18,000 word dissertation. All of these assignments arise out of the interests and concerns of the participants and are intended to focus upon issues of direct relevance to their schools or institutions as well as their own practice. A central feature of the course are the 'fieldwork seminars', where as small groups, the students act as 'critical friends' to each other's research projects. The main aim of these group discussions is to contribute to the students' progressive understanding of the research process and the development, in Stenhouse's words, of 'a community of collaborative enquirers'.

What follows is based upon conversations and written comments from a sample of twenty former students who were invited to comment on their MA course experience via the following four questions:

1. What factors contributed to making the course an effective or ineffective experience for you?
2. How useful were the assignments and dissertation in terms of contributing to your thinking and practice?
3. In what ways has participation in the course effected what happens now?
4. Is there any justification for a course of this kind in the current in-service climate?

Factors contributing to the MA as an effective in-service experience

In the context of the MA course, a number of important elements emerged as having contributed to making the course an effective experience for participants. Of considerable significance was the membership of the course itself. The course drew on people from a diversity of backgrounds and experience, with a small number from outside education (i.e. physiotherapy and radiography). As one of the respondents commented:

> The wide-ranging background of the group was most beneficial and contributed to and extended the understanding of others. The people on the course were its strength.

This is of particular importance in an in-service environment which is progressively becoming focussed on isolated schools. This trend, if allowed to continue, could lead to the recycling of inadequacies, as noted earlier. The opportunity to link with teachers and lecturers with varying responsibilities and perspectives both in and outside the education system led one person to say:

> It has reinforced the importance of seeing the education system as a whole. I hadn't realised how 'phase specific' I had become. I am now much more conscious that the problems I face are the same as for others who deal with older children and can even apply outside the context of schools.

Another contributor, who trains radiographers, commented:

> Sharing experiences with teaching colleagues from other disciplines was most helpful...I enjoyed discussing with mainstream teachers the rapid changes affecting the educational system and this has been extremely helpful to me in terms of my own work and my role as a parent and school governor.

This was reiterated by a lecturer in physiotherapy who commented that the other participants on the course,

> ...taught me a lot about their experience, which allowed me to see that within my experience of a 'narrow' speciality I had experienced problems which were common to other areas of education, and that solutions could be found from a broader spectrum of practice than I had appreciated. I suppose this gave me a feeling of being part of a broad educational community.

Similarly, many teachers commented on the benefits of being with a 'mixed' professional group, over a sustained period of time, because of the different perspectives and questions this brought to bear on their discussions. Talking with others from varied backgrounds was seen to contribute to and extend one's own understanding and emerged as another benefit of participation in the course. Over a two-year period the group members get to know each other very well. They develop contacts that are sustained beyond the end of the course and serve as an important professional support system in one's later career. One headteacher's comment illustrates this:

> The course members provided a forum for debate on many professional issues. They widened perspectives by introducing cross-county policies and practices to me and I found the shift from focussing on my own school in a parochial sense to focussing on educational establishments in the broadest sense invaluable and broadening. The networks established as a result of participation in the course continue to be a very important source of support. There is always someone that you can contact to explore current issues and concerns in an atmosphere of absolute trust and confidentiality.

The trust and confidentiality which develops as the course unfolds, also proved to be an important factor affecting many perceptions. A deputy headteacher working in a large comprehensive school commented that the course provided:

> ...the opportunity to try out my own thoughts, away from the context of my own school, in a non-threatening though nevertheless academically challenging environment, with course colleagues and tutors; then the chance to gain feedback and to stimulate further reflection in a manner which is generally impossible, in my experience, in the hectic, reactive world of the school.

A primary teacher commented in a similar way, when she said:

> The MA, as a more extended course, enabled significant interaction with colleagues. We got to know each other very well. Our shared commitment and interest made real discussion, challenge and debate possible in a way which is not possible in school. The atmosphere created and the provision of some time for sustained discussion is the best way to make people think, rather than react.... Throughout the course we were able to relate our discussions to practice, not at a simple 'tips for teachers' level, but at a deeper level of professional questioning.

As was explained earlier, one major intention of the course was the attempt to link personal and professional/institutional concerns as far as this was possible. These two elements often came together in the context of the assignments. One comment summed up the views of all of the contributors:

> The course assignments provided the opportunity to put my personal and professional context at the centre of the learning process. My assignments and dissertation all related closely to my professional work. This gave me justification for following the course. I gained, and so did the school.

The remaining factors contributing to course effectiveness that emerged from contributors concerned the organisation and structure of the course. They enjoyed the fact that there was a team of tutors who had a regular commitment to the course, which is significant as many MA courses are having to move towards a modular structure with its inherent problems of breaking group cohesion and potentially fracturing the learning experience. Many advocates of modular courses see this as a benefit however, the opportunity to meet a much wider range of people and to reduce the potential 'cosiness' of a group who have been together for a long period. Reference was made to the quality of input and the varied organisation and structure of the sessions which included whole and small group work, lectures, workshops and the use of video recordings and visiting speakers. One person suggested that the teaching on the course had provided models that had led her to change her own practice in the classroom and one comment reminds us of the effects of the market economy philosophy which currently pervades education:

> A major influence was the quality of teaching, which was excellent, both from those inside the institution and from those invited from outside. As senior professionals, we all have to think very seriously about whether participation in a course of this kind is worth the investment of our (very precious) time. It is also the case that a growing number of people are having to pay for themselves, so questions about value for money enter into the debate.

As Vulliamy and Webb (1991) found, an important factor which reinforced the course experience as something positive for the majority were the effects on perceptions of self. There were many comments which referred to the growth of self-esteem. For example, a teacher in a middle school commented:

I consider the two years spent on the course as some of the most valuable in my adult life. The course enabled me to pursue learning opportunities which had not been available to me at 21 and which I would not have recognised as being of any value at an earlier age. It developed my feeling of self-worth and self-recognition and I was able to accept myself as an intelligent being.

The contribution of the assignments and dissertation to thinking and practice

A study by Halpin, Croll and Redman (1990) comments on the lack of information about the effects of in-service experiences on teachers, schools or children. Most of the research available has had to rely upon the effects that participants say a course has had on them, their colleagues or their children. Dadds' (1991) study attempted to remedy this by following up these claims in school through observation and discussion with colleagues. The evidence presented here strongly suggests that the course experience has had a significant effect on both thinking and practice for all of those who commented. As far as the development of thinking is concerned, the importance of the writing process was emphasised as an important means by which understandings were clarified. Similar findings emerged from the study by Triggs and Francis (1990). One comment explains this:

I found that writing was the way in which I clarified my uncertainty. You could say that I wrote myself into understanding.

This process is also illustrated by another comment:

Each assignment made me think and then write in a serious, thoughtful way, gradually developing a style of my own, with increasing layers of complexity, increasingly less dogmatic, increasingly looking for alternative answers rather than just my own preconceptions. The writing process certainly clarified my own thinking on many issues.

What is being described here, is what Entwistle (1992) and others (Marton, 1988) have described as a 'deep' approach to thinking about practice rather than a 'surface' approach which relies upon a re-presentation of that which has been provided. This is what Schon (1983) referred to as 'reflecting upon action'. One course member described it in this way:

The writing process contributed to helping me make sense of situations and experiences and at times caused me to question my own beliefs, values, judgements, attitudes and approaches. Sometimes, this was quite painful, but at the same time it contributed to my own learning and caused me to think seriously about the practical implications of my findings.

Throughout the responses, there were innumerable examples of the effects on practice that were felt to have resulted from participation in the course. Of particular interest was the fact that many of the suggested effects were in the area of school organisation and policy which contrasts with the findings of Halpin *et al.* (1990), who suggested that in their study of the effects of higher education in-service courses, the greatest impact was on teachers' attitudes and knowledge levels. A senior manager in a comprehensive school describes the motivation for undertaking the course as being to improve policy.

My major reason for taking the MA course was to take a more professional approach to my decision making, to improve the quality of what underpins practice at our school. Previously, I had tended to work on 'gut' reactions. My decisions are not necessarily different, but I know they are now more firmly based on evidence.

Another secondary school teacher commented:

All my pieces of work were central to what I was doing professionally at the time; I reflected about the impact of my classroom teaching and involved my colleagues in this; my assignment on appraisal was, in part, shared with all teaching colleagues and gave me tremendous awareness of how it affected individuals as well as the whole school. This led to changes in school organisation.

Similar comments came from the lecturer in radiography:

Many small changes have been effected as a direct result of some of my research and I believe my practice has improved. Some of these changes have produced a knock-on effect and begun to influence the work of colleagues and the running of our department.

A class teacher in a middle school described effects for the pupils, as well as for colleagues and the school.

The nature of the assignments was directed at our own needs and those of the school and therefore extremely valuable. We still feel the effects six years on. I welcomed the opportunity to study issues which developed my own understanding of pupils, colleagues and the school more fully. My research led to greater awareness of individual needs of pupils transferring to the school, either as a group or separately, and as a staff we looked at the implications of my findings and set up procedures for monitoring and counselling these pupils. We set up a friendship peer-link system to assist the smooth transfer of 9+ pupils which has now been adopted by our sister school. My dissertation highlighted the connection of positive self-esteem with learning and as a staff we have adopted programmes of self-esteem enhancement for PSE and tutorial time. Drawing upon the findings of the dissertation, staff have tried positive reinforcement with slow learners with some success.

A lecturer in initial teacher training describes the effects of her dissertation on her own teaching:

The focus for the dissertation – encouraging student teachers to become independent learners has had a marked effect on my practice...it enabled me to evaluate the effectiveness of my teaching throughout the year, amending and developing a range of teaching strategies to encourage students to assume more responsibility for their own learning. The dissertation has undoubtedly affected my thinking and my practice.

A final comment comes from another class teacher who suggested that her MA experience had resulted in her being invited to become more fully involved in the development of school policy:

My assignments and dissertation were the direct result of issues that had been raised in curriculum and staff meetings which it was felt would benefit from wider research and discussion. They produced working documents on which action has and will be taken and have been built into the school development plan. I still work at the 'chalk face' but now I am often consulted at management level and invited to comment on proposals before they happen. I have led discussions in staff meetings and INSET for the school. All of which obviously does wonders for my self-esteem.

How has participation in the course affected what you do now?

One of the criticisms levelled at courses such as the one described here is that the main purpose for involvement is to achieve the award. This was disputed by respondents to this investigation, who argued that participation in the course provided the motivation for the completion of some very worthwhile studies which would not have been undertaken with the same degree of rigour without the course. One respondent who was unable to complete the course commented that even though he had to withdraw, the experience had been an extremely beneficial one. Participation has clearly had long-term effects. One primary school headteacher, who completed the course eight years ago commented:

> My whole professional life since completing the course has been influenced by the MA experience. It aptly linked practical experience of some considerable number of years with current theories of teaching and learning. The MA experience further affected me in the way I read and assimilate educational documents, which is something needed by every headteacher today. I have learned to scan text and identify important features quickly.

Other contributors described the course as 'teaching participants to think through the complexity of their work', and 'developing listening skills and the confidence to challenge, to question and to analyse', and 'less accepting of research findings, more critical of how findings have been reached'. Reference was made to participants 'having their own abilities tested', 'using time more effectively', being 'more up-to-date with educational thinking', 'more analytical and questioning of documents' and 'leading to improved presentation of documents and in-service sessions'. This can be illustrated by the comments of an advisory teacher:

> It helped me to develop a deeper understanding of my area of work and the issues that are involved and therefore greater self-confidence in discussing issues with others which improves the basis for decision-making. It has reawakened me to the importance of information, ideas and the stimulation available from periodicals and books.

The lecturer in physiotherapy felt that:

> I feel that I am now more inclined to think and plan carefully before plunging into new projects, and to base my suggestions and actions on a much more sound knowledge base. I am also more inclined to reflect upon and analyse what has happened with a view to developing it for the next time. I feel able to express my opinions more lucidly and confidently and I am more inclined to question rather than just accept.

As was suggested earlier, self-confidence emerged as a common benefit identified in many of the replies and conversations:

> The major influence of the course is my increased self-confidence. I am much more confident of my abilities and this has led to me contributing more to my work. Although I have always undertaken my work with great enthusiasm I quite often held back because I believed my contribution to be worthless. Whilst undertaking the course, I was promoted into a job which gives me much more responsibility and I am sure I would not have had the confidence to apply before participation in the course.

Increased knowledge and confidence led to involvement beyond the school for some and included participation in LEA working parties, consultancy groups, and delivery of in-service for the LEA, although as Bradley and Howard (1992) found, the systematic use of the expertise developed in such courses by LEAs was limited. Where it happened, it tended to be by chance.

One final comment relates to the effects in the classroom:

> It returned me to the learning situation, with pressures, deadlines, and an element of stress. I am better able to empathise with what pupils feel as they face assessment at school.

Is there any justification for MA courses in the current in-service climate?

As was suggested in the introduction to this chapter, the future viability of Masters' degree courses is in question, primarily because of finance. Limited resources devolved to schools means that the in-service butter is spread very thinly. Supporting a teacher on an MA course is expensive, but the evidence presented here suggests that there are considerable benefits beyond the individual. Not surprisingly, the overwhelming response from those represented in this study to the question of justification for MA course opportunities was positive and supportive but at the same time realistic. The majority of comments compared their experience with that which currently dominates the in-service scene, the short, sharp 'training experience' reported by HMI, as can be seen by the following comments.

First, the deputy headteacher of a large urban comprehensive school, who has responsibility for staff development:

> Short training courses are not staff development, they respond to immediate needs which are often short-lived. Long courses are totally different. The emphasis is on the development of professionalism. There is a place for shorter courses, but longer courses result in deeper and broader thinking. *Considered* opinions and ultimately *informed* decisions can only come from careful research, knowledge and reflection on the implications of this for practice. If we wish to raise standards, including those of management, it is essential that we provide opportunities like the MA.

One of the teachers who has funded herself for the course added:

> Funding is difficult, but I funded myself and would do so again if I had to. I have been on day and evening courses but never been impressed. The sustained nature of the MA course was infinitely more useful. Money should not govern INSET provision.

A primary school headteacher suggested that sustained INSET was especially important where there is a lack of staff movement.

> It is very easy for staff to get into a rut. You do not change people and their practice with short, one-off courses. To change people takes time and they have to be supported in the process. Recent changes in education are complex. They require in-depth professional discussion facilitated and led by people of calibre.

An in-service co-ordinator in a primary school made similar comments when she said:

> There is a vast difference between an MA course and the occasional day (or even the 20 hours over 10 weeks type of course) 'hit and run' stuff. I feel that these have minimal medium or long-term effect and reduce teaching to a craft/hobby level. Longer courses involving enquiry can contribute to the development of practical 'theory' and testing, which I think belongs with a profession.

Another primary headteacher argued that MA courses need to be seen as a part of a developmental set of in-service experiences, which in a perfect world everybody should be entitled to.

> School-based INSET has a valuable place, but you soon exhaust the possibilities that a small staff provides. Sustained courses, off-site,

with a disparate group united by their interest in further professional study has a priceless role to play and the pay off is long-term,
over a whole career, and far-reaching into the soul of the various
establishments where the 'students' will work for the rest of their
teaching lives.

The final comment on the suggested benefits of participation on
a course leading to a Masters' degree comes from Patricia Lilley,
who has recently successfully completed her course.

I believe that opportunities to attend courses of this nature are more
essential in the current climate than ever before. The opportunities
provided for students undertaking initial teacher training to read in
depth and to reflect on their own classroom practice are becoming
less and less as institutions grapple with the demands of covering
the National Curriculum and fulfilling CATE/Government requirements. Serving teachers are constantly bombarded with short INSET
opportunities related to their roles in school, attending subject spe-
cific/assessment/co-ordinators/management courses, etc. There is
far less opportunity for them to consider their own personal development. Time to stand back and think about their current practice is
at a premium. They are presented with snatches of input at staff
meetings or twilight sessions where no one is in a fit state to really
learn after a hard day at school. There is little time for sustained
reflection or study.

Attendance on the MA course has really empowered me as a
teacher. I can look at my practice in the light of my reading. I can
make informed decisions about my role and the implications of this
for my students. I have grown in self-confidence. I am convinced
that it will become increasingly important for teachers to develop
the skills that the MA course has introduced me to – to reflect,
analyse, and critique in the light of evidence; skills which will allow
teachers to view their personal practice from a relatively detached
standpoint, which should give enormous confidence when discussing practice as part of the appraisal process. This should
increase confidence when discussing, explaining and interpreting
their work on the basis of systematic evidence rather than mere cus-
tom, intuition and hunch. This would seem to be essential in the
present climate of accountability. This might empower teachers to
make a contribution to current debates about education rather than
being the passive recipients of someone else's pontifications. I feel
that teachers have been deskilled by recent government initiatives
and need to be helped to recognise their skills as practitioners, to
articulate their views in a public arena, to become involved in the
response to current proposals that have important implications for
their future role. My experience suggests that participation in a
course of sustained study contributes to the development of these

capacities. Such courses are necessary to ensure that the profession continues to include members who have a theoretical understanding of the issues that underpin practice in the classroom, who can act as critical friends to the development of thinking and who can raise important questions.

I have greatly benefited from attendance on long courses both with the part-time MA and on a secondment to study for an advanced diploma. I know that this combined experience has had a significant impact on the way that I think and teach. My hope is that as many teachers as possible will be able to benefit from similar experiences through sustained study at degree level.

References

Alexander, R., Rose, J. and Woodhead, C. (1992) *Curriculum Organisation and Practice in Primary Schools: A Discussion Paper* (London: DES).

Bradley, H. and Howard, J. (1992) 'Where are they now? – the impact of long courses on teachers' careers and development', *British Journal of In-Service Education*, **18**(3), pp.186-90.

Cooper, D. and Ebbutt, D. (1974) 'Participation in action research as an in-service experience', *Cambridge Journal of Education*, 4, pp.65-71.

Dadds, M. (1991) *Validity and award-bearing teacher action-research*, unpublished PhD thesis (Norwich: School of Education, University of East Anglia).

Day, C. (1989) 'INSET: The marginalising of higher education', *British Journal of In-Service Education*, **15**, pp.195-6.

Day, C. (1993) 'Management support for teachers' learning', *Journal of Teacher Development*, February, pp.5-13.

Dobbins, D.A. (1992) 'The effect of the Training Grant Scheme on INSET in special education in Wales', *British Journal of In-Service Education*, **18**(1), pp.42-49.

Elliott, J. (1981) *Action-Research: A Framework for Self-evaluation in Schools*, Schools Council Working Programme 2, Working Paper 1 (London: Schools Council).

Entwistle, N. (1992) Student learning and instructional principles in higher education, in the Report of a Working Party of the Committee of Scottish University Principals, *Teaching and Learning in an expanding Higher Education System* (Lasswade, Midlothian: Polton House Press), pp.52-62.

Eraut, M. (1972) *In-Service Education for Innovation*, Occasional Paper No. 4 (London: National Council for Educational Technology).

Goodyear, R. (1992) 'The in-service curriculum for teachers: a review of policy, control and balance', *British Journal of Educational Studies*, **40**(4), pp.379-399.

Halpin, D., Croll, P. and Redman, K. (1990) 'Teachers' perceptions of the effects of in-service education', *British Educational Research Journal*, **16**(2), pp.163-177.

Hammersley, M. (1993) On the teacher as researcher, in Hammersley, M. (Ed.) *Educational Research: Current Issues* (London: Paul Chapman/Open University).

Hargreaves, A. (1987) The rhetoric of school-centred innovation, in Murphy, R. and Torrance, H. (Eds.) *Evaluating Education: issues and methods* (London: Paul Chapman/Open University).

Harland, J., Kinder, K. and Keys, W. (1993) *Restructuring INSET: privatisation and its alternatives* (Slough: NFER).

66

Henderson, E. (1979) 'The concept of school-focused in service education and training', *British Journal of Teacher Education*, **51**(1), pp.17-25.

Holly, P. (1986) *The Teachers' GUIDE* (Cambridge: Cambridge Institute of Education).

Holt, L. and Johnston, M. (1989) 'Graduate education and teachers' understandings: a collaborative case study of change', *Teaching and Teacher Education*, **5**(2) pp.81-92.

James, M. and Ebbutt, D. (1981) Problems and Potential, in Nixon, J. (Ed.) *A Teachers guide to Action Research: evaluation, enquiry and development in the classroom* (London: Grant McIntyre).

Jones, K., O'Sullivan, F. and Reid, K. (1987) 'The challenge of the new INSET', *Educational Review*, **39**(3), pp.191-202.

Lewis, I. (1988) Learning together: issues arising from outstation MA course experience, in Nias, J. and Groundwater-Smith, S. (Eds.) *The Enquiring Teacher: supporting and sustaining teacher research* (Lewes: Falmer Press).

National Commission on Education (1993) *Learning to Succeed: a radical look at education today and a strategy for the future* (London: Heinemann).

Nixon, J. (1989) *School-Focused In-Service Education: An Approach to Staff Development* (Basingstoke: Macmillan Education).

Marton, F. (1985) Describing and Improving Learning, in Schmeck, R.R. (Ed.) *Learning Strategies and Learning Styles* (New York: Plenum).

OFSTED (1993) *The Management and Provision of In service Training funded by the Grant for Education Support and Training (GEST)* (London: HMSO).

Rumble, N. (1981) Whole school strategies, in Nixon, J. (Ed.) *A Teachers Guide to Action Research: evaluation, enquiry and development in the classroom* (London: Grant McIntyre).

Schon, D. (1983) *The Reflective Practitioner: how professionals think in action* (New York: Basic Books).

Triggs, E. and Francis, H. (1990) *The Value of Long (Award-bearing) Courses for Serving Teachers* (London: Institute of Education).

UCET (1993a) *Minutes of the Executive Committee*, 24 June (London: UCET).

UCET (1993b) *Annual Report*, No. 25, Summer (Bristol: GPS Publishers Ltd).

Vulliamy, G. and Webb, R. (1991) 'Teacher research and educational change: an empirical study', *British Educational Research Journal*, **17**(3), pp.219-236.

Walker, R. (1985) *Doing Research: a handbook for teachers* (London: Methuen).

Williams, M. (1991) *In-Service Education and Training* (London: Cassell).

CHAPTER 5

LINKING INDIVIDUAL AND INSTITUTIONAL DEVELOPMENT FOR SPECIAL EDUCATIONAL NEEDS

Martyn Rouse

Introduction

This chapter considers some of the lessons that have been learned from a series of staff development initiatives jointly carried out over a seven year period between a number of local education authorities (LEAs) and the University of Cambridge Institute of Education. In each case, the aim of the initiative was to develop whole school responses to meeting special needs in primary schools (SNIPS) through a process that links individual learning for teachers with the institutional development of their schools. Funding initially came from a series of government grants earmarked to help with the implementation of the 1981 Education Act (Special Educational Needs). This funding led to the establishment of in-service training courses for teachers throughout England and Wales that were designed to help with the development of whole school approaches to special educational needs in the ordinary school (SENIOS). A large number of these courses flourished and as early as 1984, Moses, Hegarty and Jowett (1987) were able to study 25 of them. The extent to which they made a difference in schools however, was unpredictable. Norwich and Cowne (1985) and Hegarty and Moses (1988) revealed a number of shortcomings in SENIOS courses. In particular these weaknesses were caused by:

- inadequate preparation and negotiation in schools;
- no expectation of commitment and involvement by the headteacher and colleagues of the course member;
- the learning often being confined to the teacher who did the course;
- the lack of impact on policies and practice in the rest of the school;
- the absence of systems of 'aftercare' and support to sustain any changes in attitudes and behaviour that might have occurred;
- many of the courses taking little account of local or LEA policies and guidelines.

In addition to these concerns, there were major changes to the funding arrangements for in-service education for teachers (INSET) which brought about a radical reappraisal of the relationship between schools, LEAs and higher education. The needs of individual teachers, their schools and LEAs were largely ignored as the government increasingly took control of the INSET agenda and budget through the training grants scheme and used it to help with the implementation of policies and practice related to the 1988 Education Reform Act.

Although the SNIPS initiatives started before many of the 1988 reforms began to have an impact, the majority took place during a time of unprecedented change for schools in England and Wales. Many of these changes were not welcomed by teachers because they were perceived as being imposed by an unsympathetic government that did not understand the complexity of schools or the nature of children's learning.

Although the turmoil created by the national reforms did not provide the ideal circumstance in which to encourage initiatives designed to improve the educational experiences for children with learning difficulties, significant developments did occur in many schools as a result of the SNIPS projects. This chapter will consider the circumstances under which progress was made, as well as describe some of the barriers that seem to prevent teachers from learning and inhibit their schools from developing. Consideration will also be given to the complex task of evaluating the impact of such staff development initiatives.

Recent trends in staff development for special educational needs

It is more than fifteen years since the publication of the Warnock Report (DES, 1978) on special educational needs, a time during which there has been considerable progress in thinking about the reasons why some children find it difficult to learn in school. In the past it was assumed that special needs existed within the child as a result of there being something wrong with the child or his or her family. When such difficulties had been labelled and categorised the child would then be taken to a different place where he or she would receive a more appropriate education delivered by experts. These assumptions and approaches led to the development of segregated forms of provision such as remedial groups as well as special schools and units.

More recent thinking has acknowledged the ecological or interactive nature of difficulties. It is widely accepted that explanations for school failure that are based upon the supposed deficits of children are inadequate. Children fail in school for all kinds of reasons. They have needs which demand a radical reappraisal of a number of issues such as the appropriateness of the curriculum, assessment, classroom organisation and management, school ethos, relationships and how students feel about themselves as learners. Clearly, it is not possible to address these issues through traditional in-service training courses that emphasise a narrow range of skills and knowledge thought to be useful when dealing with special children and their deficits.

The notion that children with learning difficulties should be taught by special needs teachers with special training and unique responsibility has been challenged by many. Ramasut (1989), Ainscow (1991), and Dyson and Gains (1992) all argue that the development of whole school approaches to special needs will only occur when all teachers accept the responsibility for all children in their classrooms. This view is based upon the realisation that learning difficulties are interactive in nature and can only be understood in the context in which they occur. Indeed it has been argued that schools can actually create special needs (Skrtic, 1991). If this argument is accepted, then it follows that any training that is provided to improve the situation should address institutional needs as well as giving individual teachers new skills and knowledge. Therefore, the agenda for such teacher education should not only include a special needs component, but also a substantial element relating to school effectiveness, school improvement and the management of change. The need to include such elements within the initiative was even more imperative given that some children who would previously have been placed in special schools are being educated in mainstream schools which took part in the initiative.

It would be easy to underestimate the difficulty in achieving such fundamental changes in the thinking of teachers and the structure of schooling. For decades the messages about children who have difficulties in learning have reinforced many teachers' views that these problems are not their responsibility. Such traditional beliefs are deeply rooted and widely held. The existence of segregated forms of special provision, local authority support services and, indeed, courses about special educational needs, all remind teachers that a particular kind of expertise is required to educate children who have difficulties. To ignore the received wisdom of many years would guarantee the rejection of new messages and insights.

The SNIPS initiatives

Whilst acknowledging and accepting the different starting point for each school and course participant, the content and style of the SNIPS initiative had to reflect the developments in thinking about special needs if it were to have an impact on promoting whole school responses. In addition, widely reported in the literature (for example, Fullan, 1982; Loucks-Horsley *et al.*, 1987; Joyce and Showers, 1988; Hopkins, 1989), is a growing body of evidence describing the nature of effective staff development. A new form of training was required in response to these influences. It was thought necessary to move from a narrow to a broad curriculum perspective that considers not just issues based upon the deficits of children's functioning but incorporates newer thinking relating to curriculum entitlement. New approaches to assessment had to be considered which not only utilise techniques designed to rank children, but also provide teachers with evidence of strengths and weaknesses for diagnostic purposes.

Course members were involved as active participants in the process and together with their headteachers they negotiated course content. Participants were expected to carry out a series of practical tasks in their own classrooms and to report back to the rest of the group on their findings. The aim of the initiative was, therefore, to produce reflective practitioners capable of collaborating with colleagues on the task of school improvement, rather than 'trained up' experts who have unique responsibility within their schools for meeting special needs. These changes in emphasis are illustrated in the table below:

Perspectives on INSET for special educational needs

Traditional	New
disability and deficit perspective	educational perspective
narrow curriculum focus (basics)	wide curriculum perspective (entitlement)
identification	observation, assessment and recording progress
development for individual teachers	development for individuals *and* their schools
passive receivers	active participants
content prescribed	content negotiated
'training up' experts	developing staff collaboration and reflective practitioners

The principles

Each of the initiatives was based upon a series of principles that broadly reflect the changing concepts of special educational needs and emerging styles of staff development that are considered to be most effective in enabling teachers to learn about how they might meet these needs. These principles are listed below.

1. The LEA has a vital role to play in providing local knowledge and support before, during and after the course.
2. Negotiating priorities for and with schools.
3. Ownership of the development to be stressed at all stages.
4. Course aims, ethos and ways of working should reflect current thinking and practice on special needs, and should incorporate and model what is known about effective staff development.
5. The course structure should stress active participation, problem solving, collaboration and support for colleagues.
6. Participants should be encouraged to involve all colleagues in their workplace to encourage a whole school approach.
7. Support during the writing process as many participants express anxiety about sustained writing for the first time since their initial teacher training.
8. Long-term review and support. INSET without aftercare is very vulnerable, so attempts to build in long-term support are central to the design of the initiative.

Phasing

There are three distinct phases to the initiative that attempt to incorporate the principles outlined above.

Phase 1. The preparatory phase during which schools are invited by the LEA to review their existing policies and practice for meeting special educational needs with a view to agreeing on an area for development. In recent years schools would be expected to link this directly to their school development plan. In many schools this initiative has become the means by which these plans have been realised.

In order to explain to schools the aims of the initiative and the nature and purpose of the policy review, headteachers together with interested members of their staff are invited to a local meeting that is addressed by the co-ordinating tutor and representatives of the LEA. This forum provides course organisers with the opportunity to stress that this initiative is not merely a course for an individual to attend but is designed to enable school development to occur. Indeed, it could be argued that it is the school that is joining the initiative and the headteacher and staffs select the most suitable colleague who acts as their delegate. Whilst many schools have selected their special needs co-ordinator to perform this function, other schools have chosen a different member of staff to represent them. It is essential that the course member should have sufficient status and credibility in the eyes of colleagues to carry out the role.

When schools have carried out their review, they are invited to make a submission outlining a proposed topic for development. An important aspect of this process could best be described as being contractual. The school is asked not only to make a commitment to work on an area of development, but also to describe how the school's representative will be supported throughout the taught part of the course and how dissemination and implementation of the project will be ensured. The submissions are reviewed by the course team and under certain circumstances modifications may be recommended. Not all applications to join the initiative are accepted, particularly when it is obvious that insufficient consultation has taken place between the staff, or when the proposed area for development is unrealistic or contrary to LEA policy on special needs.

During Phase 1, a day conference is arranged for course participants and their headteachers during which the course content is negotiated and participants are reminded about their commitment to supporting their delegate during and after the taught part of the course. Further examination of the area selected for development is encouraged at this stage.

Phase 2. This covers the taught part of the course. The pattern of attendance has varied between LEAs and is tailored to meet local needs. During this phase, participants are expected to develop, with their colleagues in school, a response to the project topic. This takes the form of action planning, meeting with and working alongside colleagues in school and regularly reporting back to the course with details of progress made and difficulties faced. At the end of this phase participants produce a written account of their project which also serves as a working document for colleagues in school.

Phase 3. The post-course phase during which LEAs provide support to course members and their schools. The extent to which LEAs have been able to sustain this support in the face of recent financial cuts and delegated budgets has varied from LEA to LEA. In the worst case, in which the LEA special needs support service has been cut from nine people to two, course members formed themselves into a group that meets regularly in their own time to help sustain each other and their school-based developments. A follow-up day conference is held after the taught part of the course. There are two aims for the day. One concerns accountability – how is the project going? What has been achieved? The other purpose is to provide participants with the opportunity to share successful strategies for overcoming barriers with each other.

The initiatives

The first of these initiatives was established in 1986 and since that time changes have been incorporated which reflect developments in thinking and lessons learned from working in this way. Other changes have been forced upon us by the tighter financial constraints of the 1990s.

Since its inception a total of eight different local authorities and nearly two hundred schools have been involved. A feature of each course has been the close co-operation of the local education authority with the Institute of Education. In most cases there has been an attempt to focus on schools coming from a small geographical area in order to provide local support networks during and after the course. Such clustering enables the time of local authority support staff to be used efficiently. The LEAs have also been able to provide local knowledge about schools and course members which enables the needs of participants and their schools to be more accurately assessed.

In each case, a course team consisting of LEA personnel and a co-ordinating tutor from the Institute is formed to plan, run and evaluate the initiative. The LEA personnel provide continuing support to participating schools whilst they are working on a substantial award-bearing INSET course under supervision. This enables them to consider and develop their own skills as providers of staff development. In recognition of their learning, the Institute's Certificate of Staff Development is available to those who wish to register and carry out self-evaluation of their contribution to the initiative.

Outcomes for participants

Although the focus of this initiative is on school development, it is important that course participants should also benefit personally. Huberman and Miles (1984), point out that motives such as professional development and career opportunities are as important as the content of innovation and its possibilities for helping students. With this in mind credits towards the Advanced Diploma in Educational Studies are awarded to those course members who wish to work towards further qualifications.

Evaluating the initiatives

Details of earlier evaluations of these initiatives which involved postal surveys and interviews are documented elsewhere by Balshaw (1990), Rouse and Balshaw (1991).

The evaluation of staff development programmes designed to bring about change in schools is acknowledged to be complex because of the large number of variables involved. These variables include, the teachers, their schools, the history of innovation within the school, the levels of support provided to the course member by the headteacher, the timing of the initiative, as well as the quality of the INSET. Robson (1993) provides some assistance in finding a way through this maze with his lucid account of research methods that are appropriate for such a task. Joyce and Showers (1988) point out that the variables are interlinked and need to be considered in this way when evaluating the outcomes of such initiatives. Evidence has been found (Balshaw, 1990) which indicates that change has occurred as a result of these initiatives. Briefly, it was found that there has been change:

for individual teachers in:
- their confidence and self-esteem
- their classroom skills
- their ability to work collaboratively with their colleagues
- their understanding of special needs as part of a wider equal opportunities debate

for schools in:
- improved INSET for special needs
- in classroom practice for some teachers
- the development of new attitudes, policies and ethos
- the deployment of support staff and special needs expertise

for pupils in:
- classroom groupings
- curriculum provision
- the location and type of support received.

There are four other issues which have arisen from the evaluation of these initiatives. The first concerns staff changes. Some schools report that personnel change, other than the course member, had a positive effect on the implementation of new ideas. This is particularly so when the teacher(s) who left held traditional views about special needs. Because these initiatives have taken place during a time of financial constraints for LEAs, the ability to provide and sustain local support has been severely constrained. Such difficulties seriously impair attempts to provide continued support to schools and has had a negative effect on the implementation of new policies and practice in schools. At the time of writing it seems increasingly unlikely that many LEAs will be capable of supporting these initiatives with advisory personnel in the way they have in the past.

The second point concerns the difficulty that many teachers have in identifying positive outcomes for pupils. They are not saying that there were no positive outcomes, but that it is difficult for them to be described. Such benefits for pupils were often explained as changes in teacher behaviour resulting from greater confidence or more collaboration. Organisational changes and curriculum developments were also likely to be suggested as bringing benefits for children. Rarely was there any direct evidence presented which indicated improved learning outcomes for children. The difficulty with identifying positive outcomes for pupils is not confined to this initiative. It is indicative of a much broader dilemma faced by those who attempt to measure and describe changes in school performance.

The third issue concerns the importance of the headteacher's active support for the initiative. Many teachers saw this as the most important factor influencing success. Although two schools were able to demonstrate significant developments in spite of their headteachers' indifference, it happened because a group of teachers within each school came together to form a 'critical mass', thus enabling the project development to take root. Elsewhere, without the headteacher's support, progress was slow, if not impossible, when compared to schools where the head provided personal, organisational and practical support.

The fourth point concerns the nature and focus of the school-based development projects. There is evidence to suggest that progress was more likely when the school selected a topic that had a clear curriculum focus leading to the development of new skills for teachers. When the project was linked to developmental work already identified as a priority by the school, then the chance of success was enhanced. This was particularly true when the projects also helped the school to make sense of some of the changes required by the Education Reform Act. Those schools that selected broader policy development projects often found it more difficult to make progress. In too many cases the course member was given the task of writing a policy document which was then filed away without it having any real impact upon the provision for pupils with special needs in the school.

A pervading theme that has emerged throughout the evaluation of these initiatives reveals that when staff development and institutional development are linked within a collaborative framework, new ways of working based on joint problem solving may occur in schools. This may play an important part in building capacity to cope with and make sense of externally imposed change. Barth's (1990) description of 'learning schools' seems appropriate in this context. We may have witnessed some schools developing the ability to solve problems as the teachers in those schools became more reflective practitioners (Schon, 1987) and increasingly were prepared to work collaboratively with their colleagues. The emergence of a school culture which encourages joint problem solving has been one of the successes of these initiatives.

Conclusion

The experience of most participants in this initiative, together with their colleagues back in school, seems to have been, in the main, positive. They seem to have experienced many of the attributes of effective teacher development programmes as reported in the literature. Loucks-Horsley and colleagues (1987) point out that staff development experiences should build upon collegiality, collaboration, discovery and solving real problems.

This positive staff development experience has facilitated the change process in many schools. Through involvement in the school-based projects ownership of the changes was ensured. Fullan (1991) stresses the importance of such involvement in managing the process of change.

The collaborative manner in which the initiative was organised and the way in which the teachers on the course were expected to work together and support each other, helped them to develop the skills for working in conjunction with their colleagues back in school. This seems to have instilled, through modelling, practice and feedback, a confidence which leads to competence. For too many years the 'special needs task' has led to a small number of teachers taking responsibility for meeting the learning needs of pupils who experience difficulty. Not only were the pupils segregated, but so were their teachers. These initiatives helped to break down the isolation caused by previous ways of working. By stressing collaboration and co-operation they have emphasised that learning is a social act and schools will be more effective in meeting a range of needs when responsibility is shared and teachers also see themselves as learners.

It is apparent that the growing literature on inclusive schools, for example Slee (1993) and Ainscow (1993), together with the evidence from the effective schools movement, for example, Mortimore *et al.* (1988), Murphy (1993) and Reynolds (1989), point to a new way of conceptualising the 'special needs task'. The schools which have taken part in this initiative have not only been engaged in improving provision for pupils with special educational needs. In those cases where success has been achieved, it has been brought about through a process which has linked school improvement, staff development and the philosophy that schools are for all pupils and are more likely to be successful for all when the learning needs of those who find learning most difficult are successfully met.

In conclusion, a set of conditions which seem to be necessary for the success of such initiatives is offered:

- initial school-based negotiation involving all staff to identify development needs;
- ensuring that the project is an integral part of the school development plan and is consistent with LEA policy on special needs;
- selecting projects which have a clear focus and will have benefits for pupils;
- active involvement by participants in the course;
- adequate time for the course and for project development;
- opportunities for participants to pursue their own profes-

sional development by acquiring additional qualifications;
* active involvement and support of the headteacher;
* a local network of colleagues working on similar developments;
* formative evaluation throughout the initiative;
* post course feedback by participants on progress of projects;
* formulating a contract between the individual, the school, the LEA and the higher education provider.

At the time of writing this chapter, great uncertainty surrounds the future funding arrangements for such initiatives. Increasingly staff development budgets are being delegated to schools and LEAs are losing the ability to take part in such collaborative ventures. The loss of these partnerships will only be minimised if schools have sufficient funds to enable substantial initiatives such as those described to continue. If we are forced into short-term, 'hit and run' INSET, then we are all likely to be losers. However, there is sufficient evidence to demonstrate that school improvement and teacher development can be successfully combined through such collaborative initiatives for the benefit of teachers, schools and especially those pupils who are most vulnerable in times of major changes and reforms.

Acknowledgement

I would like to thank Maggie Balshaw for the help and support I have received during the SNIPS initiatives and in the production of this chapter.

References

Ainscow, M. (Ed.) (1991) *Effective Schools for All* (London: Fulton).

Ainscow, M. (1993) *Towards effective schools for all – special educational needs policy:* Options Group Paper (Stafford: National Association for Special Needs).

Balshaw, M. (1990) *INSET and the Change Process in Schools,* unpublished MA assignment (Cambridge: Cambridge Institute of Education).

Barth, R.S. (1990) *Improving Schools from Within* (Oxford: Jossey-Bass).

Dyson, A. and Gains, C. (1992) *Rethinking Special Needs in Mainstream Schools: towards the year 2000* (London: Fulton).

Fullan, M. (1982) *The Meaning of Educational Change* (New York: Teachers' College Press).

Fullan, M. (1991) *The New Meaning of Educational Change* (London: Cassell).

Hegarty, S. and Moses, D. (1988) *Developing Expertise* (Windsor: NFER-Nelson).

Hopkins, D. (1989) *Education for School Development* (Milton Keynes: Open University Press).

Huberman, A. and Miles, M. (1984) *Innovation up Close* (New York: Plenum Press).

Joyce, B. and Showers, B. (1988) *Student Achievement through Staff Development* (New York: Longman).

Loucks-Horsley, S. *et al.* (1987) *Continuing to Learn* (Andover, MA: The Network Inc.).

Moore, J. (1993) How will the self-managing school manage?, in Dyson, A. and Gains, C. *Rethinking Special Needs in Mainstream Schools: towards the year 2000* (London: Fulton).

Mortimore, P. *et al.* (1988) *School Matters: the junior years* (Wells: Open Books).

Moses, D., Hegarty, S. and Jowett, S. (1987) 'Meeting special educational needs. Support for the ordinary school', *Educational Research*, **29**(2), pp.108-15.

Murphy, J. (1993) *Restructuring Schools* (London: Cassell).

Norwich, B. and Cowne, E. (1985) 'Training with a school focus', *British Journal of Special Education*, **12**(4), pp.167-70.

Ramasut, A. (Ed.) (1989) *Whole School Approaches to Special Needs: a practical guide for secondary school teachers* (London: Falmer Press).

Reynolds, D. (1989) Effective schooling for children with special educational needs: research and its implications, in Ramasut, A. (Ed.) *Whole School Approaches to Special Needs* (Lewes: Falmer Press).

Robson, C. (1993) *Real World Research* (Oxford: Blackwell).

Rouse, M. and Balshaw, M. (1991) Collaborative INSET and special educational needs, in Upton, G. (Ed.) *Staff Development for Special Educational Needs* (London: Fulton).

Schon, D.A. (1987) *Educating the Reflective Practitioner: towards a new design for teaching and learning in the professions* (London: Jossey-Bass).

Skrtic, T. (1991) Students with special needs: artifacts of the traditional curriculum, in Ainscow, M. (Ed.) *Effective Schools for All* (London: Fulton).

Slee, R. (Ed.) (1993) *Is There a Desk with my Name on It? The Politics of Integration* (London: Falmer Press).

Warnock Report (1978) *Special Educational Needs: Report of the Committee of Enquiry into the Education of Handicapped Children and Young People* (London: HMSO).

CHAPTER 6

DEVELOPING REFLECTIVE PRACTITIONERS IN SPECIAL SCHOOLS

Judy Sebba

Introduction

Staff development, as Fullan (1992) has suggested, has a history of doing things to teachers rather than with them yet the term 'staff development' implies 'growth' or 'improvement' rather than a process by which an external view of 'good practice' is imposed on the teacher which might more accurately be described as 'staff training'. Recently, the need to assimilate numerous, externally imposed, legislative changes while continuing to develop as a classroom teacher, has sharpened the distinction between training and development.

This chapter adopts the term 'reflective practitioners' to describe teachers who develop through analysing their practice in order to make better sense of the teaching and learning that takes place in their classrooms. Grimmett (1989) in analysing Schon's (1983) view of the reflective practitioner within an educational context, suggests that the reflective practitioner extracts meanings and understandings as they teach and as they examine others' teaching. Hence, developing reflective practitioners involves a process of classroom evaluation in which information is collected about how pupils respond to the curriculum as it is enacted (Ainscow, 1992). The role of staff development becomes one of enabling teachers to establish this as a continual process. The chapter begins with a justification for adopting an approach to staff development which focusses on 'developing reflective practitioners'. Examples of attempts over the past three years to do this in special school contexts are described and used to illustrate some of the tensions that arise in adopting this approach.

The issues discussed in this chapter are not specific to special schools. However, the context of special schools and in particular, the historical development of the curriculum in these schools, leads to different priorities for staff development. Attempts by LEAs to support national reforms through staff development have led to special school staff attending training events alongside representatives from mainstream schools. These experiences may have been unsatisfactory with the staff finding it difficult to extract any relevance for their own setting.

In the past, lack of appropriate curricular materials in the form of published schemes led to a strong commitment to curricular development in many special schools, some of whom clustered in order to pool their resources for this work. The introduction of the National Curriculum and its assessment has instigated this process once again, with special schools clustering to develop approaches to implementation. In some cases (e.g. East Sussex County Council 1990; Humberside County Council 1992) staff training budgets have been allocated to support these groups in their development work.

Recently, the funding for staff development has been delegated to all schools and special schools share with their primary colleagues the problem of how to allocate limited resources when the total available is, in most cases, insufficient to sustain attendance at award-bearing courses. As yet, specific allocations still exist within GEST for special educational needs alongside a small number of other areas of staff development, some of which are also targeted at special school teachers. However, the funding earmarked for specific groups changes annually, limiting the scope for long-term planning. The demise of staff development programmes provided by the local education authority has hit special schools badly since the few advisory staff who might have had more specialised support to offer have been redirected into school inspection services.

For reasons beyond the scope of this chapter, special schools have found themselves increasingly recruiting staff with mainstream teaching qualifications and experience. Planning for staff development must therefore address issues arising from recent legislation alongside an ongoing programme of developing basic teaching skills relevant to the context. In special schools, a rolling programme of development addressing physiotherapy, feeding, use of alternative forms of communication (such as signing, symbols and Braille), counselling skills and behaviour management will need to be provided.

Hence, while the issues which are involved in encouraging reflective practitioners may be similar across different contexts, there are demands on staff development in special schools which will influence the overall plan adopted.

Justification for developing reflective practitioners

Staff development is seen as a key to achieving changes in practice. However, from the reviews of the literature (e.g. Fullan, 1993; Showers *et al.*, 1987) it is evident that the relationship between development and practice is a complex one. Many factors influence the effects of staff development on practice including the characteristics of the teachers involved, school culture and the model of development adopted. Since most staff development is inadequately evaluated, the information available is limited.

Reviews of the research on the effectiveness of staff development are provided in greater detail elsewhere (e.g. Robson and Sebba, 1991). To summarise the main findings of relevance in adopting a 'reflective practitioner' approach, the initial enthusiasm of the teacher appears to be unrelated to subsequent learning (Showers *et al.*, 1987) and it is possible that an optimal level of challenge to current practice is needed. Bradley (1991) suggests:

> To have the best chance of success, it seems that INSET experiences should take participants beyond their present experiences, but not too far, and should challenge their present understanding, but not too stridently.

In addition to individual characteristics, there are features of the school associated with more effective staff development such as support from the management (Robson *et al.*, 1988), the quality of staff relationships (e.g. Evans and Hopkins, 1988) and whether the institution is currently experiencing 'innovation overload' (Fullan *et al.*, 1990). The degree to which job demands are consistent with or complement the goals of staff development is clearly an issue which schools have attempted to address through linking a staff

84

development programme to their school development plan. This leads to a crucial balance in facilitating staff development, that of:

> ... how well the school balances the needs of individual staff with whole-school development needs ... (OFSTED, 1993).

Models of staff development which plan to address this balance are likely to be more effective.

Staff development which seeks to establish negotiated objectives between those involved is more likely to lead to change since as Fullan (1992) reminds us, sustained change in curriculum and instruction depends heavily on a shared understanding about the nature of innovation and what it can accomplish. Other reviews have described in more detail the model promoted by Showers *et al.* (1987) involving a combination of theory-demonstration-practice-feedback, which is regarded as vital to ensuring the transfer of skills into the classroom. Peer coaching, in which two people observe one another's practice, is considered by Showers *et al.* to be particularly effective even when discussion between those involved is limited or absent. What clearly emerges from a review of the institutional factors is that staff development must be as close to the 'real life' situation as possible in order to maximise effectiveness.

Approaching staff development by facilitating reflective practice incorporates some of the findings regarding the most effective features of staff development. It involves teachers selecting the focus which in the light of pressures upon them is likely to involve consideration of institutional and statutory requirements. It cannot ignore contextual factors since it takes place in the classroom. The continual process of evaluation, analysis, planning, teaching and re-evaluation enables the areas to be addressed to emerge from an analysis of current learning and changes to be implemented to lead to further learning and development on the part of the teacher. The teacher as learner is therefore assimilating new practices which can be selected and modified again as appropriate.

The 'reflective practitioner' approach is an individualised activity and need not necessarily involve peer coaching. However, emerging from the examples described in this chapter are conditions which are needed for this process to occur including the identification of staff development needs, recognition of the individual's current expertise and experience, acknowledgement of the culture of the school and the provision of a flexible range of approaches to support. If these conditions are to be met, teachers cannot sustain their development as reflective practitioners in isolation. The examples of staff development described below incorporate different types of external support from consultancy provided by the Institute of Education. All the examples focussed on aspects of curricular development.

Example 1: Consultancy across an LEA's special schools

Over a period of six months in 1990 some colleagues and I worked as 'consultants' to one LEA with six special schools on curricular development. The ten day programme began with a day for the headteachers which included an activity on defining effective practice. The programme for the other nine days was negotiated with them to secure their commitment to it. We spent five days with small groups of teachers from all six schools on various National Curriculum subjects and cross-curricular approaches. Four of these days we spent working with the curriculum co-ordinators and one with the science co-ordinators. The LEA had previously funded some curriculum development work in science and our contribution was to assist them in formative evaluation of these materials.

One further day comprised a training day for all the staff of the six schools focussing on 'Integrated Schemes of Work' (see Byers, 1992, for a full account of this approach). The group numbered 140 and included teachers and assistants, some of whom had received no training on National Curriculum at that stage. The evaluation involved feedback through the curriculum co-ordinators.

Two days were spent working alongside staff in one of the schools focussing on recording progress. The schools were invited to suggest how the two days in their school could be used and the LEA selected the school on the basis of these proposals. Only three of the schools bid for this time. The school identified had a strong tradition of behavioural teaching approaches encompassing a detailed, paper-intensive recording system. They wanted to review this and to introduce recording of progress within group work in the light of the introduction of the National Curriculum. I worked alongside staff in the classroom observing and recording. Discussion with individual members of staff and at a full staff meeting focussed on the observations made, records completed and possible future developments.

I met with the headteachers for a final day in which we discussed school development planning and the link with staff development. We reviewed the work that had taken place over the nine days and shared evaluations we had received which included comments, work which had developed subsequently and suggestions for future input. The evidence suggested that the training day had been of limited use because of the varied needs of those who attended and that greatest development had occurred in the school in which we had worked alongside staff in the classroom.

It would be dangerous to assume that the staff development approach adopted was responsible for the outcomes reported. The literature on change would suggest that the school who reported the developments may have already been a 'moving' school by the definition provided by Rosenholtz (1991). Other factors such as the fact that the objectives had been identified by the staff and that the development was fully supported by the management may have been equally important. In contrast, the differing needs of the large number of staff who attended the training day could not have been met.

Example 2: Supporting staff in implementing the National Curriculum

During 1991, the National Curriculum Development Team (Severe Learning Difficulties) was set up by seven LEAs and the Spastics Society. The team consisted of 10 teachers whose role was to promote effective practice in the schools in one region, within the framework of the National Curriculum. Subsequently, the National Curriculum Council funded us to develop curriculum guidance and INSET resources for the National Curriculum (NCC, 1992). The approach taken to the development work in schools was based on our understanding of effective staff development and involved peer coaching between school staff and team members.

Each LEA invited schools in their area to approach us (in some cases via the LEA) with a suggestion of how they might use our support in school for a two week period. Three or four team members met with the staff of a school that had requested the team's involvement. Discussion between the team and staff led to the identification of one or two issues from the action plan in the school development plan. The team members then spent one day observing in the school focussing on the areas identified in order to acclimatise to the school and enable staff and pupils to meet them. Two weeks were then spent in school during which we worked alongside staff, planning sessions together, auditing the curricular coverage, considering ways of broadening current activities and varying teaching strategies to increase access to the curriculum for all pupils. The nature of the involvement varied according to the areas identified by staff as the focus for the development. During the two week period, staff meetings were attended by the team and, in most cases, staff development sessions were provided by team members.

At the end of the two weeks team members met with the staff to get initial reactions to the work undertaken. A draft report on the work was prepared by the team, sent to the staff for comment and fully discussed at a staff meeting which the team attended. Changes and corrections were made as a result of the agreements reached at the meeting and, with the school's agreement, a copy was then sent to the LEA. Where specific subject resourcing or staff development was proposed, the relevant advisory staff in the LEA were sent a copy.

Evaluation of the work of the team involved completion of evaluation sheets by school staff, discussion with staff and the collection of examples of teaching plans, recording sheets or any other evidence of developments. The feedback received through these means suggests most, but not all, schools made significant progress. Many had chosen to focus on a National Curriculum subject or on planning and recording which provided clear and practical areas of work. Particular features of the work of the team which were seen as contributing to this process included addressing priorities identified by the school, working alongside staff in context, discussion between staff and team members and review and reflection of developments as and when they occurred.

There is no doubt that the model adopted by the team exemplified some of the features of effective staff development arising from the research reviewed earlier. However, as a model of ongoing practice it may be considered too expensive. Nevertheless, the experience from other examples described in this chapter suggests that some schools might benefit more from this type of consultancy than from conventional training days. Initially in each school, both school staff and team members experienced high levels of stress as each felt judged by the other. This tended to ease as they settled into a pattern of working together and team members demonstrated that their form of support was relatively non-judgemental.

Example 3: A Certificate of Further Professional Study in managing the National Curriculum

During 1990-92 we ran two courses each involving 30 hours of taught sessions and substantial school-based work with support. It was attended by pairs of teachers, one of whom was the headteacher or deputy, from the 10 special schools of one LEA. In addition, three individual teachers attended from specialist units that were too small to release two members of staff. At an initial two-day residential conference some general input on National Curriculum issues was provided and each pair was asked to identify an area of development from their school development plan to focus upon for the rest of the course. Five tutors assigned themselves to the pairs to provide support during initial development work at the conference and for follow-up support in school.

Each pair prepared an action plan describing their current priority for development, proposed action, resources required, responsibilities and timescale. The supporters were known as 'buddies' and provided assistance in clarifying the plan, locating resources and identifying possible constraints to development. When the pair returned to school their buddy provided about 12 hours support arranged over a series of visits. Where schools were addressing similar issues these meetings sometimes involved more than one school.

The issues addressed by the schools reflected a broad range of priorities including auditing, assessment, record-keeping, specific subjects (science, history and geography), mainstream links, topic work and evaluating change. Support from buddies included reviewing developments, reading and commenting on policies or schemes of work, working alongside teachers in the classroom, providing INSET for the whole staff or attending staff meetings to discuss the priority area. At the end of the course, a dissemination meeting was held at which the participants from each school gave a brief report of their work. Written summaries of these reports were presented to governors and the full reports with any examples of work or documents were edited into a course digest which was then circulated to all the schools and the LEA.

The participants completed course evaluation sheets, evaluated their development work at the dissemination meeting and provided examples of the work completed. They also produced extensive reports for the course digests. Most of the targets set in the action plans were met and the quality of the reports and examples of work were of a very high standard. Participants reported that the aspects of the course contributing most to successful development were the commitment to an action plan supported by the management and support from the buddy for development work. Moreover, the requirements to report back to other participants, contribute to the course digest and report to governors provided the impetus to keep on task.

Example 4: Teachers swapping schools as part of an Advanced Diploma

In 1991, we began a two year, part-time, advanced diploma programme for ten teachers from special schools in one LEA. As part of this programme, the teachers undertook two placements, one for four weeks and one for three weeks in another school in order to broaden their experience. Sufficient cover was not provided for these placements so it was necessary for them to swap schools in order to complete the placement. Since they were all attending the course together they knew one another well prior to the first placement although they had no knowledge of one another's classes.

The nature of the placement varied from full-time class teaching to supporting students attending college. Support was provided within school through the appointment of 'teacher-tutors' whose role was to liaise with the staff and the management about any matters relating to the work being undertaken. Additional support was given by the tutor from the Institute who visited once a week and reviewed the placement work with the teacher. The focus of the placement was determined through discussion between the teacher on the course and the teacher-tutor and headteacher in the receiving school.

Initially, the headteachers from the schools expressed concern over the disruption the placements would cause and questioned the usefulness of the process. However, many exciting projects were undertaken during these placements including the production of a newsletter by the pupils using a desk top publishing system, learning French – which had not previously been on offer –

and gardening work. Other teachers in some of these schools suggested that projects begun by the person on placement subsequently became incorporated into the school's own developments or had provided new ideas and challenges to be considered by the staff in the future. The teachers undertaking the placements had also expressed concern prior to starting the placements but found the challenge of teaching a new class in a different school gave them a fresh perspective on their own class.

Implications for the development of reflective practitioners

These examples outline a range of ways in which staff development in special schools has taken place. Their evaluations are not extensive enough to attribute the school developments that occurred directly to the staff development initiatives. However, it is clear that they share the features of effective staff development with which this chapter began.

Identifying staff development needs

All the examples described enabled the school staff to determine the needs that should be addressed. In some cases these were negotiated with outside agencies or the LEA, in others they were determined solely by the school. It is possible for a school to fail to recognise its own needs through being too insular. This may occur more frequently than in the past as a result of delegated staff development budgets that have led to increasing in-house staff development but may be counteracted by the process of inspection which will involve an external team auditing the priorities. Conversely, less externally imposed staff development may provide greater opportunities for schools to address their own needs but ironically make it more difficult for them to identify what these needs might be.

Recognising current expertise and experience

All the examples valued the expertise and experience of the teachers involved. Teachers were expected to identify their individual needs while recognising the needs of the institution. They were encouraged to detect strengths and weaknesses in current practice by analysing pupil responses. Low morale was challenged by the staff developer highlighting aspects of effective practice which had previously remained unacknowledged. Hence, teachers did not feel de-skilled. This would appear to be a prerequisite for developing a reflective practitioner approach which might otherwise encourage further self-deprecation.

Recognising the culture of the school

In the examples given, schools were encouraged to develop approaches largely consistent with their traditions and philosophies, rather than adopt an approach externally presented as applicable to all schools. Even when the development related to recent reforms seen as being externally imposed, the staff determined an agenda which involved incorporating some of these demands into practice within the current philosophy and aims of the school. Since the culture of the school is such an influential factor in staff development, it is important to utilise this systematically at the planning stage. The examples described suggest that in order to support teachers in the process of becoming more reflective we must assist them to identify current practices and issues, including those relating to the culture of the school. Then practice can be moved forward from that point.

Providing a flexible range of approaches to support

In the examples described, the 'staff developers' (consultant, team member, buddy or tutor) were required to adapt their approach to meet the circumstances, usually with no prior warning or preparation time. This is far removed from the traditional role of staff trainer which involved giving a prepared 'speech' to a group of teachers some of whom needed a different content, some of whom required a different pace of delivery and all of whom had problems relating it to their classroom. In order to encourage teachers to observe and analyse their own practice, the staff developers may find themselves observing and recording pupil responses, analysing assessment or recording sheets, using the video camera or tape recorder, auditing the curriculum or resources, team teaching or teaching the class while the teacher observes the pupils. Interviewing skills are central to the role, since discussion of classroom practice with the teacher involves a delicate balance between listening skills and asking the right questions. Identifying which of these approaches will be required prior to arriving at the school is rarely possible, making flexibility essential.

Conclusion

This chapter describes examples of staff development activities in special schools that have attempted to develop reflective practice. The justification for this approach came from what is known about the impact of staff development upon practice. I have suggested that the examples described share certain features which appear, from the limited evaluations, to have contributed to changes in practice. These include encouraging schools to identify their needs but refining or modifying these through negotiation, recognising current expertise and experience, acknowledging the culture of the school and providing a flexible range of approaches to support. These processes are not without their tensions. In order to establish needs we have assumed a balance between institutional and individual needs to be appropriate. However, the institution is constituted of many and varied vested interests. For example, staff development needs as perceived by the governors may not match the perceptions of the senior management.

Teachers who are reflective practitioners will have access to information on classroom practice and analysis of pupil responses that can inform the school development planning process through which staff development priorities can be identified. The development of reflective practitioners often involves individual teachers actively researching their classroom practice but collaboration between teachers or between teacher and staff developer is absent from this model. To remedy this, the examples described incorporated collaborative approaches such as peer coaching in order to provide the benefits of collaboration and reduce teacher isolation. In the long term, insularity is replaced by collaboration through teachers supporting each other. However, particularly in smaller schools or where there are few staff changes, external support and development may be critical in reducing insularity. Hence, staff developers will need to reconsider the range of approaches to support that they can offer and be more flexible than was demanded by traditional methods of training. Collaborative approaches linked to reflective practice appear to offer a very effective combination in bringing about what Rosenholtz (1991) describes as:

A different and much more exalted conception of teaching, a conception in which hope replaces despair, which might begin with the core idea that professionalism is the product, not the enemy, of schools as institutions.

References

Ainscow, M. (1992) Becoming a reflective teacher, in Booth, T., Swann, W., Masterton, M. and Potts, P. (Eds.) *Learning for All 1: Curricular for Diversity in Education* (London: Routledge).

Bradley, H. (1991) *Staff Development* (London: Falmer Press).

Byers, R. (1992) Topics: From myths to objectives, in Bovair, K., Carpenter, B. and Upton, G. (Eds.) *Special Curricula Needs* (London: Fulton).

East Sussex County Council (1990) *Does It Add Up? East Sussex SLD Schools National Curriculum Guidelines* (Lewes: East Sussex County Council).

Evans, M. and Hopkins, D. (1988) 'School climate and psychological state of the individual teacher as factors affecting the utilisation of educational ideas following an in-service course', *British Educational Research Journal*, **14**, pp.211-230.

Fullan, M., Bennett, B. and Rolheiser-Bennett, C. (1990) 'Linking classroom and school improvement', *Educational Leadership*, **47**, pp.13-19.

Fullan, M. (1992) *Successful School Improvement* (Buckingham: Open University Press).

Fullan, M. (1993) *The New Meaning of Educational Change*, Second edition (London: Cassell).

Grimmett, P. (1989) 'A commentary on Schon's view of reflection', *Journal of Curriculum and Supervision*, **5**, pp.19-28.

Humberside County Council (1992) *Access to History for Pupils with Special Educational Needs* (Hull: Humberside County Council).

National Curriculum Council (1992) *The National Curriculum and Pupils with Severe Learning Difficulties: Curriculum Guidance 9* (York: NCC).

OFSTED (1993) *The Handbook for the Inspection of Schools* (London: HMSO).

Robson, C., Sebba, J., Mittler, P. and Davies, G. (1988) *In-Service Training and Special Educational Needs: Running Short, School-Focused Courses* (Manchester: Manchester University Press).

Robson, C. and Sebba, J. (1991) Staff training and development, in Segal, S. and Varma, V. (Eds.) *Prospects for People with Learning Difficulties* (London: Fulton).

Rosenholtz, S. (1991) *Teachers' Workplace: The Social Organization of Schools* (New York: Teachers' College Press).

Schon, D.A. (1983) *The Reflective Practitioner* (New York: Basic Books).

Showers, B., Joyce, B. and Bennett, B. (1987) 'Synthesis of research on staff development: A framework for future study and a state-of-the-art analysis', *Educational Leadership*, **45**, pp.77-87.

CHAPTER 7

BRIDGING THE GAP : USING THE SCHOOL-BASED PROJECT TO LINK AWARD-BEARING INSET TO SCHOOL DEVELOPMENT

Marion Dadds

Background

Several years ago a sense of professional discomfort overtook me. I had only a limited understanding of the effects of my students' INSET learning on their classroom practice or the life of their schools. Course evaluations offered some insight into ways in which teachers experienced their INSET course but this was not enough to understand the consequences for classrooms and schools.

Also, many teachers were keen to bridge the gap between their INSET learning and developments in their school; to make a contribution to their schools in return for their two year, part-time day release INSET advantages. Many were distressed when this, for whatever reason, did not seem possible. So, I needed to know how to help them to do it. But before I could help them, I needed to know what 'it' was, what it meant to bridge the gap between individual teacher development and the development of practice in school, what it looked like, felt like, how it worked, why it worked, or why it did not.

This discomfort started me on what seems to have become a life-long process of enquiry. The first phase of the research, which I began in 1985, quickly came to focus upon the Advanced Diploma INSET project or assignment – that part of the award-bearing course which most students pursue for the assessed part of their work. In those days we ran long, two year part-time courses and it was usual for students to undertake classroom or school related action research projects for their assessed assignments. The second phase took place over an eighteen month period between 1991 and 1993. By this time the 'market' had forced us as INSET providers into modularisation. Most Advanced Diploma courses had, there-fore, become modularised into sixty hour units. The projects I studied which are discussed later in this chapter emerged from two such courses.

The project assignments were as various as the nature of school-ing - gender policies; play provision; the reading curriculum; children with learning difficulties; approaches to assessment; the development of playground provision; developing mathematics and so on. These projects helped students to try to link their INSET studies to the development of their practice. My research has there-fore, focussed upon the ways in which they have fostered change in the INSET teachers' schools.

My own preferred research method in studying the nature and impact of these projects has been case study. By listening to stu-dents' stories of their projects, by trying to understand their experience of conducting them, by talking, where ethically appro-priate, with school colleagues (and course colleagues sometimes), by meeting pupils where possible, I have tried to derive multiple perspective interpretations and understandings. I have tried to reconstruct the conception, life and development of some INSET projects and I have sought tentative explanations for what I have found in these few cases. My research has been small-scale with no claim, yet, to any firm or grand generalisation. Through the exam-ination of cases, however, certain features have been seen to recur.

Vicki's case

The first phase of the research gave rise to an analysis of three cases. Ethical considerations allowed only one of these, Vicki's, to be committed to the written word (Dadds, 1991a). Vicki undertook three INSET research and development projects – a humanities policy; a study of integrating two children with special needs into her class; gender issues in her school. Vicki's case taught me a great deal about the human and institutional dimensions involved in bringing about change through the medium of the action research INSET project. Vicki taught me that more work was invested in the assessed course project than I had dreamt of; that the diligence and commitment which I had expected were exceeded many-fold; that researching and writing about the project for course assessment was but a beginning; that sharing and disseminating the project in school - the action part of the action research - was as mammoth a task as researching and writing had been and that this part of the adventure required many and different personal and interpersonal skills which the 'academic' part of the work did not. As I studied all three projects which Vicki submitted for assessment, I came to realise that each had a different impact on the school and that Vicki had employed judgement and wisdom in deciding whether, and how, to share her INSET projects with her colleagues. It was not always wise to share, but when she judged it appropriate to do so, much benefit was gained. It also seemed that much could have been lost by trying to share and disseminate at the wrong time and in the wrong way.

The practical success of her INSET projects in school was due, in good measure, to Vicki's personal, professional and historically rooted concerns and passions. She researched areas of her work to which she was deeply committed and about which she was curious. These personal qualities and resources fuelled the life of her projects. They also fuelled the school development process, since she was keen to see the world change for the better in her chosen areas of study.

Vicki's case also gave insight into the features of the school context which contributed to the successful bridging of the gap and that appeared to create a fruitful climate in which Vicki's professional passions and personal qualities could be used to advantage. There was positive support and encouragement from senior management; an 'INSET climate' in which the majority of colleagues were positive in their attitudes towards INSET and professional development; a climate of debate, discussion and exchange of ideas; organisational processes and structures that allowed external INSET to be shared and drawn upon for practical school purposes. Sharing and using staff INSET expertise was not left to chance. It was well organised. There was also open use of humour and celebration, qualities which seemed mysteriously linked to rapid change in a potentially debilitating political climate.

Vicki also taught me to think more carefully about the affective side of this work. I came to realise that a range of emotions was involved in studying and researching her projects; even more were generated in the business of sharing her project with colleagues as she organised and led a structured staff development day, an event that was designed to move her gender policy project into the minds, hearts and curriculum of the full staff group. Vicki's feelings were implicated in many ways, at many stages (Dadds, 1991b). Friendly professional support from certain colleagues helped her through these, such that negative emotion was never allowed to block the development of the project, nor her own consequential development as an agent of change. Indeed, her more positive passions and commitments were strong resources upon which she drew to drive her project forward at school level.

In the second phase of my research I decided to follow through the theme which Vicki's case had raised: that of the *personal experience* of conducting an INSET development project and of being a *potential agent of school change* in doing so. I wanted to think further about the range of demands which this placed on the INSET teachers; the qualities and understandings which managing school change through the medium of their INSET project demanded of them; the possible effects which their school context had on the development of the project.

Carol's case

This second phase has generated a case study of Carol who undertook a project on pupil profiling and pupil self-assessment which became a whole school project (Dadds, forthcoming). Carol's case reinforces much that was discovered with Vicki. Like Vicki, Carol was trusted, and regarded well, by her school colleagues. These blessings allowed her to drive the project gently but firmly forward when colleagues were feeling tired and overloaded. This was no mean feat in the more stressful national climate which had evolved since Vicki's case. Carol knew how to treat people well and understood, for example, the effect that good food and drink can have on a staff development day at the end of term. She knew that providing teacher relief time for the project was a way of publicly valuing the work; that giving regular and patient support for their questions and worries made all the difference to her colleagues, to their learning and their commitment to the project. She also seemed to understand what store people set by her unswerving public belief in the project (even though she had many private doubts and misgivings along the way). Like Vicki, Carol had the support and interest of the headteacher and the majority of her school colleagues. They provided the collective interest and motivation. Carol provided the leadership.

There were other similarities between the two cases. Like Vicki, Carol had used her time on the INSET course to enhance her own grasp of the substantive issues in her pupil profiling project. This learning brought her a new confidence. The confidence was a necessary foundation for her plans to develop the project at whole school level. This learning, and Carol's subsequent confidence, then became important resources from which school colleagues drew as they participated more fully in the whole school development. Carol drew upon her learning to create formal staff development meetings. She also drew upon it to help colleagues explore their own questions, issues and concerns about pupil profiling and pupil self-assessment.

Throughout, Carol encountered emotional ups, downs, difficulties, crises – her own and those of colleagues. All this needed handling well for the project to stay alive and to reach, ultimately, into children's experiences. She had to manage her own emotional life through these changes as well as those of colleagues, as the change impacted on them.

Carol's project also required time, patience and some faith. The eighteen months spanning this second stage of my research covered, what I came to see as, the preliminary but necessary stages of innovation. Time was needed for Carol's own substantive learning. Next a period was needed for discussion, debate, planning with the staff. Further time was then needed for preparation of materials. These processes took almost a year. In the next stage classroom practices were affected and the project began to touch children's lives. Eighteen months into the project children were able to comment upon the innovation. There were, thus, no slick, quick recipes for change here.

Colin and Sheila

This second stage of my research has also raised some less detailed but, nevertheless, telling short glimpses or cameos. These will now be shared and discussed more fully here, to complement these brief case study descriptions.

These cameos of Colin and Sheila illustrate two teachers' early experiences of their INSET projects. They are different and contrasting. They show that there is nothing standardised about the way projects start, nor the origins from which they grow. The two short cameos show the experience of initiation of a project in the INSET teachers' schools. They also show the effect of the external context and the role of the students' own developing understanding of the nature of change.

In Colin's story we see an INSET student who learnt about managing change through his first-hand experience, not through having been taught about change in the early stages of his INSET course (though that input helped in time). He learnt about managing change by initiating his INSET project in school, feeling the consequences and reflecting on what had happened.

Colin's experience of crossing the individual INSET bridge to collective school development was not a successful one. In contrast, we see Sheila starting her INSET development project with a clear advantage, with the backing of colleagues and headteacher. All seems set for success. Sheila works hard, has an impact. And then the men from the ministry arrive.

Colin's Project

Colin wanted to develop a helpful, formative, and feasible record-keeping system for the school, one that generated useful information that served teachers' purposes and enhanced children's learning. His commitment to the project was strong and was rooted in his professional history.

'Since I started teaching,' he explained to his course colleagues, 'I've had many (record-keeping) systems thrust upon me, mostly stupid, some quite good but very time-consuming, so that was something I felt I wanted to crack for myself.'

He had clear criteria that would, he felt, shape this improved system that he hoped to develop. The system had 'to be very comprehensive' and it had to inform teaching and learning. 'If it doesn't inform your teaching of the children, I don't think there's any point in doing it,' he said. It also had to go beyond the impressionistic and be 'as accurate as you can manage' whilst, at the same time, not be unnecessarily time-consuming. Feasibility was a high priority, 'an extremely manageable system that is not going to take hours and hours every day.' Feasibility also meant that it had to be possible to integrate assessment and recording procedures into daily classroom work, 'part of your everyday teaching, lesson plans...or whatever you have to do.' Thus, it would be 'formative' otherwise it would be 'a waste of time,' he believed.

With such clear criteria, such good intentions, and educational assessment high on the national political agenda one might suppose that Colin had chosen his project wisely. Time proved otherwise. What might, to some, have appeared to be a project with high development potential for his primary school colleagues, turned out to present Colin with early struggles and disappointments.

Colin would be certain to agree that his first step forward was not a successful one. 'I really haven't had a huge amount of backing from my staff,' he said, 'because it's an area they're not really interested in.'

In these early stages, his relatively undeveloped understanding of the complex forces that foster change was something of a handicap. A sound development project could not simply be generated from an idiosyncratic (Dadds, 1986) or individual interest with success following automatically, even though it may be driven by personal enthusiasm. For change to be effective and collaborative, others had to engage their own enthusiasms and motivations with the project, to feel some ownership of it. Colin had this lesson to learn and he learnt it the hard way. 'I initially went in without consulting and said, we're going to do this,' he admitted.

Not surprisingly, this 'fell on deaf ears because, in fact, they didn't want to do this.' Colin discovered that 'this was an absolute no-go area. They didn't want this at all, thank you very much.' There was, it seems, no room for the committed hero innovator here, far less a naive one.

Colin carried on despite this early discovery that colleagues did not share his commitment let alone his relish for the hard work that needed to be done. He planned a whole school enquiry on record-keeping and profiling through questionnaire and interview and, curiously, gained the co-operation of all his colleagues in this. He offered to scribe their responses to the questionnaire and this may have helped to capture their co-operation, taking some of the industry out of the enquiry for them.

During this enquiry stage, he made discoveries about colleagues' attitudes as well as their practices, attitudes which, in part may have explained some of the resistance to the intended heroic innovation. He found that 'there's a group of one or two people who won't do anything like pupil profiles'. Their resistance seemed strong, almost hostile. 'They'll avoid it until they're sacked or whatever, or they resign,' he felt. Yet this was in sharp contrast to a general belief ('all except one person') that a good record-keeping system would be ideal. The will to evolve one, however, seemed to be lacking, even though there was an almost universal disrespect for the school's current approach. 'They just looked at these tick lists that we have for these four years,' Colin added, 'and thought, like I do, that they're a waste of time.'

Perhaps the enormity of the task in evolving an alternative was too daunting for some. Perhaps the relative ineffectiveness of past and current practices was too deeply engrained to overcome the inertia needed to start a new major development. Perhaps the national political agenda at the time was too confusing and dispiriting.

Colin soldiered on. After his whole school enquiry, he discussed the next stage with his course tutor during a supervision. As a result, he suspended his whole school aspirations for a while. He elected instead to develop a more comprehensive but more effective record-keeping system for himself which he felt more firmly matched the criteria he had articulated earlier. The scope of the task was extensive and challenging, but Colin had to draw back into individualism from his collective aspirations. 'I've got a long way for myself,' he said, 'but it did not have much effect beyond that.'

Asked by Veronica, his course colleague, if he had 'something you can (now) present to the staff', he remained reticent. Although he felt that he was 'getting closer', more work needed doing. 'I haven't got to the stage yet where I'm happy with it,' he answered.

This may have been a strategy for avoiding another approach to his colleagues on a whole school basis. His earlier hero innovator experience had obviously taught him a lesson, and a new reserve. 'I don't really want to present it either,' he said. 'I don't want to say, right, this is my idea, go and try it.' This, he now knew from his abortive earlier whole school overtures 'doesn't work', not, anyway, with these colleagues in this school at this particular time. One could understand his caution.

But he clearly wanted to keep a whole school candle burning for his individualistic ideas. There were, he realised, other strategies for approaching change, and his belief in what he was doing kept him on the whole school development trail. By the end of his INSET course he was prepared to move into 'subversive' mode in order to try to promote his ideas and practices a little further.

'I'll do my usual subversive thing,' he said, which was to try to be seen successfully using these new record-keeping practices, to flaunt them, 'be blatant about it in the hope that someone would remark, "That's good" or whatever', he added. He had already 'sort of left (the materials) around', he said, in the hope that they might quietly arouse interest. He would make his work visible, without formally presenting it to school colleagues.

Course colleague Sheila encouraged him, feeding his subversive imagination. 'When you, for example, are discussing...writing a report (with your colleagues), you could say, "Well, actually I found it easier this time around because I had (these materials)".' Sheila's machiavellian appetite was whetted. 'It's possible isn't it,' she enthused, 'that somebody might say, well what did you actually do? What made it work?'

Colin seemed more than keenly interested in this potentially subversive course of action, if it would help the change and development process, especially as he saw himself as the sole shoulder behind this particular record-keeping wheel and therefore needed all the help and strategy he could get. Even the headteacher was 'very sort of non-committal', Colin explained. Like the staff, she recognised the validity of the project, 'that it's all very necessary,' Colin explained, but she was not choosing to put her influence behind it at present, 'wasn't going to push the staff along in any particular direction.'

The headteacher may, indeed, have been finding it difficult to decide on 'a particular direction', given the advice and information that was coming at schools from all quarters at that time. The LEA had 'just come out with their (record-keeping) form, for example,' said Colin. So too had the local headteachers, 'something with tiny, tiny print on the sheets,' said Sheila, 'which I actually have to put glasses on to read.' In addition, there were various changes afoot in the statutory orders for parts of the National Curriculum. These were making newly made record-keeping systems in many primary schools redundant. They were dispiriting many teachers in the process. Such conditions seemed hardly conducive for the headteacher to put the school into firm and confident gear on record-keeping at that particular point in the slippery and chaotic evolution of educational reform. So this left Colin very much on his own with his development mission. As a consequence, Colin seemed open to any good suggestions, even subversive ones, that might keep this little flame glowing for his project.

These rather abortive early moves of Colin seemed to fly in the face of the principles possibly governing initiation of change which tutors had tried to rehearse on Colin's INSET course. What the course does seem to have done, however, is provide Colin with a number of concepts and analytical tools for making retrospective sense of his first-hand experiences. Whilst unable to effect change in any significant way in these early stages, Colin became more sophisticated in his 'situational understanding' (Elliott, 1991) of the problem, seeking empirically-based explanations of the forces that moved against him.

When invited to articulate his learning as a result of his experience, he was able to give good account of the personal lessons he was drawing. First, he was fairly certain that whole school development had to mean just what it said. There had, as far as possible, to be whole staff commitment to the proposed development project, 'it has to be a total thing,' he was concluding. He had believed, at the beginning stages of this project, that he would be able to make a positive contribution in bringing people to that point of seeking totality. '(I) thought I could try and get them rolling a little bit,' he said. But his initial hopes of working towards totality, and his good, if innocent intents 'didn't really work at all,' as he acknowledged himself.

The principle of positive staff ownership had also become part of his evolving personal theory of change management. 'It can't be something that's foisted on you,' he believed, 'it has to come from them', not just 'something that you see needs to be done.' He realised that one could use negative ownership to advantage if necessary. 'If they realise it's been foisted upon them they have to do it, you (can) get the co-operation that way,' he said, but he was clearly not the one to do that, nor did he seem to have the inclination for that more authoritarian and unnegotiated approach. Some authority may, conceivably, have been helpful, he inferred. 'I suppose if I had more backing from the headteacher and deputy,' he said, 'I might have got through.'

The data do not tell us why the headteacher and deputy chose not to employ their support and authority. All Colin revealed, or perhaps knew, is that 'we were looking at other things at the same time as well.' He may, thus, have been trapped by institutional innovation overload which has been characteristic of most developing primary schools during the period of this research. Colin's project, his commitment and his enthusiasm may have been victims of those circumstances.

Colin had also reflected a little more about himself in his new role. He was giving thought to the relationship between the persona of the change agent and the nature of the colleague group. He was feeling that 'you can't force anything by personality, you have to go with the flow.' He believed that 'you can't force development'. There was here a glimmer of a 'catalysis theory' of change (Dadds, 1991a), a sense that interaction between people engaged in a change process will generate its own particular chemistry which will determine the pace and nature of the change.

His course colleagues Veronica and Sheila did not, however, seem completely satisfied with Colin's simple and relatively passive personal theory of innovation and change. They seemed irritated by the behaviour of the headteacher and deputy, for example. They felt that more forthright and public support from senior management might have breathed more institutional, whole school life into Colin's project. 'Sometimes you have to put things in front of people and say, look, this is really good, Colin has spent a lot of time on this, let's give this some positive input and see what we can do with it,' Veronica speculated. Leadership certainly had to be an influencing factor in the catalysis, and the chemistry could be changed through conscious will and effort, they inferred.

If the headteacher and deputy had fallen short in the eyes of Sheila and Veronica, Colin too came in for some firm, if gentle, criticism. They felt that he may have become a little too much of a wallflower after the abortive first heroic steps and that he might have made more progress had he marketed himself and his ideas a little more assertively in the later stages of his work. 'Perhaps Colin hasn't sold himself you see,' Sheila hypothesised. 'You haven't have you?' she added inquisitorily. 'I can see from your face that you haven't sold it to the head.'

Colin looked partially abject. Honesty overcame him. 'It's the subject I haven't sold, yes,' he said, in his defence.

We know that leadership styles and management structures can bring out the best in a shy but developing change agent (Dadds, 1991a). Conditions can be created consciously and deliberately that help latent skills and qualities to mature. In these conditions, the supported and encouraged development of the change agent can pay institutional dividends as his or her contribution is brought centre stage to fuel school developments.

There is also evidence that the regard accorded a change agent by colleagues is an important factor in his or her effectiveness (Dadds, 1991a). Colin's story offers no evidence on this and we do not know how he was perceived by those whose practices he was hoping to change. Perhaps there was some telling deficiency in trust or respect adding to the difficulties of innovation overload and lack of management support. Or perhaps he was, simply, a victim of his own initial lack of understanding of the difficult business of managing curriculum change, with no high status school colleague to support and encourage him, and to provide a platform for his voice (Dadds, 1991a). Yet in analysing his experience he had certainly developed his understanding in these matters.

There was, too, an obvious gap between the focus of Colin's interest in record-keeping and the other priorities upon which his colleagues were engaged. His dominant interest was not theirs, and he was unable in these early stages to draw them into his arena. In this, he was less lucky than others have been. Starting from personal, rather than shared or negotiated agenda, is not always doomed to failure. Some idiosyncratic and individualistic (Dadds, 1986) projects *do* 'catch on' with colleagues, despite problems of overload, but the institutional climate, attitudes and management practices have to be fertile for such a project's growth (Dadds, 1991a). Thus, Colin's work may conceivably have borne more early fruit at a different time, in a different place, with different people. As Fullan said, 'what works in one situation may, or may not work in another' (Fullan, 1991). And what doesn't work in one school may well work in another where people, attitudes, histories and management practices are different. In the institutional development game, the complex environment is all. Thus, Colin's situational understanding may have become more sophisticated as a result of analysing his experience. It had not however, been sufficiently well developed in the earliest stages to enable him to choose an appropriate focus for his project nor a suitable method of initiation. Nor, perhaps, had he chosen the appropriate historical moment.

Sheila's Project

Where Colin had put a first foot wrong in the endangered territory Sheila benefited from stepping straight on to fertile ground. From the outset it seemed obvious that Sheila's project was highly likely to have much wider influence in the school than Colin's. Sheila's challenge was, she explained, 'to write a behaviour policy for our school.' This was no idiosyncratic venture. It was a concern that the staff had identified, one that had been much discussed and one which had been on the development agenda for some time. It was a collaboratively felt need, one that was part of recent institutional history. 'I chose it because it was identified as a need by the rest of the staff,' she explained.

The project was initially conceived when the staff realised they had no guidelines or policy on behaviour in school to which they, or new colleagues, could turn for direction. Everyone had been trying to offer support to a struggling probationer last year who was experiencing discipline difficulties and this had caused them to realise that there were no formal systems for support, nor any agreed views on coping with difficult children, 'so that's where it started', Sheila confirmed.

There was a second major influence. The school was also undergoing a major cultural shift with a new headteacher whose leadership style and beliefs seemed radically different from those of her predecessor.

'Previously the atmosphere in the school had been rather authoritarian,' Sheila claimed, 'and (the new head) is a very non-authoritarian sort of person.' The new headteacher's philosophy was rooted in the concept and practice of caring. 'My headteacher is a lady who cares very deeply about children caring for themselves, caring for each other,' Sheila claimed.

Those two features, then, seemed to stimulate a desire to consider the general atmosphere and ethos of the school as well as the particular practices of which the atmosphere and ethos might be made; an opportunity to compare rhetoric and reality, ideals and practice.

If Colin's was a project not supported by the headteacher, Sheila's by contrast was a project that had the headteacher's full support. Indeed, there is a sense in which the project was used to support the headteacher and to serve her development purposes. It became an important vehicle for the changes in school practice and ethos which were motivated by the headteacher's beliefs.

The headteacher's influence upon Sheila's work became apparent, as the two of them worked in tandem. They started by looking at 'areas where there are obvious difficulties like dinnertimes and playtimes,' Sheila explained. As a result they realised that current practices did not seem conducive to cultivating the atmosphere of self-responsibility and caring in children to which they and colleagues aspired.

They identified a major lack of support for the dinnertime supervisors; they offered advice and implemented measures to give them greater control, guidance and responsibility. There was a shift towards a more consultative, collaborative and supportive way of working between staff and dinnertime supervisors.

'So we started with lunchtimes,' she explained. 'We thought we had a lot of problems where endlessly children were being brought in and (left) standing outside the head's room because they'd been naughty. So we involved the dinnerladies. First of all I sat at the meeting with the head and all the dinnerladies and we talked through with them what they thought the problems were. They obviously thought that the staff weren't supporting them, that they were out there in the lion's den for an hour every day and they just had to take all the abuse and the bad language and bad behaviour and there was nobody really listening to what they said...and we set up some sort of guidelines. So out of that came a sort of mealtime (document) – actually it's called Mealtime Supervisor Duty but it was done with them and it's a working document...they were happy with that, they're looking at it, they're working with it and we're going to come back and meet again.'

Then Sheila began to manage another major change with the full staff group, the development of 'this wonderful area...of log apparatus which the children go on a class at a time' and which is also used at playtime. Part of the explanation for aggressive playground behaviour was that the children 'were bored'. The log apparatus seems to have solved some of the problem. It has 'been very successful and (it) takes a whole class out of the playground situation.'

Then came further work with the staff, looking at 'ways of reducing friction of playtimes...because very often the confrontations that occurred at playtime spilled over into the classroom and (the children) would come in so wound up and (that would create) problems.'

The log apparatus initiative had helped. Other structured play opportunities were created, together with plans for a 'written up code of behaviour (it isn't typed up yet because we're still talking about it)'. Also systems were being evolved to provide better support and supervision for 'children who don't go out to play because they're ill'.

Developing the project with colleagues was not totally trouble-free for Sheila, even though she had ready co-operation from the majority. She, too, had to deal with resistance, though not on the same scale as Colin. One particular colleague, it appeared, took an habitual oppositional stance, which seemed characteristic of her normal response to change. She was a colleague 'who never goes along with anything anybody else does,' Sheila said, 'who automatically...says, I wouldn't do it like that'. The resistant colleague seemed to bear a personal grudge towards Sheila and 'certainly resented (her) appointment' though for what reason is unclear. In managing her project, it was clear that Sheila was taking account of this negative interpersonal agenda and was seeking ways of avoiding potentially unhelpful conflict with her colleague. 'I always try to get someone else to suggest something,' Sheila explained. 'She's much more likely to take it on board if it comes from someone else than if it comes from me,' she added. Over a period of time, communication and empathy between them improved but these initial hurdles and blockages had to be negotiated sensitively for that to happen.

Here, we see the need for the effective change agent to have her own theories of others' behaviour as part of her situational understanding. It is useful to understand how others operate, how they tick, how the change agent can work with, and around, their motivations. In general, however, the development of Sheila's project in these early stages seems to have been eased significantly by the willingness of colleagues, and by their general commitment to the direction of the change. But in meeting, and working with, this initial resistance, Sheila shared a common experience with Vicki (Dadds, 1991a), Carol (Dadds, forthcoming) and Colin.

But staff involvement alone was not enough and Sheila worked 'to try to get the children involved.' This she achieved in several ways. There was, for example, encouragement of good practical ideas for improving behaviour through 'a sort of campaign (in which) they've been writing up lists of things that they think will help'. There was a whole school approach to this through the highly visible medium of the school assembly in which children were made aware of, and invited to reflect upon, the bad experiences suffered by bullied and teased children.

These were early beginnings, as Sheila recognised, though there was evidence that some children were already assimilating the new practices and values of this changing culture. 'The children did seem to be becoming aware of guidelines,' Sheila explained, 'and when I said to them what would help in school to make this better, they said things like, Be kind, make friends.' She continued, 'They didn't say you have to stand outside the head's office if you're naughty. They actually were talking about positive things.'

Sheila was not complacent though, and she could see that this kind of change was neither consistent nor easy. It was subject to other influences which were, perhaps, too powerful to be within her, or her colleagues' total control. She admitted, honestly, 'I thought we were winning. We're getting towards the end of term. We've got children who are about to leave because they move on towards the end of...year four, and it's getting a bit dire again.'

One step forward, five back. Such is the fragile nature of much school development. Sheila may well have gained a little hope, in this early process of development slippage, at the thought that:

> ...whatever the circumstances of a school, the process of becoming whole and of developing a whole school curriculum is generally slow and halting, is sometimes subject to decay, yet may occasionally move forward at a surprisingly rapid rate. (Nias *et al.*, 1992)

This was not the only factor that slowed the development of the project which had, otherwise, made a constructive and successful start. There is evidence that external forces can stop an insider school development project in its tracks (Dadds, 1991a) and Sheila's was no exception, as an HMI inspection called a halt to her behaviour policy project. She admitted that 'everything's been delayed because of the HMI inspection.' And she did not seem happy nor relaxed about this. 'People weren't really prepared to think about anything else for about the last five or six weeks,' she grieved. 'Everything else went out of the window.'

This tension and conflict between internal growth and external accountability highlights something of a power struggle for the change agenda. We do not know what positive impact the inspection may have wrought on Sheila's school and it may well have been substantial in the longer term. We do know, however, that it caused stress and anxiety in the short-term and arrested sound developments of the behaviour policy over which the staff had gained a sense of positive ownership, control and commitment.

Nor does it seem that HMI's views about school policy development sat comfortably with those explored on Sheila's INSET course and which had been informing her and her colleagues as she developed her project. For example, the course had considered the role of whole staff consultation, participation and 'ownership' in the policy making and change process. Many course members had made brave attempts to foster these ideas in practice through their INSET projects with their school colleagues. Yet Sheila reported, 'HMI told us that (the curriculum co-ordinators) had better go away and write them all (policy statements) and present them to the staff and we didn't have time to mess about with all this consultation.'

It is little wonder that this contrary perspective caused stress and anxiety for Sheila and her school colleagues, as it negatively critiqued their existing practices and perceptions of policy development. It also interfered with processes which Sheila was adopting for her school-based INSET project.

Sheila was, however, prepared to accept partially HMI's point of view that the school needed to move along rather more quickly with policy formulation. On the other hand, she felt policy could not be fixed for all time and it had to be responsive to practice and to wisdom generated by use.

Here, then, was a temporary but major source of tension and challenge which Sheila had handled whilst undertaking her project. In addition, the political macro-climate was having a continuing major impact. Throughout her project work on the course, Sheila was well aware of the effect of multiple external changes on her school colleagues as well as upon herself. Attitudes to change were being shaped negatively because of overload, rather than because of irrational resistance. 'We've had too much change lately, haven't we,' she said rhetorically, 'that's why people are beginning to crack because we've had too much change in too short a time. It's not that we don't want change,' she added, 'or that we're not prepared to change, but we're having difficulty. I'm having difficulty coping.'

In her own case, the change overload had taken its toll on her sense of personal confidence, as she had been forced to examine and re-examine her work in response to government curriculum reforms. 'I think (too much change) can lead to a considerable lack of confidence. It's eroded a lot of my confidence,' she admitted. 'I've been through quite a lot of heart searching.'

She seemed, then, to have this in common with Colin, and, like Colin, the experience was being stored in the form of accumulating professional reflection and understanding. In turn this store of accumulating knowledge was being turned into professional practical wisdom as she reflected upon her role as curriculum co-ordinator and change agent in conducting her project. '(The curriculum co-ordinator) needs to know that change can be threatening,' she reflected, 'so when you sit down in a staff meeting and present new things to people you have to be very sensitive and tactful, and know that people are feeling unsure.' She continued, as if from the heart, 'Even experienced teachers are sitting there wondering whether or not they can actually do...whatever it is.' And to show that she believed professional change to be a steady and slow process, she added, 'You can't expect them to flick a switch and change the pattern, the way they've been doing it for the last ten, fifteen, twenty years.'

In this brief insight into Sheila's INSET project work, we can see a multiplicity of challenges and demands which have confronted her. We have seen her taking the lead on the development of a major whole school issue. In taking the lead, Sheila worked at various levels within the organisation and with different groups. She worked in partnership with the headteacher; she helped to change the working circumstances of the mid-day supervisors much to their satisfaction; she encouraged and led the whole staff in developing the play opportunities for the children and in devising strategies for supporting children unable to play outside; she tried consciously to steer the project around the sensitivities and hostilities of a resistant colleague. With the children, she began to raise new moral awareness and discourse. As changes in thinking and practice were being sought, the development of others was implicated - development of teachers, support staff and children. Sheila had a key role in promoting and supporting these multiple developments.

In these ventures, Sheila took a lead in the conscious articulation of agreed policy decisions and their realisation in practice. In return, she had to face the stress and pain of external feedback from HMI, however courteously and constructively this may have been expressed, on the methods by which she, and her colleagues, attempted to develop policy. Sheila had been caught in a contradiction between the ideas of the course, and the ideas of HMI; trapped between two competing external 'expert' views.

Perhaps it is to Sheila's credit that she began to formulate and articulate her own middle ground, to find her own way of passing between the experts, assimilating the laudable ideals of participation and ownership to the harsh demands of externally imposed change, much of which was badly managed at national level and which had eroded her self-confidence.

Still she carried on learning. And she seemed prepared to make constructive use of that learning in order to develop her role as curriculum co-ordinator and in order to handle her colleagues' change processes in the best way she knew. The experience was highly charged, emotionally, for Sheila along the way, and required skills of emotional self-management, as well as support. Managing one's own change in such cases may mean handling substantial upset and grief (Dadds, 1993) and without support, further development may be impossible. These demands on the curriculum co-ordinator, and the personal qualities they require, cannot be overlooked. Perhaps this was Sheila's most significant new professional learning.

Conclusion

Together with Vicki's and Carol's stories, these two cameos reinforce my view that managing change through the INSET project is a complex and demanding task. It requires understanding and strengths at many different levels. It requires an understanding of one's colleagues, how they think, how they tick, what motivates them, how they feel, why they embrace change, why they do not. It requires some grasp of the organisation as a whole within which the student is trying to effect change; a 'situational understanding' (Elliott, 1991) which also has to be matched with the ability to make judgements and take action in the light of that understanding.

Managing change through the INSET project also requires self-understanding; the ability to see oneself in the situation in which one is working, to understand how one is perceived by others, how one is regarded, how one's motivations are construed, how one's enthusiasms and passions are shared by others or not, as the case may be. It requires the willingness and ability to reflect upon the potential effect of oneself on the situation and to be able to account for that in managing the change process. It requires one to handle the many and different emotions which may be encountered as one tries to encourage change and its many consequences (Dadds, 1993), some of which will be self-confirming, some of which may be potentially destructive of self-confidence and self-regard. If one cannot manage these many, varied and turbulent emotions, one is probably not able to manage a development project either.

Perhaps more than any of these qualities, managing a school-based INSET project also requires fortitude. An INSET project that is to effect improvement in school requires much hard work. It requires one to study, and be knowledgeable about, one's chosen area; to know how to share one's knowledge and to help colleagues use it as a resource for their own learning. It requires one to study, and come to understand, the nature of change; to help one's colleagues with their own change and development as well as managing one's own at the same time. It requires one to understand oneself, the ups and downs, the highs and lows, the successes and the knocks along the way, the delights and sheer exhaustion which may rain down.

For some it is lonely and dispiriting. Some find themselves swimming against other tides of change in their schools. Some drown. Some have their development project cut down prematurely by forces well beyond their control.

The more fortunate see improvement in their schools as a reward for all their hard work and fortitude. They may struggle, they may sweat, they may often want to abandon their project (Dadds, forthcoming). But they carry on. They endure. They succeed in their small way in their small corner of the world. Colleagues benefit. Children benefit (Dadds, 1991a; Dadds, in progress).

The extent to which all this learning can actually be applied to new practices is still partly a mystery, though it does seem clear that the school context plays its part in the scope offered for applying one's INSET learning, as does the confidence, judgement, wisdom and, probably, maturity of the student. Support, encouragement and 'value congruence' (Kinder and Harland, 1991) from the course may be another key factor. Even one's spouse can be a help (Dadds, 1993).

We cannot assume that the understandings, qualities and abilities which the successful INSET development project seems to need come automatically or easily. The luckier amongst the INSET students may be endowed with ready insight; gifted with empathy and compassion; remain strong and cheerful in the face of antag-

114

onism, resistance and hostility; smile and forgive in response to backbiting and betrayal; stay alert after the midnight oil has seen them create further forays into their INSET studies and understandings. The naturally blessed students may pick themselves up after the heavy gusts of overload and political abuse have felled their colleagues; offer a hand to those who stumble more readily; bend, banter and cajole with those who are unyielding.

These blessings seem not to be the norm, however. It seems that the qualities required of the INSET change agent have to be learned by most. Some learn through the hard school of experience. For some, the path is smoothed by positive, encouraging and humane school colleagues. For most, the journey is probably a long one but it seems, too, that much can be learned along the way. We do not have to rely totally on the fate and fancies of the gods and the accidents of genetic endowment.

Managing the INSET development project is a rich source of professional growth in itself for the INSET teacher and many grasp the opportunity with both hands, thorns and all, in their bid to cross the bridge from their individual INSET learning to their collective school development responsibilities and commitments.

References

Dadds, M. (1986) 'The school, the teacher researcher and the in-service tutor', *Classroom Action Research Network Bulletin*, No.7, pp.96-107.

Dadds, M. (1991a) *Validity and award bearing teacher action research*, unpublished PhD thesis, University of East Anglia.

Dadds, M. (1991b) *Passionate enquiry: the role of self in teacher action research*, paper presented to Classroom Action Research Network Conference, April, Nottingham University.

Dadds, M. (1993) 'The feeling of thinking in professional self study', *Educational Action Research*, **1**(2).

Dadds, M. (forthcoming) Becoming someone other: teacher professional development and the management of change through INSET, in Southworth, G.W. (forthcoming) *Readings in Primary School Development* (London: Falmer Press).

Dadds, M. (in progress) The nature and use of the personal INSET project in short award-bearing courses at UCIE, Research Report (Cambridge: University of Cambridge Institute of Education).

Elliott, J. (1991) *Action Research for Educational Change* (Milton Keynes: Open University Press).

Fullan, M. (1991) *The New Meaning of Educational Change* (London: Cassell).

Kinder, K. and Harland, J. (1991) *The Impact of INSET: the case of primary science* (Slough: NFER).

Nias, J., Southworth, G.W. and Yeomans, R. (1989) *Staff Relationships in the Primary School* (London: Cassell).

Nias, J., Southworth, G.W. and Campbell, P. (1992) *Whole School Curriculum Development in the Primary School* (London: Falmer Press).

CHAPTER 8

LOCAL EDUCATION AUTHORITY AND HIGHER EDUCATION PARTNERSHIP IN SUPPORT OF SCHOOL-BASED DEVELOPMENT PROJECTS

Mary James[1]

Context

As the 1990s advance, the idea of LEAs and university depart-ments of education choosing to work together to provide in-service education and training for teachers might seem improbable. We live in competitive times when the rhetoric of market economics has come, through deliberate policy measures, to pervade the whole of the education service. The Government has taken the view that the quality of education can best be improved by subject-ing educational provision to the disciplines of the market. Fundamental to this conception are the principles of choice and diversity. It was no coincidence that these two terms provided the title of the White Paper which preceded the 1993 Education Act, which was designed, among other things, to reduce drastically the power of the local education authorities. Other legislation, being

[1] This chapter draws substantially on the PIER documentation to which the whole team of teachers, advisory teachers and consultants contributed. My thanks go to them for allowing me to use it here. Any errors and misunderstandings are, however, mine alone.

debated at the time of writing, could equally diminish the role and influence of university departments of education.

LEAs and HE have therefore been put in a similar position. Although there are still some services they are expected to provide, these have been markedly reduced and they are forced to compete for funds that are increasingly controlled by schools. The Government's view is that this will stimulate the market in training provision by encouraging diversity and competition and enable schools to chose what best matches their needs. This may be very healthy but there is another side to the coin. Rather than stimulating innovation and true diversity, these changes could merely encourage competition between agencies providing essentially similar services. There are already numerous short courses offered by LEAs, HE and the growing band of freelance educational consultants bearing the same titles and having similar content. The logo and design of the boxes may be different but the soap powder inside may be indistinguishable.

This kind of 'regression to the mean' undervalues the particular skills, knowledge and situation of different groups of providers. It also lays upon them expectations to undertake activities for which they are not best suited and can dissipate energies which they might properly direct elsewhere. For example, teacher educators and researchers in universities usually have a deep knowledge and expertise in a specific field and this extends beyond the parochial to the national and international. They will often have close working contacts with a considerable number of schools and schoolteachers but because of the other demands of their job, especially research and scholarship, they will not have the day-to-day dealings with schools that has been a feature of LEA advisory services. LEA staff, on the other hand, have some form of direct access to all the maintained schools in their area (albeit diminishing) and through proximity and contractual and professional responsibilities have opportunities to build relationships for medium and long-term support. Like university educators they have expertise in a specific area, usually subject or phase related, but because of the location of their work and the terms of their contracts they cannot be expected to possess a deep knowledge of current developments much beyond the bounds of their authority. Many do, but this understanding can be patchy. Moreover, there may be particular demands from schools, say, for research, evaluation and accreditation, which they cannot easily meet.

Given the different but complementary qualities and competencies of educators in LEAs and HEIs there would seem to be a good case for working together in mutual support to meet the development needs of teachers and schools. This chapter describes one such partnership which had its fullest expression in 1991 although its origins were in the late 1980s and it continued in a modified form into 1993.

PIER

PIER stands for Partnership In Educational Research and was the acronym given to an initiative involving eight schools in the London Borough of Enfield, Enfield's advisory service and the Cambridge Institute of Education during 1990-1. The 'prime mover' was Martin Brown, advisory teacher and co-ordinator of a unit for developments in assessment and recording achievement in Enfield (DARE). He was supported by Sandra Knott, the advisory teacher for assessment in the primary sector, and by Jane Reed the senior adviser for assessment and evaluation.

At that time the pressure to 'train' teachers for National Curriculum assessment was increasing but, alongside more conventional forms of training, Enfield advisory staff wanted to preserve a place for research-based projects on assessment issues identified by schools.

Antecedents

In earlier years a number of Enfield's advisory staff had pursued Masters' degrees with the University of East Anglia at Norwich and had been influenced by an approach to educational change drawing on Lawrence Stenhouse's ideas about research as a basis for teaching and on Michael Fullan's work on the management of the change process. In 1988-9 and 1989-90 respectively, Enfield embarked on two pilot projects looking at pupils' involvement in their learning (PILS) and developing school-based projects in assessment (SCUBA). Both of these projects involved a group of teachers as researchers in their own schools supported by the LEA's advisory service which provided project management, organisational structure and assisted with the provision of resources. The Centre for Applied Research (CARE) at the University of East Anglia was the third partner and was asked to assist with initial planning, to contribute an understanding of classroom research methodology and to provide an external evaluation.

The SCUBA documentation made reference to the influence of Fullan quite explicitly. In relation to the theme of this chapter it may therefore be helpful to look again at what, in 1982 in a seminal text, Fullan had to say about support agents for development in schools. He wrote about 'internal and external consultants' and discussed their roles and relationships in the various phases of the change process. (By 'internal consultant' he meant local school district personnel, the North American equivalent of our LEA advisory staff.) He stressed the importance of the implementation and continuation phases of the change process and argued that:

> ...the consultant, whether internal or external, who gets a new program 'adopted' may do more harm than good if little effective implementation follows. Put differently, in deciding on or in assessing the role of consultants, we should have in mind not only whether they obtain or provide good information on given occasions (e.g. a workshop), but also whether they or someone else follows through to provide support for the use of that information. (Fullan, 1982)

With this in mind, he then went on to classify the types of roles that 'consultants' or 'change agents' might perform. Drawing on the considerable research evidence currently available, he identified roles of resource finder, information linker, technical assister, process enabler and helper, solution giver, generalist and communicator, which he reduced to two basic categories: solution giver and facilitator. He concluded that:

> The resolution to the problem, as one might suspect, is not to choose between supplying content expertise and facilitating; both kinds of help are needed and may be offered by the same person or by a combination of people. (Fullan, 1982)

The dilemma for LEAs – one that Fullan identified – is between expertise-seeking and self-reliance. On this matter, Fullan argued that:

> The primary task of the [LEA] should be to develop its own internal capacity to process needed educational change, relying on external assistance to train insiders and to provide specific program expertise in combination with internal follow-through. (*ibid.*)

The choice of external consultants is, of course, crucial and Fullan counselled districts [LEAs] to select those who possess both technical competence and the commitment, knowledge and energy to spend time on-site to assist during implementation. Ideally:

> When external consultants are used, they should be used in combination with some internal team or personnel with some specific design or plan to follow through on the ideas. (Fullan, 1982)

There was evidence that Enfield's advisory service had all of this guidance in mind when planning SCUBA and the PIER projects that followed in 1990-1.

Rationale

The value of working with teachers on problems that they identify in consultation with colleagues in their schools, using a research-based approach, was also a prime consideration. This derived very much from the influence of Lawrence Stenhouse and the classroom action research movement that had grown since the mid 1970s. There was also a sense in which PIER was conceived as an antidote to the known shortcomings of the cascade mode of INSET that was everywhere in evidence at the time. The PIER report gave the following as the rationale for the projects:

> Traditionally, much of in-service training has involved teachers attending central training courses and lecture programmes, often as passive participants. The onus has been on the individual teacher to return to school to share information and skills with colleagues. Without support, the teacher is often required to write reports and duplicate materials which are then formally shared during staff and departmental meetings. Informally, teachers will have discussions with colleagues willing to listen and share experiences they have gained. Obviously, this cascade method of disseminating information, skills and understandings, has strengths as well as the weaknesses outlined, but many people have identified some serious limitations on this means of development and dissemination of information.
> In recent years, many well-documented projects involving hybrid forms of school-based INSET have been developed. In Enfield, the PIER project seeks to develop a school-based approach to research, training and development. It combines the training, planning and evaluation aspects of a centrally co-ordinated and managed project with the accepted value of building on school-based research.

Teachers value research work which they are involved in within the context of their own school and where the process and outcomes can be shared directly with colleagues. This approach allows priorities identified within the school to be researched and results used to inform future developments. Teacher-researchers often show a willingness to share their work 'warts and all' with colleagues and feel confident to modify the process used for the context in which they work. (Enfield, 1992).

Roles and responsibilities

In September 1990, work began on planning the projects that became known as PIER. On the basis of the SCUBA pilot, both the focus of the work and the roles of participants had been clarified. Teachers were to be invited to identify issues for investigation 'centred on the integration of assessment processes with day-to-day classroom practice to enable effective learning'. They would be expected to develop and refine their ideas in consultation with senior colleagues in their schools and with the LEA project management team and 'external consultants' and tutors. They would attend twilight, residential and workshop sessions to find out about research methods and the ethics of research and to work on analysis and writing up with the support of other teachers and the LEA/HE project team. The data would come from two concentrated periods of data collection in schools during the spring and summer terms, 1991. After the first short period in the spring term they would come together for preliminary data analysis, and refocussing if necessary, then they would do the major part of their research in the summer. Within the space of the school year they would share the results of their work with invited colleagues from their schools and the LEA at a formal presentation. This dissemination would be supported by materials – posters, booklets and a project report – designed for wider distribution. If these tasks were satisfactorily completed, individual teacher-researchers could also expect to be awarded the Certificate of Further Professional Study by the Cambridge Institute of Education.

At school level, obligations were not only placed upon individual classroom teachers. Evidence concerning the impact of classroom action research (e.g. Elliott, 1993) suggests that the management structures of schools can help or hinder the pay-off in terms of effective change. The LEA management team therefore regarded it as important to involve schools' senior management teams at the outset. They were not simply expected to take an interest but to draft initial proposals with teachers and refine and, if necessary, refocus school projects after the initial training sessions. They were also expected to support release for training and for data collection and analysis and to enable the sharing of outcomes of the research in the school.

The LEA project management team – principally Martin Brown and Sandra Knott – continued to define their role in terms of providing project management, organisation and resources. Although one of these project managers was quoted in the evaluation report as saying that 'the LEA role is minimal' this role nevertheless entailed:

- negotiating with other LEA personnel such as officers and advisers and the INSET Unit to secure moral, material and financial support for the projects;

- preparing invitations to join PIER and visiting schools to discuss possible projects with senior management and would-be teacher-researchers;

- developing 'contracts' for support and dissemination with selected schools and making arrangements for supply cover for the release of teachers for training and for school-based research (a maximum of four half-days were allowed for the latter);

- organising project team events including a twilight session to refine initial ideas, a two-day residential training session, a one-day workshop for data analysis, and a half-day preparation for a further half-day public presentation of outcomes;

- supporting teachers in their schools by providing resource support in terms of equipment, but also providing practical help in collecting data by operating a video recorder, for example, or assisting with micro-processing;

- documenting the whole project and producing both a 'glossy' interim newsletter and an attractive pack of project materials including a general report and booklets for each of the teacher's projects;

- arranging an evaluation which on this occasion was not conducted by the HE partner, although CIE acted as a critical friend, but by Ian Terrell, an advisory teacher with experience and responsibility for evaluation within the LEA.

An interesting feature of this project was that the 'external consultants' in this partnership were not only drawn from HE. A key participant in the PIER project team was Graham Hiles, an independent media and education resources consultant. He was a former teacher and media resources officer in London but now worked freelance. He was primarily engaged to help with IT support and the production of materials for the projects but his wide-ranging skills led to his involvement in all aspects of the work. He worked with teachers to help them produce individual project plans on a computer data base. Few of them had computer expertise so this entailed a good deal of informal training. He also contributed to the training session on research methods by leading a session on the uses of video data. He provided practical help to teachers by supplying technical assistance with data gathering and analysis and he compiled and produced most of the PIER documentation.

Representing the Cambridge Institute of Education, I was the second 'external consultant'. As had previously been the case with SCUBA, the role of the HE partner was to assist with planning and to act as a 'critical friend' to the project management team, also to provide input at training sessions on methods of doing classroom research. This time, however, the HE institution was not asked to carry out an external evaluation of the project *per se* but rather to monitor the evaluation that was provided within the resources of the LEA. This seemed appropriate because a number of the post-experience courses provided by university departments of education are now designed to provide teachers and advisers with the skills of self-evaluation. A number of Enfield advisory teachers have had experience of these, including Ian Terrell. Having a 'watching brief' with regard to the evaluation was also sufficient to meet the requirements of course accreditation which was a new feature of PIER. There was another evaluation task, however, and this was a more direct responsibility for CIE. Both the LEA and CIE were interested in the value of this model of LEA supported/HE accredited school-focussed INSET. In a sense this was a 'meta-evaluation' task.

At an early point in partnership negotiations, the possibility of providing teachers with some recognition of their individual efforts had arisen. In earlier phases of work the benefits for teachers, schools and the LEA had been evident but it was felt that teachers would appreciate some more tangible recognition of their personal professional development which might benefit their future careers. Moreover it was calculated that the expectations of the project conformed to the requirements of the Certificate of Further Professional Study offered by the Institute. Therefore an additional role for me was to become the CFPS course co-ordinator, tutor and assessor. Although much of the actual 'tutoring' was carried out by the Enfield team, this probably led me to have a more ongoing involvement than previous HE partners. As before, the planning and teaching on the residential training workshop was a major responsibility but support for other off-school-site sessions was also important. The assessor role came to the fore in the final public presentations of teachers' work, at the end of which they were awarded their certificates.

A diagrammatic representation of the sequence of events and the contribution of each of the major partners in PIER can be found in the table below.

Dates	Event	Schools	Project Management Team	CIE	Monitoring/Evaluation
Sept 1990	Project Brief		Discussion LEA/HE	Joint planning of structure, content and timing with LEA	**Antecedents and intended outcomes**
Dec 1990	Draft proposals sent to schools		Criteria produced / Initial 'talk through' with schools	Identification of purposes, time resources, quality, use of outcomes	Establishment phase / Field notes, discussions, interviews
Jan 1991	Responses from schools	Schools send response to Project Management Team	Check initial match with selection criteria		Documentation: minutes, project outlines, timeline
			Check Fit with IDP		
Jan 30	Twilight session / Meeting: Teachers / Senior Management Team / Meeting: Teachers / Senior Management Team / Project Leaders / Project selection / Contract drawn up	To draft initial ideas for research	**Talk through with group** / **Discuss project commitment** / By Project Management Team / **By Teachers / Project Management Team /Senior management team**		
March 14/15	Residential Powergen Cockfosters / Project management document produced / Project outline document produced	To include dates / administration of project / To focus directly on project		Supporting and monitoring of: research methods, interpretation / analysis of data, consideration of appropriate dissemination	**Processes** / Interim phase / Interviews with participants
		Meetings between all parties to refine and review proposal			
March 22	revised project outline	From schools	To project Management Team		Review meeting
April 25	Workshop E.T.C. 9.00 – 3.30	Initial data produced	**Support to schools over whole research period**		Refocussing projects / Refining / Management
June 27	Preparation for presentation E.T.C. ½ Day 9.00 – 1.00	**Decision on type / form of presentation, Preparation of summaries of research for publication, Materials sent for design / production**			organisation, support / Production interim report
July 11	Presentation / Evaluation E.T.C. ½ Day 9.00 – 1.00	**To colleagues and Heads of school, LEA guests**			**Outcomes** / End phase / Presentation of projects
	Dissemination through INSET		Accredited school-based model to: Sector specific instructions Officers, advisers, National groups / individuals	Produce evaluation of model of LEA support / HE accredited school-focussed INSET. View to future development. Role of 'critical friend'	Reflexive accounts / Audience evaluation / Questionnaire / Interviews with participants

The PIER projects

PIER intended to work with a group of approximately ten teachers across phases to encourage sharing of experience and to highlight issues of continuity in teaching, learning and assessment. By the end of the scheduled period for research and development, nine teachers from eight primary, secondary and special schools had seen their projects through to fruition and been awarded a CFPS. Although the intended focus was the relationship between assessment and teaching and learning, teachers were allowed to interpret this broadly in the light of current school concerns. Therefore projects ranged from one teacher assessing special needs provision by shadowing one child and another teacher diagnosing the specific difficulties of one child in mathematics, to two teachers collaboratively researching target setting in a teaching group and another looking at different teaching, learning and assessment styles across a humanities faculty.

In most cases only one teacher-researcher was involved in each participant school, but where two teachers were able to work collaboratively there was evidence of considerable additional benefit. No extra resources were made available to them – they had to share out attendance at training sessions and release from teaching for research – but the opportunity to discuss a common issue and share data was highly valued and the results were impressive. The project management team quickly came to the conclusion that, if PIER was to be repeated, pairs of teachers from schools should be encouraged.

All of the teachers' projects were different but their flavour might be captured by the following account taken from one of the booklets produced by the teachers to report their work. The teacher is Paul Barraclough who was then a Year 6 class teacher, special needs co-ordinator, teacher-governor and RE co-ordinator at Walker Primary School.

The PIER project appealed to me immediately because it offered guidance and facilities for classroom research and assessment. I saw the project as a means of receiving the guidance I needed. I was also keen to learn the skills of assessment as they related to a boy in my school who desperately needed more individual attention.

It was agreed between the senior management team and myself that the best use of time – both for the school and myself — was to focus on an issue that would give definite support to a child in school. I had responsibility for children with special needs so the study would be relevant and practical. A child (Gary) was selected who would benefit particularly from a detailed assessment of his difficulties in maths.

My aims were to:

(a) assess the child's difficulties;
(b) discover what number concepts and knowledge he did possess;
(c) analyse his learning style and strategies;
(d) look for ways to give greater breadth to his maths experience;
(e) build on his enjoyment of the subject and develop his confidence.

I worked with Gary individually and videoed all four sessions. The video gave me time to focus carefully on the activities and proved useful for Gary to watch and assess himself. It also proved to be a useful means of communicating to his parents what I was doing.

Gary obviously enjoyed this individual attention and gained from it. He needs much more of it – as do most children. He needs lots of small group and individual work and lots of practical experience of applying the mathematics he knows in different contexts. He needs help in using mathematical language appropriately and he needs a wider experience of maths. His experience through the published maths scheme used in the school was mainly of computation. This had highlighted his weaknesses, but had done little to put things right. It had just compounded his belief that he couldn't do maths. This had undermined his confidence. Therefore, the value of the maths scheme has to be looked at and a more individualised programme needs to be designed to met Gary's special needs.

The National Curriculum mathematics rightly emphasises a broad approach to the subject – a breadth which is often lacking in the schemes, particularly in the area of using and applying maths.

Issues related to class management, organisation of the curriculum and staffing will be important in ensuring that the needs of a child like Gary are met.

Paul Barraclough's account provides a clear description of the sequence of development that started with the identification of a need relevant to the teacher and his school. This was followed by a refinement of focus, then a period of data collection and analysis drawing on the training received. Finally, and most importantly, the findings were reflected upon and conclusions drawn about action that the school would need to take. (Shortly after the end of this project, Paul was appointed to a deputy headship in a Cambridgeshire primary school. He keeps in contact and is looking for another involvement of this kind.)

Evaluation

Evaluation of the principles, process and outcomes of PIER were carried out by Ian Terrell, advisory teacher for evaluation, throughout the life of the project and two drafts of an interim report were produced in May and July 1991. Data were collected by means of evaluation sheets completed by participants, field notes of observations of PIER activities, document analysis, review discussions with teachers and the planning team, interviews with senior managers in schools and LEA officers, and evaluation sheets collected from the audience at the project presentation.

Much of the detail in the evaluation report covered issues already mentioned in this chapter but, additionally, there were perceptions about the project *process*. (Much of what follows in this section is drawn from the report.) The programme was generally regarded as flexible and adapted to the needs of the whole group: 'One interesting aspect was the devising of a menu based on the needs of participants. The needs were met through tutoring and consultancy.' More directly taught sessions on research methods and ethics were found to be useful although 'on the whole there was more to cover than the time would allow'. Towards the end of the project it became clearer to the project management team that more time could have been spent on preparing for reporting and dissemination. This was rather hurried and much of the work on materials eventually fell to Graham Hiles.

Teachers were at first tentative in their approach to the project. There was some concern about the scale of the work and the idea of a formal presentation. The first ideas for projects were large-scale. Later the focus became clearer and more limited in scope. Teachers valued the time spent in 'thinking things through' and became happier as a result.

Some of the first attempts at data collection proved to be difficult. There were some technical problems with using recording equipment but these were mostly overcome with practice and support. The benefits eventually outweighed the difficulties and the revelations in the data generated a great deal of enthusiasm: 'The interview was...probably (one of) the most influential experiences of my educational life'. However, such insights sometimes created new problems of their own: 'The tape identified a brilliant sexist incident...but I don't know what I am going to do about it'.

Some of the results were more mundane and confirmed existing understandings: 'These issues are known; I've known them for years'. Other research raised ethical and professional difficulties for teachers because of implied criticism of the organisation of learning in their schools. However, teachers had an opportunity to discuss the meaning and implications of their research with others in the project team and this exchange was valued. As one teacher said of the project:

> It has made me use my powers of reflection and analysis that I have not used for years. It has given me a clearer understanding of the nature of my school's particular situation and it has helped me to plan a way forward.

Benefits of the partnership model of INSET

At some point in the development of PIER, someone in the project team (the details are now lost in the mists of time) produced a list of purposes that the initiative was intended to fulfil. This still offers a useful summary of the benefits of this model of INSET to each of the partners in the project. This summary is reproduced below:

For individual teachers involved:
- method of researching concerns/issues
- accredits classroom research.

For schools involved:
- provides accredited staff development
- provides a managed and resourced framework for carrying out an identified task
- provides school-based INSET data and materials.

For LEA:
- creates an INSET model of teacher-led research and development that arises from perceived needs (i.e. identified within IDP) of individual institutions
- produces research data in context that informs LEA decision-making in areas such as curriculum management, policy formulation and is available for sharing across institutions
- provides professional development which is based in teachers' own institutions and is accredited by HE.

For project management team:
- provides a managed and resourced structure to produce research data with a particular focus.

For Higher Education Institute:
- provides a model for 'distance' research
- provides a closer link with research and development in schools
- accredits teacher research
- provides research data for publication.

Is there a future for this approach to INSET?

However convinced the project team was, and is, of the value of INSET initiatives such as PIER, we are also aware that the world has changed since 1991. Enfield LEA has attempted to reserve some resources for work of this nature and a similar project was mounted in the following eighteen months, jointly funded by CIE, to encourage teacher-research on curricular issues in the education of 16 to 19 year olds. This was smaller in scale, involving only three schools, but it was interesting that one of the PIER teachers participated again because, she said, she had become addicted to teacher-research.

The maintenance and support of this kind of work has, however, not been easy. It is more difficult to argue for resources for this

130

more flexible and open-ended approach, despite the evidence for its benefits, than it is to create programmes of courses to 'deliver' National Curriculum training. The greatest threat however has come from uncertainty concerning the continuity of tenure of the LEA staff who were the key to project management. On a number of occasions the advisory staff have received redundancy notices as a result of pressure from Government to cut back drastically on LEA services. Sometimes money has been found, at the eleventh hour, to retain their services for a while longer but none of this is conducive to the provision of a planned, coherent and effective service. Undoubtedly, HE could take over the management role but it would be a difficult task to develop the same degree of access, in-school support and follow-through that was regarded as one of the greatest strengths of the partnership with an LEA in PIER. Until the future of LEAs, and indeed university departments of education, becomes clearer, it is difficult to make any predictions about the future scope for such partnership approaches. We have evidence to say that it works and has long-term value to participants. The question is whether policy makers are listening.

References

Elliott, J. (1993) 'What have we learned from action research in school-based evaluation?' *Educational Action Research* **1**(1), pp.175-86.

Enfield LEA (1992) *PIER 1991: Report* (London Borough of Enfield: DARE).

Fullan, M. (1982) *The Meaning of Educational Change* (Toronto: OISE Press).

CHAPTER 9

JOURNEYING AS PILGRIMS: An Account of the 'Improving the Quality of Education for All' Project

David Hopkins

During the past three years or so we have been working closely with a network of thirty or so schools on a development project known as 'Improving the Quality of Education for All' (IQEA). We often use the metaphor of 'the journey' to describe our work in the project, in an attempt to capture the non-prescriptive and invest-igative nature of our collaboration. There is however another, perhaps more important, aspect to our approach to school improvement as a journey. The image was beautifully captured by a headteacher of a large Catholic secondary school recently, when he said at one of our meetings 'that we journey as pilgrims, not as nomads'. What he was so evocatively reminding us of was that our collaborative approach to school improvement was based on a set of values that characterised and disciplined all our work. So although we had all rejected the 'blueprint' or 'top-down' approach to change, we were not lurching from 'fad to fad' on a whim or impulse. Rather we were journeying in a direction that was, although not always well signposted, informed by goals or by a vision that reflected a core set of values. In other words, we were following a star.

At the outset of IQEA we attempted to outline our vision by articulating a set of principles that provided us with a philosophi-cal and practical starting point. Because it is our assumption that schools are most likely to provide quality education and enhanced outcomes for pupils when they adopt ways of working that are consistent with these principles, they were offered as the basis for collaboration with the IQEA project schools. In short, we were inviting the schools to identify and to work on their own projects and priorities, but to do so in a way which embodied a set of 'core' values about school improvement. Originally, there were ten such principles, but during our period of working with the schools we have found ourselves 'reorganising' these into the following five statements. They represent the expectation we had of the way project schools would pursue school improvement, and act as an *'aide memoire'* to the schools and ourselves, about principles that are likely to foster enduring school improvement initiatives. The five principles of IQEA are:

- The vision of the school (the school-in-the-future) should be one to which all members of the school community have an opportunity to contribute, and most will seek to.

- The school, because it has its vision, will see in external pressures for change important opportunities to secure its internal priorities.

- The school will seek to create and maintain conditions in which all members of the school's community can learn successfully.

- The school will seek to adopt and develop structures which encourage collaboration and lead to the empowerment of individuals and groups.

- The school will seek to promote the view that the monitoring and evaluation of quality is a responsibility in which all members of staff share.

We feel that the operation of these principles creates synergism – together they are greater than the sum of their parts. They characterise an overall approach rather than prescribing a course of action. The intention is that they should inform the thinking and actions of teachers during school improvement efforts, and provide a touchstone for the strategies they devise and the behaviours they adopt. It is in this sense that we journey as pilgrims. If we are not always clear as to the exact path to take, we are becoming increasingly skilled as travellers – in telling the lie of the land, in reading the contours and in locating the most appropriate staging posts along the way.

Creating the conditions for school improvement

So what does the journey of school improvement look like in practice? Although there are many faces to success we have noted some patterns and trends which we believe can apply to other schools and other systems. A key finding from the early phase of the project was that *school improvement works best when a clear and practical focus for development is linked to simultaneous work on the internal conditions within the school*. Such school improvement efforts appear to include:

- reconstructing externally imposed education reforms in the form of school *priorities;*

- creating *internal conditions* that will sustain and manage change in schools.

Identifying priorities

Development planning is an important preliminary to school improvement. Whatever method or approach is adopted, the planning cycle is likely to involve the school in some form of audit – revealing current strengths and weaknesses; and in generating a number of 'priorities' for action – often too many to work on. This means that decisions about 'priorities' must be made – moving from the separate, perhaps even conflicting priorities of individuals or groups, to a systematically compiled set of priorities which represent the overall needs of a whole school community. Elsewhere, we have suggested that two principles should guide this process of choice amongst priorities (Hargreaves and Hopkins, 1991):

- *manageability* – how much can we realistically hope to achieve?

- *coherence* – is there a sequence which will ease implementation?

To these principles we would now add a third:

- *consonance* – the extent to which internally identified priorities coincide or overlap with external pressures for reform.

We believe that there is empirical evidence that those schools which recognise *consonance*, and therefore see externally generated change efforts as providing opportunities, as well as (or instead of) problems, are better able to respond to external demands. We also believe that it is as important to be clear about what is not a priority as what is – otherwise it is possible to dissipate staff effort and enthusiasm across too many projects or in discussions about initiatives which we have neither the means nor the inclination to implement.

Developing the conditions

It is essential that some aspect of the *internal conditions* within the school are worked on at the same time as the curriculum, or other priorities the school has set itself. Without an equal focus on conditions, even priorities that meet the criteria outlined in the previous paragraph become marginalised. When circumstances exist that are not supportive of change, it is necessary to concentrate much more in the initial stages on improving the conditions in the school and limit work on the priorities. Although the list of conditions represents our best estimate of what the important factors are at present, rather than a definitive statement, we believe that there is both research-based and practical evidence to support them. Broadly stated the conditions are:

- a commitment to staff development;

- practical efforts to involve staff, students and the community in school policies and decisions;

- effective leadership, but not just of the head – the leadership function is spread throughout the school;

- effective co-ordination strategies;

- proper attention to the potential benefits of enquiry and reflection;

- a commitment to collaborative planning activity.

The following accounts of school improvement journeys illustrate how priorities lead to school improvement strategies which operate on the conditions and culture of the school. These accounts are organised around the conditions for a number of reasons. First, because these conditions identify those key areas where management arrangements influence the school's capacity to engage in improvement activities. Second, experience tells us that in many cases it is necessary to start by building one or more of these conditions before substantive improvement effort is possible. Third, although it is the school's priorities which drive improvement, rather than, for example, 'doing staff development', we expect each school to have its own unique priorities, and are reluctant to suggest any 'ideal type' set of priorities as organising categories. Nevertheless, we hope that in each case, the link between priority and condition can be discerned by the reader in what follows.

Staff development

In the quest for school improvement powerful strategies are required which integrate staff development and school development in a way that is mutually supportive. These powerful strategies, that link staff development to school improvement, need to fulfil two essential criteria: first of all they need to relate to and enhance ongoing practice at the school; and, secondly, they should link to and strengthen other internal features of the school's organisation.

We could quote many examples of schools that have used staff development as a central strategy for supporting teachers as they have attempted to engage in improvement activities. All of them work from an assumption that attention to teacher learning is likely to have direct spin-offs in terms of pupil learning. All of them demonstrate the pay off of investment of time and resources in teacher development.

An excellent example is that of Village Infants School in Barking and Dagenham. There, over the last couple of years, a sophisticated strategy has been adopted to create conditions in the school that support the development of the staff. At the outset there was a concern with how to find time to observe children in the classroom for the purposes of new assessment requirements. With this in mind a staff development day was led by an external consultant. This event had an enormous impact on staff thinking. Specifically the consultant led the staff through a series of problem-solving processes focussing on the arrangement of one classroom. Gradually the teachers rearranged functions and resources in order to make the classroom more autonomous. Subsequently similar activities have been carried out in other rooms.

Overall the evidence suggests that the strategy has had a significant impact. Specific changes in teaching style are evident in all classrooms; there is clear evidence of increased pupil autonomy in learning, even with very young pupils; and the quality of dialogue about teaching and learning amongst the staff is very striking to the outsider. Indeed it does seem that the strategy adopted has brought about a significant change in the culture of the school.

What follows is a brief account of these by the headteacher, Jan Featherstone, and deputy head, Lyn Newman, of Village Infants. It gives a real sense of the evolution of their work over the two year period.

(Following the initial staff development day, one class had been changed)…there were seven more to go! We now wanted to work on the remaining classes but like Rome we couldn't do it in a day. However, we adopted the 'strike while the iron's hot' approach. Over a period of a few weeks and working in teams we moved from room to room. The team system meant that everyone had their turn and could benefit from advice, muscle power and one child-free day to reorganise their room. It was dynamic and it did work!

Meanwhile, what was now happening in the classrooms? Children were gradually being encouraged to help and think for themselves. Simple systems for handling equipment and resources were introduced throughout the school with slight variations according to the experiences of the children.

We had worked well as a large team but now we adopted a smaller, more intimate grouping to look at how the 'work station system' was operating in the classroom. Peer observation, peer coaching or 'Tweedling' as we nicknamed it (as in Tweedle-de and Tweedle-dum), was introduced. However, it was not without its teething problems. We didn't know how to observe and we certainly didn't know how to record it so we could draw conclusions. We enlisted the help of an expert. Armed with a bit of theory we focussed on the success criteria we had identified. ... Although we were not finding many answers, the questions that were raised stimulated lively debate and helped to clarify our thoughts and map out a way forward.

So into another year we go. We are learning all the time. The children are becoming more independent in the way they use the classroom and their time. Now, we will focus our observations on what the children are doing rather than how. What are they learning? How much are they learning? Are they learning what was intended they learn?

Involvement

In the research literature on effective schools there is strong evidence that success is associated with a sense of identification and involvement that extends beyond the teaching staff. This involves the pupils, parents and, indeed, other members of the local community. It does seem that some schools are able to create positive relationships with their wider community that help to create a supportive climate for learning.

Pupil involvement seems to be a particularly important factor. The research suggests that this occurs at an organisational level, by involving pupils in decision-making and by encouraging them to take responsibility for day-to-day routines. At the classroom level this occurs when pupils are encouraged to take responsibility for their own learning and, through involvement, to learn organisational, planning, discussion, decision-making and leadership skills.

In the IQEA project we have observed how a number of schools have used the power of pupil involvement to support their development activities. A particularly good example of this approach occurred at Sanders Drapers Secondary School in the London Borough of Havering. During the academic year 1990-91, a cross-curricular group was established on 'open learning'. It had two aims: the organisation of a flexible learning week, and the development of a Learning Resources Centre (LRC). The existing school library was book based, located at the back of the school and used mainly by the English Department; it was felt that this was a poor use of resources. It was decided to move its site to a more central location being vacated by the sixth-form. Besides extending the range of resources in the LRC, the group realised that if they were to succeed in raising the quality of education offered at Sanders Draper, they had to do more than simply create a physical area. Therefore, in September 1991 they began a programme of staff development aimed at enabling and encouraging staff to widen their range of teaching approaches.

In this account, Gill Daley who co-ordinated this initiative explains what happened.

By the summer of 1992 we felt that we were ready to launch our work school-wide. We organised a whole staff INSET day for the Autumn term to investigate teaching and learning style. During the day staff were exposed to a series of experiences such as working out their own preferred learning style and learning that a wide range of preferences existed amongst the staff. Pupils were used as witnesses during the morning session helping staff to reflect on what it was *really* like to learn at Sanders Draper School. Towards the end of the day, departments were asked to respond to what they had learned by drawing up action plans to meet the needs of all the pupils.

Throughout the project we have tried to involve students. As their role developed they have taken on a variety of tasks:

1. *Monitors of the classroom impact of the project.* Year 9 pupils were asked to complete a questionnaire in June 1992. The aim of this exercise was to detect a shift in pupils' perceptions of how they learned. Almost all noticed a change in the ways in which they had worked.

2. *Motivators.* Staff were encouraged by the response of pupils. Transcripts of the pupils' conversations with the IQEA team were made available to staff and governors – positive pupils' comments had far more effect than we could have made.

3. *Resources for staff development.* Pupils at work in the LRC were videoed and this was used to sharpen our classroom observation

skills. In November 1992, students were used as 'witnesses' as part of a whole staff training day.

4. *Practical helpers*. Students were invited to apply for the posts of Resource Assistants to help with the day-to-day running of the Learning Resources Centre. A pupil chairs the regular meetings on LRC issues.

Enquiry and reflection

School level evaluation will not of itself improve schools. There needs to be a commitment to scrutinise data, to 'make sense' of it, and to plan and act differently as a result, if we are really going to make the exercise worthwhile. In practice, this means that school improvement activities are frequently small-scale and focussed. In the current climate it is more advisable to carry out a series of small-scale focussed investigations in key areas and implement the action plans that may result from these enquiries. A planned series of specific audits creates a *rolling programme* which provides a picture of the school built up over successive years.

The following account demonstrates how powerful a force for improvement school-based enquiry can be, underlining the sense of empowerment teachers feel when actively involved and able to influence. It also illustrates the importance of a school-wide strategy for review and development. The 'answers' the teachers came up with were their own, grounded in their own enquiry and interpretation processes - but the impetus to engage in enquiry stemmed from a school-level commitment to quality review. King Harold Grant Maintained School, Waltham Abbey, is one of the first secondary schools to achieve BS 5750 registration. Frances Howarth and Malcolm Wright describe how the school's commitment to the identification of quality systems took them, via an initial focus on teacher appraisal, into the scrutiny of one aspect of the school's performance – the development of pupils' basic numeracy skills.

Background to process. The school was looking for a TEAM approach to teacher appraisal – that focused on outcomes for pupils. The Maths team selected one of the vision statements and identified one or two main targets that would be the focus of their work over a specified and agreed period of time.

140

Vision Statements selected. 'The Quality of education and commitment to academic achievement encourages students and staff to achieve their highest potential.'

Team target. 'To raise the standard of basic numeracy across the curriculum for Years 7 and 8.'

Two key result areas.

To improve numeracy test scores by 10%.

To enable pupils to feel more confident and secure using numeracy skills across the curriculum

A Base Line Test was administered to all Year 7 and 8 pupils to establish a measurable starting point that would be used in the evaluation.

The team came together and discussed what evidence they would expect to see to ensure that the basic level of confidence and competency had increased. Good practice was shared in terms of strategies staff had used in the past which could now be formalised and used across the whole team.

Individual staff set individual targets related to the team targets together with the evidence they would bring to a final review meeting when the team would assess the extent to which the team target had been met.

A range of strategies was devised.

- Staff generated specific work sheets to target pupils, groups of pupils, classes who from the test had been diagnosed as having a weakness in certain areas.

- Specific lessons on aspects of numeracy skills that would be used across the curriculum.

All pupils were tested.

There had been an 18% increase overall, one class went up 37%.

The review meeting took place – at this individual staff members publicly reviewed their targets and the extent to which they had been realised.

Why was it successful?

- The vision statements were generated by all the staff and made them feel they were all moving in the same direction. It gave cohesion to the work of their team.

- From the onset staff had a very clear idea of what was expected in respect of the given area.

- The focus is outcome for students – so that the quality improvement focusses on the classroom and curriculum delivery.

- Staff reflect on their own practice and select their own targets in relation to the team target set – the motivation comes from the staff member themselves.

Leadership

Research into effective schools provides clear evidence that promoting a more dynamic and decentralised approach to leadership is associated with school improvement. Such leadership by a headteacher involves a significant shift away from structures as 'control'. Rather, structure becomes the vehicle for empowering staff, a network which informs and supports staff as they seek to bring to life the values and goals of the school community in its day-to-day activities. The building of a school culture in which individuals at all levels enjoy a degree of autonomy in relation to their own work, and the possibility of bringing their own knowledge, skills and creativity to bear in resolving problems and pursuing opportunities is the challenge facing school leaders. Of course, decentralisation of decision-making within the framework of agreed and clearly communicated school goals and priorities will not of itself improve schools – we need to be assured that staff do indeed possess the relevant knowledge and skills. Our own experience is that 'capability' is widely distributed within schools.

In the following account, Carol Robinson, Headteacher of William Ford C of E Junior School, Dagenham, underlines the importance of relationship building – the mutual trust which is needed for genuine empowerment to occur hinges on the quality of the relationship between head and staff – and also shows how trust builds once relationships are right. Communication is clearly important here too, the creation of new opportunities for staff to meet and talk about what is happening. But, better quality communication does not mean universal agreement – indeed it has been 'very uncomfortable at times'. What is important is that although certain issues or discussions create discomfort, the staff still feel able to raise them. This leads to a much healthier environment for handling conflict (i.e. by acknowledging and exploring it) than is usually the case in leader-dependent cultures, where differences in view tend to be minimised or hidden, rather than viewed as opportunities for growth.

But to leadership. I believe that everyone in a team has something to offer. Sometimes we need to listen to experience, sometimes to the person with expertise, sometimes to the person with vision and sometimes to the person who feels they're going under because they don't know what they're supposed to do. The leadership pattern established in the school was of the 'pyramid' type – head then deputy head then senior management and so on. What we discovered was that there were a few 'powerful' members of staff (not necessarily members of the senior management team) with the majority seeing themselves as powerless. There were two sections to the school with Upper School and Lower School and the planning, except for one year group, was done very much by the individual for their own class.

It seemed that the people with posts of responsibility had been given little opportunity to develop their own expertise or to learn the management skills needed for the post. They also had not been given the opportunity to decide on resources in their own areas.

We soon identified the fact that although we were increasing the 'power' of the majority we had taken away some of the power of a minority. I believe that this must have caused distrust and uncertainty for those teachers. However all of these influences were happening below the surface. There was still not trust to speak openly.

The belief that a team committed to working together with the same aim has more to offer than an individual wielding power is a very basic belief. It is also very uncomfortable at times because the team can propose some things that the head does not totally agree with and yet the style of management means that we 'try it'. So much is discussed and honest opinions are exchanged – we are not afraid to challenge one another and yet all of the time there is this interdependence – an essential ingredient of this development from hierarchy to team.

Co-ordination

Schools are not just buildings, curricula and procedures such as timetables. *Much more importantly* schools are relationships and interactions amongst often quite large groups of people. How these interpersonal interactions are carried out largely determines how successful a school is in achieving its purposes. Despite the rhetoric of curriculum aims and objectives, schools consist of groups of people who may have very different values and, indeed, beliefs about the purposes of schooling. How, then, can such an organisation be co-ordinated in order that those involved can work in a more efficient way?

Within the IQEA project we have recommended that schools should appoint at least two co-ordinators, one of whom at least being a member of the senior management team. These co-ordinators, referred to as the 'cadre', take responsibility for the day-to-day activities of the project in the school. In the following account, Les Fearns, Deputy Head of Marshalls Park Secondary School, reflects upon the way he has carried out his co-ordination roles. The school's work within IQEA has involved a fundamental rethink of the use of staff task groups. This has, at times, led to some 'turbulence' as the staff have become more involved in policy development. In particular the emergence of new, more widely representative staff groups has had implications for the responsibilities of existing structures such as the senior management team and heads of faculty group. Les and his two co-ordinator colleagues have been particularly successful in supporting this restructuring process.

What I did.

• Acted as a link person between senior management and the project and facilitated similar linking between the project and the staff in general.

- Provided for direct access to the management structure of the school for the project (e.g. for resourcing, meeting times).

- Lead a cadre of three and provided with the other two members initial frameworks for both the management of the project and the issues to be focussed upon.

- Helped facilitate amendments to the school management and development structure which would enable the outcomes of the school's involvement in the project to be more effective and which would also be of benefit in making the planning process in the school more effective, open and accessible to all staff in general.

What I learned from my involvement.

- There is a need to work with a supportive team who get on with each other personally as well as professionally. The cadre was made up of staff who knew each other socially and who had already worked together on school visits. This made the management of the project much easier and allowed each cadre member to be that much more supportive of the others.

- Staff scepticism can be overcome but only through involvement and trying to present as much professional integrity as possible. This means taking time to communicate and interact with staff, informally as well as formally.

- The need for long term planning was reinforced, especially where different groups of staff are concerned. There needs to be some concept of where you are going eventually.

- The need is to communicate fully with everyone involved. One cannot rely on assumptions or perceptions being shared implicitly. Time needs to be spent cultivating staff at all levels.

- It is important to the project to have the support of senior staff, both in a personal and structural sense, to help ensure the effectiveness of what is being implemented and for what is being done to be seen as a whole school programme.

Collaborative Planning

The quality of school-level planning has been identified as a major factor in a number of studies of school effectiveness. Sometimes 'excellent planning' is frustrated by a failure to communicate planning goals to those who will be working towards them – staff can only work on those plans they know about. Successful schools are more likely to work towards general goals and around general themes than with 'polished' mission statements, implying that it is a broad understanding of where the school is going that matters, rather than one clear image.

On the ground, the various stages constantly interact, seem often to spill over into one another and come together in an apparently seamless cycle of thinking, action and reflection. There is a continuous process of planning and re-planning going on in the school. We may well, at particular points in the school year, wish to take stock, to set down what we hope to achieve in the following year; but this must not be seen as the first point when planning goes on, and once the plans have been drawn up, the end of the exercise for another year. Such points merely bring the school's planning activity into focus – providing one 'still' from a continuous movement; they are frames drawn out of the film – not composed photographs which summarise or portray.

In the account that follows, Monica Adlem, Deputy Headteacher at Britannia County Primary School in Ipswich, describes how this approach to planning is reflected in her school.

We are a large primary school with 24 staff. The use of staff groups has developed as an effective way of enabling staff to focus on planning and be engaged in the development of specific curriculum areas while maintaining their involvement in the development of the whole curriculum and whole school issues.

There are three parallel, mixed ability classes in each Year Group. Each year team of teachers is released for one half-day towards the end of the summer term so that they can make an overall plan of work for the coming year. Our school curriculum framework outlines the content for their plans.

At the end of each term they are also released to make detailed plans for the coming term. One hour per week is included in the time budget for year team meetings. This enables them to refine and adjust their plans as well as to discuss any problems. The strength of the year team is in mutual support and inspiration.

The time spent on planning is valued as enabling the more efficient use of time and resources during the term. It is also seen as helping to raise the standard of work produced in the classroom.

All staff are involved in producing the school development plan. The curriculum groups and subject co-ordinators produce their own plans for the coming year. Whole school issues can be raised by any member of staff.

All staff discuss all aspects of the development plan. We regard this as essential if all staff are going to be committed to implementing the plan. After the whole staff discussion, the plans are discussed by the senior management team and the middle management team so that the advantages and disadvantages of each element can be discussed and prioritised.

This format is not static but developing. Each year refinements or changes are made, either in response to staff requests or in anticipation of future needs. Our aim is to improve the quality of the education for our children. In order to achieve this we need all of our staff working together to provide a stimulating and cohesive curriculum with a happy and structured environment.

Working with, rather than on

So far the broad IQEA approach to school improvement has been summarised through the school's own stories of their journeys of change. Something now should be said more explicitly about how we support the schools through this complex process. Our current thinking is best represented in a strategy which consists of seven elements.

The first element of our strategy is the *contract* between the partners in the project – the school and in some cases its teachers, the LEA or sponsoring agency, and ourselves. The contract defines the parameters of the project and the obligations of those involved to each other. It is intended to clarify expectations and ensure the conditions necessary for success. In particular the contract emphasises that all staff be consulted, that co-ordinators are appointed, that a 'critical mass' of teachers are actively involved in development work, and that sufficient time is made available for classroom observation and staff development. For our part, we co-ordinate the project, provide training for the school co-ordinators and representatives, make regular school visits and contribute to staff training, provide staff development materials, and monitor the implementation of the project.

The second element of our strategy is our *knowledge of the change process*. The 'framework for school improvement' that we have developed maps the territory of our engagement with the schools, and is described in detail elsewhere (Hopkins *et al.*, 1994; Hopkins, 1994).

The third element of the strategy is the *manual* that we have produced to support our staff development work with the schools. The manual contains our best shot at summarising the conditions necessary for successful school improvement described earlier, and includes training exercises and support materials (Ainscow *et al.*, 1994).

From the beginning of the project we were determined that we would attempt to affect all *levels* of the school, and this is the fourth element. One of the things that we had learned from the research and our previous work is that change will not be successful unless it impacts, and is owned, at all levels of the organisation. The key ingredient in this approach was the *cadre*. In many schools members of the cadre established an *extended cadre* which served to extend the project in a more formal way within the school.

Fifthly, there is a strong emphasis on *reflection and enquiry* within the project. Reflection is the essential building block of professional competence and confidence.

Sixthly, from the teachers' point of view it is appropriate that involvement in school improvement should be acknowledged. An advantage of the school-university collaboration is the opportunity for teachers to *accredit* their school-based professional development activities through a series of academic awards.

The final element in our overall strategy is the nature of *our own intervention*. As is by now quite obvious, we have explicitly chosen an interventionist role. We work with the cadre and in the schools and while trying to assist, facilitate and support, we are also trying to research and evaluate this approach to school improvement.

Our commitment to *working with rather than on* schools, presents many difficulties and dilemmas. In a more traditional project we might well have chosen to introduce the schools to an existing model of development based upon previous research activities. Then, having set the initiative going, our task would have been to stand back and record the process and outcomes of the intervention. In IQEA we have deliberately chosen to adopt a very different approach, based upon an alternative perspective as to how change can be facilitated. Rather than seeking to impose externally validated models of improvement we are attempting to support schools in creating their own models. Our assumption is that such an approach, that builds upon the biographies and circumstances of particular organisations, is much more likely to bring about and help sustain significant improvements in the quality of schooling.

Finally a comment on the metaphor of the *journey* that we have been using when talking about the progress of development over time. It is a helpful image, implying as it does a dynamic view of development and change. But, to be literal, where does it lead? One of the problems with previous approaches to school improvement is that they have taken a short-term view of change. In many cases this has meant focussing on the implementation of a single issue or a given curriculum development. We now live in a 'change-rich' environment, where multiple policy initiatives and innovation overload can easily oppress schools. In order to cope with change of this magnitude and complexity, we need to adopt a long-term perspective. We need to focus on the *management of change* in general, on the creation of effective and flexible structures and on the empowering of individuals, rather than on the implementation of specific, but usually minor, changes. This is why we have chosen to journey with our schools rather than to search for 'quick-fix' solutions. It is inevitable that this account of our travels with the moving school is reflective and interim, because there is no clearly defined beginning or end to our work together. Simply, we journey on.

Note

This chapter is based on more detailed descriptions of our school improvement work found in the articles and books referenced below. In this respect, I am most grateful to my colleagues, Mel Ainscow, Michael Fielding, David Hargreaves, Judy Sebba, Geoff Southworth and Mel West, for sharing their own school improvement journeys with me.

149

References

Ainscow, M. and Hopkins, D. (1992) 'Aboard the Moving School', *Educational Leadership*, **50**(3), November, pp.79-81.

Ainscow, M., Hopkins, D., Southworth, G.W. and West, M. (1994) *Creating the Conditions for School Improvement* (London: Fulton).

Hargreaves, D.H. and Hopkins, D. (1991) *The Empowered School* (London: Cassell).

Hopkins, D. (1994) 'Yellow Brick Road', *Managing Schools Today*, **3**(6), March, pp.14-17.

Hopkins, D. and Ainscow, M. (1993) 'Making Sense of School Improvement', *Cambridge Journal of Education*, **23**(3), pp.287-304.

Hopkins, D., Ainscow, M. and West, M. (1994) *School Improvement in an Era of Change* (London: Cassell).

CHAPTER 10

SCHOOL IMPROVEMENT AND STAFF DEVELOPMENT:
The Thurston Development Project

Mel West

In the Autumn of 1992 Thurston Upper School joined the
'Improving the Quality of Education for All' (IQEA) Project which
is based at the University of Cambridge Institute of Education.
This chapter however is not about the IQEA project (a description
of the aims and approaches adopted in the IQEA project can be
found elsewhere in this book), but about the progress of a school
development initiative in one school. It happened that the school's
development work was connected via the IQEA project with a network of schools similarly engaged in school improvement efforts,
and with an LEA partner offering external support. There have
clearly been occasions when the school has made use of this support framework, drawing on members of the IQEA project team,
drawing in the LEA adviser linked with the initiative, drawing
from the experience of colleagues undertaking parallel activities in
their own schools. The IQEA team like to believe that such contacts
have offered both stimulation and practical support to the school's
own efforts. Essentially though, this is the story of one school finding the space and time to look at itself, reflecting upon the images
it saw, and beginning to consider how it might create brighter and
sharper images in the future.

This focus on a real development in a specific school context
argues for practical and pragmatic criteria for evaluating the success of the project as a staff development exercise. Accordingly, the

following are suggested as features of effective staff development to which the reader might refer. They are not intended to offer a theoretical framework – there are already quite enough 'models'. Nor do they pretend definitive advice – lists of 'dos' and 'don'ts' are also widely available elsewhere. They are offered rather as a series of observations about what happens when school-based staff development seems to be working.

- Effective staff development starts from *where the teacher is*, though it is informed by a view of where he or she is going. It is therefore a 'building from' rather than a 'deficit' approach.

- Effective staff development involves teachers recognising that they can and do learn 'on the job' – the classroom is an important development centre for teachers as well as pupils.

- During the development process, feedback is available to stimulate and to reassure teachers who are experimenting with new behaviours.

- Individual learning in practical settings is related to key concepts and ideas which facilitate generalisation.

- The best opportunities for staff development relate to those activities which teachers find meaningful and satisfying.

Of course, in one short chapter, it is not possible to recount all those conversations and activities which contributed to the Development Project. Accordingly, this analysis is limited to an outline of the project goals, and to the perceptions which various members of staff hold as to its impact on the school.

The School

Opened in September 1973 in pleasant purpose-built buildings Thurston Upper School is a 13-18 comprehensive school serving a rural community of 210 square miles. There are 1,300 on roll including 300 in the sixth form and a staffing establishment of 82.7. It sees itself as a 'Community Committed to Success' and places considerable emphasis both upon the quality of good, caring relationships and the partnership with the local community.

Commitment to the highest standards of teaching and learning throughout the school is seen as vital to individual success. In 1990 Thurston received the Schools Curriculum Award for being at the 'heart of its community' and it was one of the first schools in the country to be awarded development funding under the Technology Schools' Initiative in 1992. It was invited by the Suffolk LEA to participate in the IQEA project as a pilot school in 1992 and was fortunate to receive some additional INSET monies from the authority to support the venture in the first year.

The Project goals

The success of Thurston Upper School's bid to become one of the Technology Schools' Initiative (TSI) pilot schools meant that in the 1992-93 academic year the school would receive a grant of approximately £250,000 to improve the availability of and the access to technology resources in the school. It was recognised that this rapid expansion of the technological base, coupled with the commitments to develop a broadly-based 14-18 vocational /technology-related curriculum would mean changes to teaching and learning in the school. Indeed, the school development plan had identified as a priority:

> ...improvements to support the development of student-centred resource-based learning, improving the quality of teaching and learning for all.

Consequently it was not difficult for the IQEA cadre group in the school to identify an area of the school for systematic review and development. When, early in the Autumn term, the Thurston Development Project was launched within the school, departments were invited to join in a process of enquiry into the quality of learning experience currently made available to Year 9 pupils. Year 9 was selected because the implementation of Key Stage 3 was already raising questions about how quality might be maintained in the face of national curriculum requirements. The enquiry would involve a number of elements including:

> – A review of departmental schemes of work in light of national curriculum requirements and the notion of 'quality' implicit in the school's policies and documentation.

- 'Pupil pursuit', so that some members of staff could experience first-hand the quality of learning available to Thurston pupils.

- Paired observation of classroom practice (cross-curricular) to help identify existing strengths and opportunities.

- Interviews with a sample of Year 9 pupils so that their views on learning quality and on their experiences at Thurston could be established.

- A survey of parents' views about their children's progress in the school.

These activities were to be supported in a number of ways. The LEA link adviser would play a major role in the review activities and help staff to prepare for the observation sessions. He would also undertake the student interviews and feed back findings to the staff. Planning and training days for the members of staff (cadre group) co-ordinating the project would be available under the IQEA programme. IQEA team members would be available to help the co-ordinators to develop their own thinking and planning, and to assist in the whole staff training for classroom observation. INSET for participating staff would be made available, and time for paired observation would be funded from the INSET budget. All staff would be kept informed of progress through a series of reports produced by the co-ordinators, beginning with a description of the project's aims, rationale and scope.

The Thurston Development Project

What is the Project?
The Thurston Development Project is designed to explore what we at Thurston understand by the term 'Quality Learning' and what this means for the pupil in our classrooms.

Initially the Project will focus on our work with pupils in Year 9.

Why has this Project been chosen?

In our School Development Plan we had already identified the need to look at our use of resources, styles of teaching and learning and at the enhancement of student-centred learning. Good schools like Thurston are committed to doing the best possible for their pupils, and, at a time of great change, we must ensure that we identify, preserve and build upon our existing good practice. It is in this way that we can carry forward into whole school and departmental developments clear notions of what we believe the quality learning should be that leads to individual and school success.

Why focus on Year 9?

Several departments at Thurston have already expressed a desire to develop new schemes of work and teaching resources for this year. We are experiencing the effect of KS3 for the first time and there is much to learn and cope with here. Some departments are concerned that what they believed represented quality learning experiences are threatened by the demands of the National Curriculum.

It makes sense to examine the issues at KS3 as a whole staff working together and not just in departmental isolation.

How will the Project be carried forward?

As a group of staff we must explore what we mean by 'Quality Learning' as it applies to curriculum areas and to our own classrooms.

What are the outcomes looked for in the Project?

The process of working together as a staff to decide what quality learning is and how we can protect and enhance it will undoubtedly have real and positive benefits even though these may not lend themselves to easy measurement.

Departments involved in the Project should be able to apply what we learn to the development of any schemes of work which they have in hand or intend to start.

Staff will have the opportunity to examine and try a variety of teaching and learning styles.

There will be structured staff development opportunities focussed on what is central to schools, that is learning in classrooms.

Pupils should have even more opportunity for interesting and successful learning experiences.

As a staff we will have had more structured opportunities to focus on our vision of what makes a school successful.

Is there an underlying philosophy of approach to the Project?
Yes, that it should focus on our work in the classroom. Also central is the assumption that teams of staff working together on school development is most likely to bring about success ful implementation of desired change.

What are the first steps of the Project?
1. For interested groups of staff to be introduced to the ideas underpinning the Project.

2. For groups of staff from different curriculum areas to consider what is meant at Thurston by 'Quality Learning'.

3. To apply agreed notions of 'Quality Learning' to our own departments and classrooms through action research so as to identify the qualities and good practice we already have.

4. For pilot departments to link notions of 'Quality Learning' to Year 9 developments they have in hand or wish to pursue.

What is the length of the Project?
Initially one year but undoubtedly we will wish to review progress and continue to learn from experience. It looks increasingly as if some development time will be required in the academic year 1993-94.

Are the desired outcomes and the shape of the Project open to change?
Yes, we need to feed back what staff are thinking and feeling about the Project so that it can be managed to meet real needs and not imagined ones. The emphasis must be on the process of working together to look at pupil learning rather than on a list of predetermined outcomes.

However, the Project should not be so woolly that there is no way of measuring if it has achieved anything.

Will staff outside the pilot departments get to know what is happening?
We hope to evolve a way of sharing what is going on so that all staff are aware and can learn from and contribute to the Project. It is hoped the Staffing & Resources sub-committee will be actively involved in monitoring the Project and disseminating ideas.

We plan to use part of the second Staff Development Day in January to work with all staff on the Project.

Planning for, carrying through and evaluating the significance of this enquiry into the quality of learning became itself a major staff development exercise. For example, almost fifty members of staff became involved in cross-curricular working groups identifying what 'quality learning' meant in Thurston, providing the criteria for subsequent classroom observation sessions. The classroom observation programme itself involved a similar number of teachers, drawn from all levels and subject backgrounds. In these pairings teachers who would not normally have opportunity to share one another's ideas were frequently brought together. Feedback from the pupil interview programme and review of departmental policies combined with findings from the teachers' own enquiries to suggest new priorities for the school. This, in turn, has led to a significant revision of the school development plan, and (in the following year) to wide consultation and information gathering (for example, a major survey of parent views) and to adjustments in staff structures and roles to reflect the new priorities. Above all, the Thurston Development Project provided time and space for busy teachers in overcrowded days to share practice and ideas, discuss needs and opportunities and focus energies around the classroom.

This has resulted in staff recognising that their contact with and work in collaboration with colleagues is a valid and important vehicle for school development. It has underlined that most staff development takes place in and around the school, and as a direct consequence of engagement in work as an activity. Courses, and conferences have a role to play – indeed, the Thurston Project has sometimes used professional development days for training purposes – but central to any notion of continuing growth and development in the School is a commitment to see the classroom and the staff-room as key centres for teacher development.

But, such conclusions are often more readily offered by 'outsiders'. There are times when those who work inside the school are rather less sanguine about development projects than those who are observing the process from a comfortable distance. Yet, what we need to identify is what is happening in the perceptions of those directly involved. In an effort to tap into these internal responses, an interview programme was carried out with a number of staff from the school at the end of the 1992-93 school year.

The perceptions of staff in the school

In any development project it is to be expected that, even over a relatively short period of time, individuals will engage and progress at different rates. It is also to be expected that staff will hold different views, both about what has taken place and about the importance or significance of particular developments. Given the spread of responses which can be attributed to these factors, it is not possible to claim that a small number of staff in any sense 'represents' a group of more than eighty. Nevertheless, there are views which may be considered important, either because they come from those who are well placed strategically to influence the course of events or because they offer a yardstick against which impact can be gauged. The following interviews are focussed on such a group – the headteacher, who can decide whether the project is to be continued or discarded as unsuccessful, the co-ordinators who have had almost daily involvement in the management of the project and who have monitored its progress most closely, and the teachers, who are best placed to estimate the extent to which a particular development leads to any real change in practice.

The headteacher's perspective

The headteacher felt that the Thurston Development Project, with its emphases on enquiry and on classroom practice, would help the school to increase the level of involvement of all staff in the thinking and planning processes which guide the school. The classroom focus would also be empowering, since those involved would be able to set their own agenda and work on their own priorities with the 'school need' in mind. He felt that staff were ready for this kind of development, and hoped that the resources provided for the scrutiny of their own practice and the systematic analysis of pupil-based data would underline the importance attached to the teacher-pupil relationship by the school's senior management. Beyond this, and the need therefore to lend his (public) support to the goals of the project, he felt that the co-ordinators would see it as 'their project to manage' - keeping the senior management team informed but devising their own strategy. Where a senior management team decision was required (e.g. a questionnaire to parents) he felt that support had been offered. Despite this 'hands off' approach, he felt a number of staff had probably regarded the project as a 'Trojan Horse for the SMT' at the outset.

However, he was extremely happy that 52 members of staff had been drawn into the project, at least at the level of paired observation, with many having a much more extended involvement. This seemed a tremendous achievement at a time when so much else was going on – and it was clear evidence of the co-ordinators careful and constructive planning. He felt that the spread of involvement had introduced many colleagues to the idea of working constructively with each other – an important staff development outcome, even though it might not always lead to consensus.

Most interesting, the project had raised issues which had caused the headteacher to think again about his own role, to question his own priorities and goals. This was not always comfortable – he felt that the staff had, through their enquiries brought a new dimension to evaluation in the school – similar in some ways to inspection, but self-critical, coming from within, and addressing the 'foundations of what we are about'. He was confident that the senior management team would respond to this new focus and a new sense of alignment was already emerging, but it had reminded him of the need to continually question his understanding of 'headship' and been professionally very challenging. The involvement of partners from outside the school was seen as a significant stimulus to this reconceptualisation of his own role, but also as a source of information which could offer reassurance.

He felt that the sense of challenge that he had experienced was paralleled at head of department level. Some of the findings there too would be uncomfortable, 'we have created pressure, we need to ensure support', and in this case the findings were hard to dispute as they came from many sources and were, for the most part, teacher initiated. The breaking down of boundaries would be helpful here – allowing advice to move along previously unexploited routes.

Of course, levels of engagement varied – even amongst heads of department. It was hard to maintain uniform levels of involvement at any one level, but there did seem to be examples of commitment at all levels.

The most important outcome was the consensus arising from the working groups about the school's priorities. Several of these issues would transfer into the school development plan, with linked resourcing, demonstrating support and creating the possibility of observable outcomes. This made school priorities the staff's priorities, though the SMT would need to negotiate the rate of transfer in light of other initiatives, and external pressures.

The co-ordinators' perspective

The Thurston Project was jointly co-ordinated by a deputy headteacher and a head of department. Both describe the early weeks as a time of confusion and frustration, before they could see how best to identify a quality focus which would offer possibilities for wide involvement. They felt that the key event came about half-way through the term when the headteacher published the school's mission statement, which concentrated attention around the core purposes of the school. Linking the Thurston Development Project to the core purposes on the one hand and the need to review curriculum processes because of other pressures (National Curriculum and Technology Schools Initiative) on the other hand provided a solid basis for the venture. The initial reactions of the staff were encouraging, with enough volunteers to run six workshop sessions during the autumn term.

The involvement at this stage of the LEA link adviser was seen as crucial. His involvement was seen as 'legitimating' teacher enquiry by some. His working sessions with the staff were well-received and reassuring. As an outsider, his compilation of pupil views was seen as objective. As an OFSTED registered inspector, his comments on the schemes of work and other departmental documentation were authoritative. As a presence in meetings he increased the status of the project amongst senior management. As a source of advice and support to the co-ordinators his role was much appreciated and helped increase their confidence and sense of direction. Contact through the IQEA project with colleagues from other schools, and the sessions offered to support school co-ordinators seemed timely and relevant to their needs. The three-cornered partnership between school, LEA and IQEA team provided the co-ordinators with an important reference framework.

The quality of work produced in school by the volunteer groups during this stage was high, and was fairly readily adapted into a schedule which could be used for the paired observation. Paired observation was important because it was the major form of teacher data, to set alongside the positive (from parents) and less reassuring (from pupils) images of the school which were emerging from the other aspects of the enquiry. Involvement in determining the criteria to be used in observation was empowering, as was the freedom to select a partner with whom you were comfortable. The numbers engaging in the paired observation programme (26 pairings) were higher than expected, and the activity which this occasioned carried the project through to the summer term.

Processing this new mass of data about the quality of learning was a difficult task, and 'a huge responsibility'. But the resulting reports have had a profound effect on the school's priorities. It was difficult not to address the reports when they were based on data produced from such a wide base, and so many colleagues had contributed to the processes of data collection. As a result of the findings, working parties had been established to follow up the main issues (schemes of work; differentiation; marking policy, etc.), and already the senior management team had shown a willingness to modify the development plan in light of the emerging priorities and issues of concern.

As a side-effect, staff from different curriculum areas seemed to get together or even 'just talk' more than they had previously and when co-ordinators felt things had been grinding to a halt, the staff had kept things moving. However, 'organising' volunteers was not always straightforward. Some 'volunteers' had been less willing than others, imagining they were under pressure to come forward. Co-ordinating a development project also gave insights into how easily the perceptions of the senior management team and the perceptions of the 'staff group' could differ.

Resources had been central to the strategy for involvement. In the end, the willingness to fund the paired observation programme probably gave a clearer notion of the importance the senior management attach to quality improvement than all the papers produced, but those involved tended to use the papers once they had decided to opt in. The co-ordinators felt that their own skills in working with colleagues had developed significantly. They hoped that this was a general outcome from the project. They felt that staff had developed ways of looking at things, insights into evaluation as a process and into the quality of experience Thurston offers its pupils. These were attributes likely to be useful in other contexts. There was however a possible point of tension. The co-ordinators themselves were clear that the Thurston Project had only been a 'beginning' – it was what they did next that mattered. They felt that the senior management recognised this in principle but might show less enthusiasm in practice. For some of the teachers involved however, the project was seen as an 'end' and, by implication therefore, that was 'development' taken care of for a while.

The teachers' perspective

Teacher views differed somewhat, though there were some areas of general agreement. The focus on classroom practice was one such area, though for some this emphasis only became apparent later on. Some had felt that the project was a senior management initiative, rather than an invitation to staff to join in and contribute to the school's development. Others were just 'too busy' to take much notice, so long as it did not effect them. From the participants point of view, the clarification of the paired observation programme which took place at the beginning of the spring term was a key point (i.e. some two months after the point of 'lift-off' for the co-

ordinators). Certainly, the opportunity to engage in paired observation was a major incentive for involvement.

The actual experience of classroom observation was universally
welcomed as beneficial – 'finding out about teaching approaches in
other subjects', 'seeing how the motivation of pupils you 'know''
changes between teachers'; 'having someone come in made me
really think about my teaching', 'feedback was really useful', 'I felt
I got some gentle but important reminders', 'it is probably good
preparation for appraisal'. The sessions where staff had collabo-
rated to identify criteria for classroom observation and the
contextualising/guidance from the link adviser were good preparation. Though some felt that the impact would be short-lived,
others felt that classroom observation should be a regular feature
of the school's staff development programme.

Other forms of enquiry carried out during the project were less
well-received. Staff were very sensitive to the 'criticisms' they
detected in some aspects of the reports, leading some to question
the 'evidence', whilst others accepted the evidence but questioned
the method of reporting. Certainly, staff generally seemed much
more aware of the issues raised by the project, and much less
aware of the strengths the project had revealed, than were those in
senior or co-ordinating roles.

Many staff felt under pressure, from curriculum change, from
parents, from 'league tables', from senior management initiatives.
In such a climate, with a premium on time, it was queried whether
enough time could be found to address the issues which had
emerged, however important these were. In particular there was
confusion about the machinery (if any) through which project outcomes would be processed, and some doubt about the extent to
which any 'whole school' initiative could be successfully implemented.

It was felt that most staff already worked 'desperately hard', and
that not much more could be fitted in. Some individuals were 'constantly evaluating' their teaching – the barriers to improvement in
the quality of learning provided were to be found in the policies
and attitudes of senior managers, not in any lack of awareness
amongst teachers.

But for others the project had produced 'sound evidence'; 'the
first time we have had real evidence of what is going on'. It had
resulted in 'the best report we have ever produced in this school',
and in the identification of 'priorities' which were seen as 'the

important things we all need to concentrate on'. While some teachers reported little or no impact on the day-to-day life of the school, others were able to point to significant outcomes ('we have begun to consult with students'; 'we are beginning to talk about a whole school ethos'; 'since the observation I have deliberately tried to extend my teaching approach'; 'pupil-pursuit fascinating, we must do more...').

Some wondered how the development would be sustained. There was a need for senior management to pick up the findings and make sure that momentum was maintained. Though 'opposition' from a small number of staff who 'don't want to know' could be anticipated, senior management should stress the positive outcomes and use the consensus emerging from the whole staff meetings to drive the school forward.

The Thurston Development Project and staff development

Returning to the criteria for effective staff development activity suggested earlier, it would seem that the Thurston Project has been successful. The project deliberately started with enquiry, mapping current experience and approaches, underlining the importance of looking at what staff currently do and think. Drawing on an increasingly large participating group, the project has begun to shape ideas of how the school might develop which are grounded in the real day-to-day experiences of the teachers.

The role of teachers as data collectors, data interpreters and as resources to one another has also been clearly established. Classroom contexts have been placed at the centre of development effort, and the role of staff as mirrors to one another's practice and (in some cases) 'critical friends' has increasingly been recognised. Teachers report that feedback from colleagues has been available and useful. There has also been important 'conceptualising' going on – both of frameworks for specific behaviours, such as classroom observation and pupil-pursuit, and of the conditions necessary to support long-term improvement – such as the way leadership operates in the school, the potential of school-based data, and the role of staff development itself. There has also been a definite sense of engagement – the project has identified an area for development which most of the staff see as central to their work. This has added a sense of purpose, and, sometimes a degree of stress, to the activities.

As a staff development exercise then, the Thurston Project would seem to be generating responses which tend to be associated with real changes in staff attitudes and behaviour. To that extent, it can be considered a successful venture, which has provided development opportunities for most of those involved. However, it has also resulted in a substantive agenda for the school.

The issues identified by staff from their enquiries and deliberations do, as the headteacher noted, 'go to the foundations of what we are about'. Such issues demand attention – whether through a continuation of the project or other means. The school has now begun to address these issues, in part through extending the Project into another year, in part through a reordering of priorities, in part through a reorganisation of roles and structures. It can expect some difficult as well as some exciting times ahead. The very changes staff are seeking will create a turbulence from which some will wish to turn back. The empowerment which has proved so stimulating initially will inevitably mean an accompanying responsibility which may seem rather harder to accept.

But there are also strengths which the school can carry forward. The relationship with and support from the LEA link adviser has been enormously beneficial (a point worth particular note, as government legislation continues to erode the role of the LEA), and the school has accumulated experience of how to use such support purposefully and to its own agenda. The amount and the quality of discussion about school priorities, student learning, teaching approach, has increased at all levels – creating a vocabulary which will make future dialogue and debate easier. Staff are beginning to recognise that empowerment in relation to and 'ownership' of school policies brings with it the need for commitment and the willingness to share in the responsibility for the school's development. Most important, it has become plain that a school that tries to 'stand still' will in fact be going backwards. However difficult it seems, continuous improvement is the only way to avoid decline. The Thurston Development Project has signposted the route. It is now time to travel the road.

Note

My thanks are due to the following members of staff from Thurston Upper School who contributed their views to this chapter: Al Brown, Stewart Chenery, Juliet Ecclestone, Richard Fawcett,

Martin Goold, Muriel Lawrence, Sally MacDonald, Gary Mills, Rebecca Offley, David Perry, Tony Sear, David Sixsmith, Shena Waitkins, Wendy White, and *especially* Nick Pavitt and Joy Tubbs.

CHAPTER 11

DEVELOPING OWNERSHIP OF A NATIONAL INITIATIVE

Howard Bradley

The introduction of appraisal and the need to prepare teachers for it makes an interesting case study because the conditions surrounding the change ran counter to all we have learned about successful implementation of change. At the time the national requirement was introduced there was little evidence that school staffs either felt ownership of the scheme or recognised appraisal as a desirable aspect of their work. In some cases there were very definite statements of the opposing view. There was also no evidence that in many schools the organisation and culture were such that appraisal would fit naturally and productively into the schools' systems, nor did the Government's time-scale allow an approach which might attempt to develop organisation, culture and appraisal together. Equally there was no time available to build up a partnership between the external consultants and the individuals who form a school staff. At best there was time to forge a good partnership with the LEA and to make more tenuous contacts with the senior staff of each school. In effect, the Government's demand for speed, coupled with the suspicions surrounding appraisal, threw schools directly into the phases of destabilisation described by Hopkins and Ainscow (1993) when change hits the wall of institutional and individual resistance and momentum is lost. In the case of appraisal, change often began at the foot of the wall without any momentum.

The nature of the problem

Perhaps more than any other initiative pressed upon schools from outside, the introduction of appraisal raised fear and suspicion among teachers. It could truly be said to be born of adversity for its origins lay in a labour dispute. Moreover, its principles were fundamentally liberal at a time of intense conservatism. No surprise then that teachers found it difficult to reconcile the developmental tenor of the regulations introducing appraisal with well-publicised statements of ministers, from the weeding out of poor teachers advocated by Sir Keith Joseph to the league tables promoted by John Patten.

Surprisingly, the National Steering Group for Appraisal, representing the Department of Education and Science, the local education authorities and the teacher associations, was notable for the collaborative tone of its work. Relationships were always delicate; at different periods two associations withdrew from the negotiations. Nevertheless, the final report had support from all parties.

There was then an unfortunate hiatus while successive Secretaries of State considered the scheme. Finally, in August 1991, appraisal was launched formally at a time when teachers were already struggling with the introduction of the National Curriculum. For many teachers, appraisal, instead of appealing as a support mechanism, seemed to be just one more imposition. At least one of the teacher associations had by then faltered in its support for appraisal. At the point when the associations could have promoted actively this model of appraisal as central to professional development, and when they could have taken great credit for its subsequent success, some nerves failed.

As a result, the advice available to teachers in the same school from their various associations differed considerably. For example, those reading the Regulations themselves (DES, 1991) or the commentary upon them agreed and circulated jointly by the six teacher organisations (The Six Teacher Organisations, 1991) learned that:

(3) Appraisal procedures shall in particular aim to-
    (a) recognise the achievements of school teachers and help them to identify ways of improving their skills and performance;
    (b) help school teachers, governing bodies and local education authorities (as the case may be) to determine whether a change of duties would help the professional development of school teachers and improve their career prospects;

   (c) identify the potential of teachers for career development, with
       the aim of helping them, where possible, through appropriate
       in-service training;
   (d) help school teachers having difficulties with their performance,
       through appropriate guidance, counselling and training;
   (e) inform those responsible for providing references for school
       teachers in relation to appointments;
   (f) improve the management of schools.
 (4) Appraisal procedures shall not form part of any disciplinary or dis-
     missal procedures, but appraisal statements may be used for the
     purposes specified in Regulation 14.

However, the purpose of appraisal was presented by the
NASUWT to its members as follows (NASUWT, 1991):

   (a) identifying in-service training needs both for their own benefit
       and that of the school;
   (b) identifying where a change of job would be appropriate;
   (c) identifying candidates for promotion;
   (d) identifying those with capability problems;
   (e) evidence in disciplinary cases;
   (f) evidence in dismissal cases;
   (g) evidence in the withholding of increments;
   (h) evidence in the awarding of discretionary payments (e.g. extra incre-
       ments, incentive allowances, inter incremental 'dollops', extension
       of the standard scale by, currently, up to £3,000).

Teachers need to bear these purposes in mind when participating in
appraisal. Appraisal can no longer be presented as exclusively
intended for professional development. Appraisal is essentially about
collecting information on a teacher's performance. The information
gathered can then be used for a variety of purposes including more
pay, disciplinary warnings, dismissal on grounds other than disciplinary (e.g. redundancy) and in-service needs.

There were similar differences between the associations concerning the elements within the appraisal process, particularly those
which were not made compulsory by the Regulations. Considering
the initial meeting, self-appraisal and debriefing meetings after
observation, AMMA held the view (AMMA, 1991):

AMMA considers that without the initial meeting, and the meetings
before and after classroom observation, appraisal cannot promote a
teacher's professional development, will not be supportive and cannot
achieve the aims envisaged in the Regulations.

The NUT is equally strong in its commitment to the initial meeting
(NUT, 1991):

It is *vital* that the initial meeting is a significant stage in the process in your school, so that the appraisal process is based on clear initial objectives.

but more cautious about self-appraisal:

Although the Government scheme does not make self-appraisal compulsory, you may find it helpful...If appraisal is being used as a control mechanism, you should consider carefully what you say. Remember that you do not have to give your appraiser any report of your self-appraisal.

The NASUWT Report takes a different view:

NASUWT believes that schemes of appraisal ought to be kept as simple and mechanistic as possible in order to reduce the workload demands on teachers. To this end we have advocated a tick box approach to appraisal together with a minimal number of meetings.

On the non-compulsory meetings, it said:

NASUWT believes that teachers would be better served if appraisal were confined to what the law requires rather than to 'desirable additions'.

and on self-appraisal:

The Regulations do not require self-appraisal. Bearing in mind the uses to which appraisal can be put, NASUWT opposes such self-appraisal.

In view of this spectrum of advice, in the context of unsympathetic political attitudes towards teachers and the demands of implementing the National Curriculum, it is not surprising that teachers approached appraisal with considerable uncertainty, suspicion and in some cases fear.

Such a climate was not the most propitious for an innovation which was expected to come very close to the heart of teachers' practice. It is more typical of those situations in the past when educational innovations have failed than it is of success. Rudduck (1991) reports difficulties when teachers are:

...exhausted by the demands of multiple initiatives whose coherence and whose relationships to their own values they haven't the time, and sometimes the energy, to work out.

She agrees with Poppleton (1988) that these pressures lead to what the latter calls a 'militant conservatism' which is characterised by reactions which are anti-innovation and anti-bureaucracy. Rudduck suggests that if teachers are to be able to cope with innovations that threaten their professional status and confidence they need to feel that:

> ...change is not something that happens to them, and which they cannot control, like bereavement, but instead something which they are in principle seeking and welcoming.

The first requirement therefore was to increase the belief that teachers could control this innovation. Fullan (1982) remarks that in the early stages of an innovation teachers are much more concerned with the way in which the proposed changes might affect them personally than they are about the potential benefits of the innovation. He said that change must 'take into account the subjective reality of teachers'. Bradley (1991a) suggests that 'INSET experiences should take participants beyond their present experience, but not too far, and should challenge their present understanding, but not too stridently'.

The second requirement was to demonstrate that the innovation could take account of subjective reality. Bradley (1987) deduced from the evidence of curriculum change projects that successful institutionalisation of projects was slow and uncertain and that the more innovative a project was for the school concerned the less likely it was to succeed. He identified as important the following climatic factors:

(i) awareness that there is a problem;
(ii) willingness to do something about it (often influenced by what happened when previously they tried to solve a problem);
(iii) attitudes of senior staff towards change;
(iv) availability of support and resources.

Although some schools approaching appraisal could demonstrate positive scores on all these factors there were many where that was not the case. The third requirement for the implementation of appraisal was therefore to create a sufficiently positive climate in schools to allow the innovation to develop as the school itself wished it to do, and to flourish. As Fullan (1987) says:

What is at stake is how to improve the very professional culture of the school toward (depending on one's emphasis) such norms as increased collegiality, experimentation and continuous assessment and reflection.

The conundrum is, as Bradley *op. cit.* points out, that a climate supportive of innovation is, at one and the same time, a goal for staff development and a prerequisite for it.

Strategic questions for the INSET programme designer

The three requirements noted above led to a series of strategic questions for us as we developed the appraisal training programme. In moving towards a strategy of support for schools implementing appraisal, decisions were based upon exploration of these questions.

(i) *Climate.* How to utilise, and indeed strengthen positive climates where they existed and how to build a sufficiently positive climate where none existed? How to develop in teachers the belief that in this innovation lay a powerful weapon to support them and their schools?

(ii) *Knowledge.* How to present the features of the national scheme in a way that encouraged the school to make the most of this opportunity? How to dispel the myths, the fears and the negative thinking which was associated with appraisal and how to help teachers to the point where they could reap maximum benefit from skills training?

(iii) *Skills.* How best to develop in particular the skills of interviewing and classroom observation and how to follow up with reinforcing experiences?

(iv) *Institutionalisation.* How best to cross the threshold from training to implementation? How to help schools develop an effective structure for the appraisal process and how to ensure that appraisal becomes an integral part of the school planning and development structure, ensuring access to resources and effective use of resources?

(v) *Volume and funding.* How to prepare every teacher in England and Wales in a period of under four years? In the case of the University of Cambridge Institute of Education, this meant training every teacher in each of a number of local education authorities (LEAs), training the trainers in others. In doing that, how to strike the balance between training appraisers and appraisees and how to do it all with at most two days per teacher available for training?

The Evaluation of the School Teacher Appraisal Pilot Study (Bradley *et al.*, 1989) provided guidance on some of these strategic questions. The Study, involving more than 1,000 teachers in over 150 schools in the six pilot LEAs, makes a series of points which are helpful to programme designers:

(i) The role of the LEA co-ordinator, someone seen as trustworthy and credible by teachers, is of key importance in addressing the questions of climate and institutionalisation.

(ii) The provision of well-produced, practical documents to explain the principles and practice of appraisal is important in helping teachers after training to put appraisal into practice.

(iii) The view of training shifted during the Pilot Study away from that of a preparatory training course making people ready for action. This view was replaced by the concept of the whole implementation period as a training experience, with training at appropriate points. This led us to produce distance-learning materials for use by teachers in schools at times they judged to be appropriate.

(iv) The Pilot Study pointed to the need for more training for appraisees than some originally envisaged. There was considerable support for appraisees and appraisers having the same training for at least part of the time on two grounds: the first that appraisal is a one-to-one process and both need the skills; the second that if they are trained together there can be no possibility of there being conflicting messages or agendas for the two groups.

(v) The Pilot Study demonstrated the need to engage not only in awareness-raising, which was regarded as a vital stage in the pilot LEAs, but also in skills development, which is seen as central to the success of implementation. Skills development tended to demand more time than is available in the introductory training for appraisal. Paraphrasing the work of Joyce and Showers (1980), Bradley *et al.*, *op. cit.*, suggested one could:

(i) demonstrate skills to people and hope they will replicate them;

(ii) give them the chance to practise skills in the hope they will recognise their deficiencies and repair them;

(iii) give them repeated practice and coaching on the job to improve the skills.

There is seldom time in training sessions for repeated practice and coaching, yet we know that is most effective.

Strategic decisions

In the light of the data from the Pilot Study and in discussion with LEA officers and co-ordinators, a common programme was agreed:

(i) Support for the co-ordinator, LEA officers and local union officials in devising an LEA policy.

(ii) A handbook for every teacher containing as an *aide mémoire* a page about each element of the appraisal process, as well as the training materials (Bradley, 1991b).

(iii) A much larger pack of distance-learning materials to be distributed at least one to each school (Bollington and Bradley, 1990).

(iv) Two half-day briefings for senior management in schools, with time between for discussion with their senior staffs.

(v) In the first year of implementation, a half-day awareness-raising session for all teachers, conducted with very large numbers so as to leave resources for small group skills training. Later in the programme of implementation, when anxiety levels had fallen and there was adequate local experience to call upon, schools did their own awareness-raising with the help of this local experience.

(vi) A day of skills training concentrating on two major areas, the interview and data collection, particularly classroom observation.

(vii) Continuing support from co-ordinators by means of clinics and further visits to the schools.

This programme was designed to encompass the transmission of knowledge, individual reflection, group decision-making and the development of confidence and capability. It fits with Joyce and Showers' (1980) analysis of the desirable components of training:

- presentation of theory, strategy or skills,
- modelling or demonstration of skills,
- practice in simulated or classroom settings,
- feedback,
- coaching.

It also matches Binsteed's (1982) description of three different forms of learning, usually going together:

(i) a discovery cycle; characterised by experimentation, trying things out in practice and seeing what happens;
(ii) a reflection cycle; assimilating new information or experience into existing practice, plans or beliefs;
(iii) an input cycle; involving the giving and receiving of information.

Binsteed suggests that a learning design is a combination of these three, determined by the preferred learning style of the individual and the particular learning objectives of the activity. In this case the preferred learning styles of the individuals were unknown and had to be assumed to be widely varying. The learning objectives were determined in consultation with LEA officers and representatives of the schools and teachers and were presented to every teacher in the handbook as follows:

At the end of the introductory session group members should have a good idea of the major principles involved in appraisal and will have discussed the issues arising in different parts of the appraisal process.

Between the first session and the skills training day it is hoped that colleagues will examine their own practice and undertake a short self-appraisal limited to one area of their work which they are prepared to discuss with two colleagues.

The self-appraisal exercise will form the basis of the appraisal interview practice which is central to the next session.

During the skills training day, we will concentrate on observed interview practice with feedback and on collecting data through classroom observation in preparation for an appraisal interview.

After the second session, colleagues will be asked to undertake some experimental data collection. Further support will be available in the form of a 'clinic', to which one or more people from a school will be able to bring issues and difficulties and we will join them in attempting to find solutions.

Content and approaches

The first management briefing contained short inputs from the presenter on :

(i) getting ready; climate setting; using working groups and co-ordinators; briefing governors; and,
(ii) points that need to be discussed with the staff before reporting back to the next meeting.

These were accompanied by small group work exploring case studies of matching appraisers and appraisees and larger group discussion in which members were asked to devise the concrete steps needed to carry out the management tasks required by the introduction of appraisal.

The second management briefing began with a clinic session, discussing issues raised in the individual schools, followed by activity sessions concerned with introducing classroom observation and other forms of data gathering, monitoring the school's programme and evaluating its impact.

These briefings were well-received and were found to be helpful by headteachers in thinking through their approach to the introduction of appraisal and in clarifying their understanding of its role. Their impact on the climate towards appraisal in the school more generally were less sure. Success depended on the existing climate in the school, the relationship between headteacher and staff, and the existence or not of active doubters among the staff. The same variables affected the impact of the awareness-raising half-day, which typically consisted of a presentation explaining the scheme and an opportunity for school staffs to discuss how they could make it work to their benefit, individually and as a school. Some schools laid here the foundation of their future discussions, others compounded their fears, reinforced their suspicions and speculated about how a future Secretary of State could use appraisal for malign purposes. In the most rewarding sessions, presenters watched doubt giving way to understanding. At the other end of the spectrum, presenters sometimes felt they were seen as Government agents and were unable to crack teachers' disbelief that appraisal could be developmental. As successful experience of appraisal grew in each LEA and as the credibility of the LEA co-ordinator became established, the need for awareness-raising sessions decreased and it was with some relief that they were replaced by more informal approaches.

Of all the elements of appraisal training, there is no doubt that the most successful in bringing home to teachers the value of appraisal as a process was the simulated interview. There have been attempts to train for interviewing by watching video tapes but the weight of opinion during the Appraisal Pilot Study and since supports what are often called 'triads', three people who in succession act as appraiser, appraisee and observer during three 15 minute discussions. These triads exercises are not role-play. Teachers are asked to bring with them an issue which they would like to explore with the help of a colleague. One of these forms the basis of each discussion, so reality is very close. The observer notes how the appraiser handles the discussion, then observer and appraisee feed back to the appraiser on his or her performance. As the process is repeated three times, groups are able to aim to improve skills from one discussion to the next. Interview training brought home the essentially developmental basis of appraisal, as well as developing the skills needed. It was not always anticipated with pleasure but evaluation afterwards reported widespread satisfaction with its outcomes.

The success of the interview training lay in its closeness to the real thing. The best format for training for classroom observation was more difficult to find. Ideally, the process would have involved repeated observing in the classroom with feedback on performance as an observer. Some schools in the Pilot Study were able to achieve training on this scale and the evaluators found this always led to satisfaction. In the limited time available for formal training during the implementation of the appraisal scheme, no parallel was found to the 'triads' activity which brought the training so close to reality. If video taped lessons were used for observation training they often led to generalised judgemental criticism of the video taped teacher. Even when specific issues were targeted, for example questioning techniques or use of praise, the teachers emerged trained in only a very narrow field of observation because of the lack of time for repetition. These problems led finally to a break away from the video tape to a different approach concentrating on reaching a satisfactory design for an observation, leaving it to be carried out later in the classroom. The new approach was a small group activity in which each person in turn identified an area of their work which might be focussed on during appraisal and challenged the others then to work their way down the following chain:

What kinds of information would help us in our discussion?
Which of this information could be collected through observation?
What would the observer need to do to collect it?
How should the observer record it so that it will be most helpful to the discussions?

This exercise proved difficult for teachers to do and it relied heavily on follow-up by the school but it did get closer to the major issue, the strategy for observation. In recognition of the fact that real learning would only ensue when ideas were put into practice, schools were encouraged to create space for short 'dummy run' observations after which discussion of the observation strategies could take place. To support this work, schools were given distance learning materials to help them extend their experience of classroom observation and of task observation. They were also given access to 'clinics' where issues could be explored further.

Outcomes

By the summer of 1993 about half the schools had experienced their first round of appraisals and LEAs carried out their evaluations (McLaughlin, 1993; Vince, 1993; Heywood, 1993). There were some heartening outcomes:

(i) Almost all teachers taking part in these evaluations reported benefits from their appraisal, among them better understanding of roles, clearer priorities and greater confidence and self-esteem.
(ii) What is more the initial apprehension, still well remembered, had almost completely disappeared.
(iii) Headteachers too believed their schools had benefited, quoting as evidence greater openness and collaboration, more

focussed staff development and greater cohesiveness in addressing school goals.

(iv) Self-appraisal and the interview had gone well. Classroom observation had been carried out satisfactorily but many felt more could yet be gained from it.

(v) In some schools the integration of appraisal into the planning and development process of the school had already taken place, with significant impact on effectiveness and morale. For many schools, however, the need for integration was just becoming apparent and it remains to be seen how well they will succeed.

(vi) The training programme itself was well-received. Evaluating responses from 1,602 teachers in Hampshire's third cohort of training, Vince (1993) reported 94% of teachers found the training helpful or very helpful.

What have we learned from the exercise?

Four major points emerge from our work which have wider applicability. First, that it is possible for external consultants to help schools to introduce a change, even if initially it is not seen as a particularly desirable change, provided the innovation is intrinsically worthwhile and the consultants believe its integrity can be demonstrated. Second, that the role of the external consultants, both trainers and LEA co-ordinators, is not easy when teachers are suspicious of the Government's motives and their associations are uncertain whether to maintain those suspicions or dispel them. Third, that although the benefits for individuals seem immediate and widespread and schools are believed by their headteachers to have gained, the extent to which appraisal is integrated into the working structures of the schools depends very much on their culture and organisation. Fourth, our work with appraisal has shown us that it is possible to help schools across the threshold of change, even when the staff has no initial ownership of it. This is perhaps the first time this has been demonstrated so clearly. However, once across the threshold, the conditions for maximising the benefits for the individual and the school are those concerned with the organisation and its culture. There is no short cut.

References

AMMA (1991) *Appraisal and You: AMMA Advice to Members* (London: AMMA).

Binsteed, D. (1982) 'Design for learning in management training and development: a view, *Learning in Management Training,* **4**(8), pp.1-31.

Bollington, R. and Bradley, H.W. (1990) *Training for Appraisal* (Cambridge: Cambridge Institute of Education).

Bradley, H.W. (1987) Policy issues concerning staff development, in Wideen, M.F. and Andrews, I. *Staff Development for School Improvement* (Lewes: Falmer Press).

Bradley, H.W. *et al.* (1989) *Report on the Evaluation of the School Teacher Appraisal Pilot Study* (Cambridge: Cambridge Institute of Education).

Bradley, H.W. (1991a) *Staff Development* (Lewes: Falmer Press).

Bradley, H.W. (1991b) *Ready for Appraisal* (Cambridge: Cambridge Institute of Education).

DES (1991) *The Education (School Teacher Appraisal) Regulations 1991* (London: HMSO).

Fullan, M. (1982) *The Meaning of Educational Change* (Ontario: OISE Press).

Fullan, M. (1987) Implementing the implementation plan, in Wideen, M.F and Andrews, I. *Staff Development for School Improvement* (Lewes: Falmer Press).

Heywood, J. (1993) *Teacher and Headteacher Appraisal: Evaluation Report* (Cambridge: Cambridgeshire County Council).

Hopkins, D. and Ainscow, M. (1993) 'Making sense of school improvement', *Cambridge Journal of Education,* **23**(3), pp.287-304.

Joyce, B. and Showers, B. (1980) 'Improving in-service training: the messages of research', *Educational Leadership,* February, pp.379-385.

McLaughlin, C. (1993) *Evaluation Report on Cohorts One and Two of Teacher Appraisal in the London Borough of Havering* (Cambridge: Cambridge Institute of Education).

NASUWT (1991) *Coping with Appraisal* (Birmingham: NASUWT).

NUT (1991) *Appraisal: Your Rights and Expectations* (London: NUT).

Poppleton, P.K. (1988) 'Teacher professional satisfaction: its implications for secondary education and teacher education', *Cambridge Journal of Education,* **18**(1), pp.5-16.

Rudduck, J. (1991) *Innovation and Change: Developing Involvement and Understanding* (Milton Keynes: Open University Press).

The Six Teacher Organisations (1991) *Appraisal - Report of Six Teacher Organisations* (London: The Six Teacher Organisations).

Vince, B. (1993) *Headteacher and Teacher Appraisal: Evaluation Reports* (Winchester: Hampshire County Council).

CHAPTER 12

HEADTEACHER MENTORING: Insights and Ideas About Headteacher Development

Geoff Southworth, with Ruth Clunie and David Somerville

Introduction

The focus of this chapter is headteacher mentoring. The chapter is divided into three parts. In section one we outline the nature of the mentoring initiative and explore the concept of mentoring. In the second section Ruth and David describe their experiences of mentoring and being mentored. These accounts provide first hand data for analysis and discussion and we do this in the third section.

Throughout the chapter we have attempted not only to identify some of the key issues in headteacher mentoring, but also to base our thinking and subsequent analysis upon our respective experience and to tease out some of the main points for the professional development of headteachers.

Background to mentoring: the scheme and definitions

In 1991 a joint DFE and School Management Task Force initiative established a pilot mentoring scheme for new headteachers in England and Wales. The scheme was devised to complement existing arrangements in LEAs for newly-appointed heads. In other words, the scheme was set up not to replace LEA induction programmes, but to supplement them by offering additional support for new heads in their first year of appointment.

Responsibility for setting up the national scheme was devolved to regional consortia of LEAs. Each regional consortium was to be governed by an executive committee made up of LEA officers and headteachers. The DFE also specified that this committee had to be chaired by a headteacher. As the regional executive committee in East Anglia began its work, it invited the Cambridge Institute of Education to assist them in designing and providing a preparation programme for headteacher mentors in line with advice received from the DFE.

One of the significant features of this initiative is that the DFE is not only supporting it financially, but also has provided 'notes of guidance for regional executive groups' and these have proved to be valuable. The guidance makes a number of points. First, although it suggests that in some senses 'mentoring is whatever the two people involved regard as appropriate', a survey of existing schemes notes that mentoring is one or more of the following roles:

guide	tutor
coach	confidante
role-model	sounding-board
listener	sponsor
door-opener	counsellor
facilitator	networker
protector	trainer

Second, that in respect of headteachers, mentors should be neither judgemental nor over-protective of the new head. Third, mentors need to work to some model of adult learning. Fourth, that the mentor and new head establish, at the outset, a learning agreement which makes it clear to both parties the basis on which they will work together for the year-long process of mentoring.

Whilst the DFE advice is useful, it is apparent that the concept of mentoring is rather opaque. Moreover, the scheme is starting from a relatively low knowledge base in this country for two reasons. First, there has not been a great deal of headteacher mentoring reported in the literature. Second, little research has been conducted into the needs of new heads, the specific issue of how individuals become headteachers or the more general issue of leadership succession. Weindling and Earley's (1987) research is an exception to this statement, but, being confined to secondary heads, it means we do not know very much about the first year of headship for primary, special and middle school leaders. By contrast, there has been some valuable work conducted into mentoring in the USA and it is instructive to review this work to advance our thinking about the topic.

The work of Daresh and Playko (1993) suggests that the first year of principalship is 'marked by considerable anxiety, frustration and self-doubt'. As Weindling and Earley (1987) have noted in their research in England, many heads feel isolated from their former peers and have to accept that headship can sometimes be a lonely position. Elsewhere, Daresh (1986) has argued that beginning principals need to resolve for themselves 'who they are, now that they are principals, and how they are going to make use of their new authority'. In other words, during the first year of headship new heads are coming to terms with the nature of the role and their own professional identity.

Daresh and Playko (1990) clearly believe that the novitiate head's search for a role and an identity is assisted by mentors who fulfil certain criteria. These criteria include mentors:

- being willing to accept 'another way of doing things';
- wanting to see people go beyond their present level of performance;
- modelling the principles of continuous learning and reflection.

Indeed,

> ...we have discovered that, above all, mentors must be caring and giving people who are truly committed to the enhancement of the professional lives of the beginning administrators. (Daresh and Playko, 1990a)

In the light of their investigation and experience Daresh and Playko understand mentoring as:

> ...the process of bringing together experienced, competent administrators with beginning colleagues as a way to help them with the transition to the world of school administration. (Daresh and Playko, 1992b)

It is important to note these emphases in Daresh and Playko's work because they show that mentoring is not a substitute for headteacher induction, nor preparation for headship, neither is it management training. Rather, mentoring is a finite (e.g. year long), enabling and supportive activity which helps newcomers deal with the initial and transitional experience of becoming a head.

What a review of the literature concerned with mentoring discloses is that there is no single, agreed definition of the term (Stott and Walker, 1992). Mentoring means different things in different contexts. For example, in industry and commerce, mentoring often means a hierarchical relationship between a manager and her or his protege. Even within education mentoring is likely to mean different activities in relation to mentoring for initial teacher training and for newly qualified teachers.

Given that the term has shades of meaning, we have made the search for shared and common understandings a key part of the mentoring preparation programme at the Institute. Each cohort of heads who are preparing to be mentors spend the morning of the first day of the programme exploring as a group what headteacher mentoring is (and is not). Using the word list from the DFE (see above) as a prompt list, colleagues are asked to select the three words they most favour and to discuss them with their fellow programme participants. Following this process they are then invited, in small groups, to set down in less than 25 words a definition of headteacher mentoring. What is encouraging is the high degree of similarity between these group definitions as the following sample demonstrates:

— A mentor is a sympathetic trusted colleague or friend available to respond in confidence to the new head's needs by listening, observing and offering support in a non-judgemental way.
— A mentor is able to listen and observe within a sensitive, non-judgemental, confidential relationship, being a sounding-board as necessary to enable the mentee to find his or her own solutions and directions.
— A mentor is someone outside the immediate situation who is non-judgemental and is a listener, sounding-board and confidant.
— Mentoring is the art of listening without judging, enabling without guiding, exploring without directing. The art is in the relationship.

These four definitions are broadly congruent with the ideas of Daresh and Playko and are in line with the main emphases of the DFE guidance. In other words, it seems that mentoring is taken to mean, at least by the first cohorts of heads who have volunteered to be mentors in East Anglia, a professional relationship between two heads where one acts as a listener, enabler and sounding-board for the other in a non-judgemental way.

If the preparation programme is helping to provide a clearer definition of mentoring, it is also the case that we can now draw upon the experience of those who have worked together as mentors and new heads. In the next section Ruth and David describe what the year of their partnership as mentor and new head was like. Each has written an account based upon their individual experience. Together these accounts provide an empirical basis for generating some insights into mentoring in action and this we attempt in the third section.

Headteacher mentoring: a case example

The mentor's account: Ruth Clunie, Headteacher, Beech Hill Community Infant School, Luton

'New head syndrome' can be described as a state of well-disguised anxiety. It stays clearly etched in my memory with its ever attendant feelings of vulnerability, accountability and isolation overlaid with excitement and exhilaration. In its early stages it is difficult to discuss the symptoms with others for fear of risking loss of credibility but there is, nonetheless, a very real need for consultation and appropriate support.

Time, experience and emerging confidence have been the traditional forms of treatment but in January 1992, the regional Management Unit wrote to heads inviting applications for a pilot scheme for mentoring new headteachers. I was immediately attracted by the outline of the mentor/mentee roles. New heads would be enabled and empowered while experienced heads would themselves develop through the process of analysis. This two-way relationship also offered a heightened awareness of the fast changing role of the head with the opportunity to analyse the individual elements of headship in a structured situation.

Acquiring counselling skills and working in a small group were long held interests which I hoped would be as relevant as my headships throughout the primary age range. They included a nursery school, JMI and nursery school and presently a community nursery and infant school in a densely housed inner urban area. As a newly-appointed head I experienced the usual nut-and-bolts-meet-the-Inspectors-Advisors-and-LEA-hierarchy induction course. INSET over the years added curricular, cross-curricular and management skills, but there had been no specific focus on the needs of newly-appointed heads, and certainly no opportunity for new and experienced heads to learn together.

I was part of the first cohort of mentor heads who were prepared at the University of Cambridge Institute of Education in March 1992. During the first two days of the programme we examined mentoring, moving from role definition to theory and practice. Group activities and discussions consolidated sessions on adult learning, consultancy skills and active listening. They were an effective vehicle for establishing group trust and confidence in each other. Working in threes on reflective listening enabled personal risk-taking and developed a sense of mutual trust, a sound basis indeed for the subsequent days when the roles of mentor and mentee were practised.

The trio of which I was a member visited each other's schools. We felt it important to find a non-threatening way into the process which would set a relaxed yet purposeful climate. Shared commitment to the mentoring process and a willingness to refine skills resulted in the following approach. After a relaxed welcome the 'mentee' described the school, its setting and the staff, with a map or plan of the school to put it in context. The mentee shared an area of concern and added reality with a guided tour of the school and appropriate introductions. We returned to the head's office to review the tour, discuss the chosen problem further and identify possible solutions. It was both challenging and stimulating, particularly in terms of improving our listening skills and posing open-ended questions. On the fifth day of the programme members exchanged experiences, refined our mentoring skills and matched our practice to the theory of the first two days of the course. Thus prepared we awaited our mentees.

It had been proposed that cross-county mentor/mentee pairing could provide a useful comparison to the planned in-county partnership. A phone call from the local Bedfordshire co-ordinator for mentoring invited me to be part of the experiment and to meet

David Somerville at Cambridge on the bonding day. At that first meeting we talked of background, careers, our experience of education, and our feelings about the scheme. We ranged around families, music and travel, finding that we had much in common. Drafting a 'contract' or learning agreement was a tangible starting point. As part of the 'contract' we defined terms and expectations and then moved to discussing the probable content specifics which covered areas such as school organisation, the school development plan, staff meetings, financial planning and governors' meetings.

In retrospect it was our shared expectations discussed and negotiated in the 'contract' that set the climate for our future half-termly meetings. We wanted quality time, and recognised that through sharing concerns and successes and confronting anxieties and problems we would reach a clearer understanding of headship. Meetings were held alternately in each other's schools so we could experience one another's problems in different settings.

I was aware that in David's first year he would be breaking new ground in his professional life. Our first meeting at David's school followed the pattern that my trio had found to be effective on the preparation programme. David had thought through the main foci of his first year recognising that it was important to make haste slowly. It was exciting to share his fresh approach to headship and hugely energising for me and it became natural during our meetings to examine and question my attitudes as well as his. The reflective process was a positive way of moving ourselves forward while approaching situations from many angles.

We talked at length about school climate and ethos, about the messages staff receive from us as heads and how to develop both schools and all who work in them. We reflected on appropriate approaches and tried to walk in each other's shoes. Our discussions centred on areas where we felt vulnerable, rather than on those areas where David received adequate support from colleagues and his LEA. As trust grew we were both able to take risks with our insecurities. This is not to say that we have worked with great intensity and seriousness gazing avidly at our navels all the while. There has been much laughter at ourselves and situations, and much telling of stories, which has lightened the all too prevalent pressures.

It has been a privilege to be allowed into David's professional life through his first year of headship and to be able to re-examine my own role. Heads need time to look at themselves and their schools. This scheme has been an effective way of finding that time. It has also been a constant reminder that there is no ideal school! Heads receive strong messages on courses, from the LEA and the DFE that there is an ideal world in which all teachers are expert practitioners. Not only that, but they are all well-motivated, hard-working, positive and happy to implement each and every initiative. In their scenarios there are not teachers who are utterly resistant to change, who are negative, or who present heads with problems.

The mentoring process has been a great opportunity to look at the realities of headship in a constructive proactive way. It was significant that David and I were from different LEAs and brought no hidden agendas or preconceptions to our meetings. We knew no one in common so a neutral approach was easy and there was no anxiety associated with discussing (in confidence) personalities. In addition, our schools were different in every conceivable way. This had implications for my security. It could have been threatening to work with a new head in a similar school who had what could be perceived as a 'better' approach, 'better' ideals and a 'better' way of developing the school, giving rise to a whole range of insecurities. We have celebrated our differences and shared the common ground. So feelings of vulnerability, well known to heads at whatever stage in their career, did not emerge or develop.

Being a mentor has added an extra dimension and depth to my work. I have learned from David's approaches to initiatives and problems and my reflective process is more finely tuned, enabling me, I believe, to be a more effective head. I can recommend this process to all experienced heads. It revitalises!

The new head's account: David Somerville, Headteacher, William Westley Primary School, Cambridgeshire

In February 1992 I was successful at the interview for the headship of William Westley Primary School and was to take up my new post the following September. I had much to do in the intervening period as deputy head with full-time class responsibility at my then school, and used the time as best I could to prepare myself for my new job. During the summer term I was contacted by the area co-ordinator of the New Headteachers Mentoring Scheme with a view to joining the project. I knew little of what it would involve, but I was enthusiastic about it, knowing that I would be faced with many new challenges as I moved from being primarily a classroom teacher to taking on a managerial role. At that point it was not clear if the LEA would be able to organise any support targeted at new headteachers. I was grateful for the chance to be involved in something that I was confident would be valuable. I have been involved in support groups of various types before, and I know how powerful such non-hierarchical groups can be for personal development.

Most of the pairings for the scheme for the year had already been organised by this time, and I was given a choice between two experienced headteachers who had offered to be involved in the project but who had not yet been paired up with a new headteacher. One was the head of a secondary school in the same county, and one was the head of an inner urban area infant school in a neighbouring county. Neither was a person known to me personally. As my new school was to be a small Church of England village primary school, I was faced with a choice of possible mentors from rather different backgrounds. I decided that it would be more sensible to choose someone who had experience of a similar age range of children. I was not moving far geographically and I knew I would be able to contact my previous headteacher about matters relating to the LEA if the need arose.

At a meeting at UCIE a few weeks later I met Ruth Clunie for the first time. The group of newly-appointed heads had spent the morning together discussing with Geoff Southworth what we thought were the hallmarks of a good mentor/mentee relationship and what we hoped to gain from the project. At lunch our mentors arrived and we spent the rest of the day together. Discussion with Ruth ranged widely. We sketched out our respective careers to date, established mutual agreement on fundamental issues such as confidentiality, the non-hierarchical nature of the relationship, our expectation that Ruth, with many years of headship behind her, would learn much from the project just as I would. We talked about families and holidays and discovered many shared interests. We drafted a formal 'contract' that would guide us through the project, established an agenda of possible topics that we would consider in our time together, and then arranged a date for Ruth to visit me early the next term.

The contract (or learning agreement) we negotiated comprised both an agreement about the principles that would inform our relationship as mentor and mentee and a list of possible discussion topics that we could cover during the year. We agreed that the mentor/mentee relationship should be based on confidentiality, mutual respect and a commitment to the building up of trust. We expected that the relationship would:

(a) enable both of us to grow professionally and personally through sharing concerns, ideas, problems and successes;
(b) provide quality time to reflect and develop;
(c) allow me to share my inevitable anxieties at starting a new job with a colleague who had already 'walked the path';
(d) allow us to work to an open agenda with broad aims and a time for reflection.

We identified the following as specific areas for possible future discussion: organisation for reception intake; planning for rising roll; parental involvement; school development plans; staff meetings and INSET; governor meetings and governor involvement; staff development and financial planning.

As arranged, we met early in the autumn term at my new school. We started with a tour of the school, meeting staff and children, talking about the history of the school and issues I had inherited. After a hectic first few weeks of term I started realising how pleasurable it was to have someone to show the school to. I remember feeling as excited as I had done when I showed my parents the first house I bought! As so often happened in our subsequent meetings, I was finding that explaining the school to a friend who was genuinely interested in it, allowed me the chance to see it in a new light. It gave me the time to reflect on the place and the people working in it, and on my own feelings about what I was doing. It was a time to talk in an honest and relaxed way about what we both felt effective leadership entails. I was able to discuss some of my hopes, some of my worries, and to explain the strategies I was adopting. Some of these were things that it was too early to be able to discuss so openly with my colleagues at the school.

Later in the term I spent a similar day at Ruth's school in Luton. Ruth gave me a tour of the school and I met the staff and children. Although her school seemed so different from mine – a large infant school, all of whose children are from New Commonwealth families, in old buildings and in a different LEA — the similarities, of course, soon became more important than the differences. I believe that it is because our two schools are different on the surface that so often in our discussions together we have focussed on deeper and more significant issues, notably the notion of effective leadership, and the related issue of staff development.

Through the year we continued to meet every half term, taking turns to be the host. Our discussions (once we had had an update on any holidays taken!) often returned to those issues indicated above. I realised how much I was looking forward to these intense and rewarding discussions. I would prepare myself for them by storing up anecdotes – 'I must remember to tell Ruth that – she will be interested,' I often found myself thinking. Through the sharing of such anecdotes we moved to a deeper understanding of the issues underlying them. The meetings were an important motivation for continuing reflection and personal appraisal. They helped me to keep a long-term view of what was going on at a time when it was so easy to get completely immersed in short-term detail. Our initial agenda of discussion items proved to be unnecessary. We found that we did not need to talk about topics such as 'Writing the School Prospectus' or 'Budget Planning'. When I needed advice on such topics there were people closer to home who could provide it. I was helped by the fact that clearly Ruth was finding the relationship as valuable as I was. It seemed as if it was helping her to relive that time when she had been a new head, and to evaluate what she was now doing in the light of this. During the year Ruth had to deal with a difficult personnel issue and I know that being a mentor helped her in this.

My first year of being a headteacher was a very happy one, despite times of exhaustion, uncertainty over what I was doing or anger directed towards higher authority. I was lucky in that I faced no major crises. As a result, the mentor/mentee relationship was not so much one of giving advice, but of confirmation that my broad aims were sound. When I started the job I had little idea of what the detail of the job would be, but I had firm ideas about what I broadly wanted to achieve as regards finding the right way to motivate people so that they will willingly give of their best. I was lucky to be paired up with Ruth, a person who shares similar ideas and who has much greater experience than I have at implementing them. One of the reasons that the relationship has worked so well is that Ruth does not tell me what to do when I am sharing a problem with her, but probes and questions until I have found a way through it for myself. This has been fortunate, for I do not like being inundated with advice – it usually makes me feel inadequate for not having thought of it in the first place!

There are particular ways in which the scheme has helped me. First, when we met together, we met as equals. There were aspects of my new job that made me feel vulnerable, and it was difficult or impossible for me at that time to discuss these openly with my colleagues at school. With Ruth I could be honest. Secondly, our meetings were 'quality time': we were able to think through issues in depth and with sufficient time to reflect at length, something that normally we have too few chances to do. This allowed us to explore solutions to problems in a measured way, resulting, of course, in those solutions becoming better. Thirdly, Ruth helped me to focus on what I had achieved, and helped me to avoid feeling guilty at all those things that had been left undone. Fourthly, Ruth helped me to confront the fact that I sometimes found it hard in my new and unfamiliar position of authority to praise and encourage staff. I had been able to do this as a deputy head, but something about my new role created barriers that took time to remove. I needed an external person to talk this through with, to help me understand what was going on, to try out new approaches and then to report back on what had happened. Lastly, Ruth is someone I could laugh with. We could laugh at ourselves and at the irony of the situations we sometimes found ourselves in.

Now I am in my second year at the school. Ruth and I still meet. For us the mentoring scheme has not ended. Instead, it has developed into an important part of the network of professional friendships that I have, friendships which give me a range of different types of support. I know that one reason our partnership has worked is the fact that Ruth, notwithstanding her many years of experience as a head in three different schools, is still able and willing to learn new things. That she has developed as a result of our partnership is proof of our original intention to make the relationship non-hierarchical, a meeting of two equals.

Analysis and conclusion

Arising from Ruth and David's experience of mentoring there are six sets of points we now want to highlight and briefly discuss.

The first set of ideas arises from the fact that mentoring is beneficial to both the mentor and the new head. Mentoring has made a difference to both David and Ruth. Indeed, other mentors have made similar discoveries. As one mentor recently said to a group of prospective mentors, ' I cannot stress enough the benefits mentoring has brought to me.' Moreover, these findings in England parallel those in the USA. Daresh and Playko (1992c) have identified three rewards for mentors: increased peer recognition, potential career advancement and improved job satisfaction. Whilst the first two have not as yet come to light in our experience, it is clear from Ruth's testimony that being a mentor has increased her job satisfaction.

Daresh and Playko also note a number of gains for the new heads. They suggest that mentees benefit through:

- increased confidence
- expressing important ideas and thoughts
- feeling 'connected' with at least one other person who understands the nature of the world in which they must work.

Whilst all three correspond with David's account, the last one is worth emphasising here because it relates to points raised earlier in the chapter. Given the comments in section one about new heads experiencing strong feelings of isolation when they first take on the mantle of headship, then it is clear that the availability of a mentor helps to reduce the feeling of being on one's own. Indeed, David has elsewhere remarked that having a mentor 'broke down my loneliness'. It seems, then, that the presence of a mentor helps the new head deal with the initial solitariness of headship. Mentoring does play a part in helping newcomers make the transition into headship.

The second set of ideas centre upon the finding that mentoring is professional development for both players. Mentoring is not merely support for one person, it can extend the new head and the mentor. We say this because when the pair work productively together, they challenge each other. The newcomer has to articulate his or her ideas and concerns and can use this process as an opportunity to think out aloud and rehearse propositions. We regard this process of articulation as immensely beneficial to new heads since it provides them with a chance to explain, as much to themself as to another, what they think and why. Essentially, new heads are 'meaning making'; that is, they are making sense of what they see and know, organising it into some intelligible whole and working out what to do next. Such activity is vital since heads who make meaning:

> ...achieve mastery over the noisy, incessant environment – rather than simply react, throw up their hands and live in a perpetual state of 'present shock'. (Bennis, 1984)

In addition to helping the new head, it is clear that the mentor is also challenged by listening to their partner's accounts and ideas. As Ruth has said, working with David has made her 'look anew at what I am doing'. Clearly, then, mentoring simultaneously provides both support and challenge. Given the former, the challenges that arise to one's assumptions and customary approaches can be faced in a way which is not personally threatening but professionally enriching.

The third thing we wish to note is the issue of match between mentor and new head. Ruth and David were not as closely matched as they might have been. Their respective schools were situated in markedly different locations, served contrasting communities, covered differing key stages and were not in the same LEA. In some ways David and Ruth might be described as a 'poorly' matched pair. Yet none of this seemed to harm their partnership; if anything these differences seemed to enhance rather than impede their relationship. We take from this then, the idea that mentors and new heads do not necessarily need to be closely matched in terms of school types, phase of school or LEA. However, where they do need to be congruent is in respect of educational values and in terms of what each wants the mentoring process to be. As David says, 'we shared similar ideas.'

The significance of this finding is that it suggests that the time and effort David and Ruth put into drawing up their contract or learning agreement was time well spent. The process of devising a learning agreement enabled them to negotiate expectations, clarify assumptions and work out together what they thought they would be doing and sharing. In short, the learning agreement helped them to clarify for themselves what they thought mentoring should involve and embody. Just as it is important for mentors to think about the nature of mentoring, so too is it useful for the mentor and new head to do the same. Establishing shared understandings is crucial.

Fourth, it is clear from Ruth's account that the preparation programme played a part in helping her to become a mentor. It gave her opportunities to practice and prepare for the role and these she valued and drew upon when she began to work with David. It is also apparent that David could have benefited from some greater knowledge of the mentoring process. Whilst he attended the introductory session at UCIE, this served only a limited purpose and was barely, if at all, adequate. If new heads are not offered any opportunities to explore the idea of mentoring they are likely to enter the process with a very low knowledge base and understanding, at least until the process becomes established and a normal feature of promotion and entry to headship. Mentors *and* new heads need to be prepared for the process.

Fifth, the approach to mentoring adopted here by Ruth and David and implicit in both the DFE's original guidance and the definitions held by heads who have participated in East Anglia's preparation programme, is one which fosters a reflective approach to headship. In other words, the process of mentoring encourages heads to be reflective practitioners. The idea of reflective practitioners is derived from Schon's work (1983, 1987). Schon has argued that practitioners, in dealing with the problems of the real world, are faced not with clear and neat problems, but rather with 'a complex and ill-defined melange' (1987) of factors from which the individual has to 'construct' the problem. Practitioners, such as heads, need to be able to 'name' and 'frame' problems before attempting to find technical solutions to them. Moreover, the process of naming and framing often takes time and means that for a period of time the individual has to tolerate the uncertainty of not yet fully recognising or understanding or comprehending the situation. Practitioners need to work through this 'indeterminate zone' (Schon, 1987). They also need to reflect on their knowledge of the situation and their initial efforts at naming and framing. If this is true for experienced practitioners it is even more true for novitiate heads.

New heads, often lacking long and close acquaintance with the schools they are now leading, are frequently trying to make sense of their new contexts and are trying to name and frame the problems they are encountering or beginning to perceive. The opportunity to talk to a mentor is an occasion when the new head can share his or her framing of the situation and is a time when the mentor can help them to reflect on this provisional articulation of the issue or situation. Through the exercise of such skills as reflective interviewing, the mentor is coaching the new head to work in a way which encourages them to analyse situations, to read their workplace as a text and to develop and articulate the meanings they place upon what they see and know about the circumstances.

In which case, the earlier point that mentoring is professional development needs to be revisited. Whilst mentoring offers support and challenge and encourages the individual to appraise his or her situational perceptions and understandings, it also cultivates reflective practice. Mentoring can help those in positions of authority to examine their assumptions and to reflect on their values and beliefs about leadership. Mentoring can play a part in developing critical, reflective leaders.

The sixth point is that mentoring for new heads clearly needs to continue. The support which David received helped him to make the transition to headship and contributed to his capacity to reflect upon the issues and problems he encountered and wanted to understand more fully by sharing with a trusted colleague. Equally, the process was beneficial for Ruth. She was able to give something to a colleague and, in turn, received some help and support from David. So saying, we are not simply reiterating the first point in this section, rather we want to use these observations to preface the realisation that mentoring is a process where the medium is also the message. The meta-message of mentoring is not that newcomers need help, it is that reflective practitioners are lifelong learners. What David and Ruth have tacitly demonstrated to each other and to their colleagues, is the importance of lifelong professional growth and development. Mentoring is not so much a one year event, but more a long-term process of professional exploration and learning about one's tasks, workplace and, ultimately, oneself.

Indeed, one of our conclusions is that mentoring should help heads to recognise that all members of staff need to be supported. Mentoring should increase heads' awareness of the need for teachers to have the opportunity to reflect on their work and to share their concerns with others. Everyone needs a mentor.

Mentoring may also play a part in increasing headteachers' appreciation of the fact that professional development is adult learning. As such, this awareness should foster the view that staff development involves a personal dimension, since it is concerned with identity and feelings as well as skills and knowledge. Through the process of mentoring we might be encouraging heads to be more empathetic towards their colleagues' professional development needs and more in touch with themselves. Mentoring may play a part in enriching the nature of staff development in schools by deepening headteachers' understandings of the personal dimension of professional growth.

References

Bennis, W. (1984) Transformative power and leadership, in Sergiovanni, T. and Corbally, J. (Eds.) *Leadership and Organizational Culture* (Chicago: University of Illinois Press), pp.64-71.

Daresh, J. (1986) 'Support for beginning principals; the first hurdles are the highest', *Theory into Practice*, **25**(3), pp.168-73.

Daresh, J. and Playko, M. (1990) 'Mentoring programmes: focus on the beginning principal', *NASSP Bulletin*, **74**(527), pp.73-7.

Daresh, J. and Playko, M. (1990a) 'Mentoring for effective school administration', *Urban Education*, **25**(1), pp.43-54.

Daresh, J. and Playko, M. (1992) 'Mentoring for new headteachers; a review of major issues', *School Organization*, **12**(2), pp.145-52.

Daresh, J. and Playko, M. (1992b) 'Entry year programmes for principals and other forms of professional development', *Catalyst for Change*, **21**(1), pp.24-9.

Daresh, J. and Playko, M. (1992c) 'Perceived benefits of a preservice administrative mentoring programme', *Journal of Personnel Evaluation in Education*, 6, pp.15-22.

Daresh, J. and Playko, M. (1993) 'Aspiring and practising principals' perceptions of critical skills for beginning leaders', *Journal of Educational Administration*, April.

DES/School Management Task Force (1991) *Mentor Scheme for New Headteachers: notes of guidance for regional executive groups* (London: DES).

Schon, D. (1983) *The Reflective Practitioner* (London: Temple Smith).

Schon, D. (1987) *Educating the Reflective Practitioner* (San Francisco: Jossey-Bass).

Stott, K. and Walker, A. (1992) 'Developing school leaders through mentoring: a Singapore perspective', *School Organization*, **12**(2), pp.153-64

Weindling, D. and Earley, P. (1987) *Secondary Headship: the first years* (Windsor: NFER).

CHAPTER 13

STAFF DEVELOPMENT AND CHANGE IN THE SPECIAL SCHOOL

Tony Bowers

The context

Most readers will be familiar with the story of the man who went to see a psychiatrist about his brother. 'I'm really worried, Doctor,' said the man. 'My brother thinks he's a chicken.'

'Thinks he's a chicken? Tell me more,' said the psychiatrist intently, stroking his beard.

'He struts around the house clucking incessantly. He won't eat anything except cereal. And at night, he doesn't go to bed – he perches on the back of the settee until daybreak.'

'This sounds very serious indeed,' said the doctor. 'Your brother is suffering from delusions, indicating a deeply-seated neurotic regression. He needs immediate treatment. You must bring him to my clinic for assessment.'

At this the man looked worried. 'Will he have to stay away from home, Doc?'

'Of course,' came the reply.

'Then I think you'd better forget the whole thing. You see, we need the eggs.'

The same ambivalence – wanting something to be done while at the same time needing to preserve the status quo – can be discerned in the special educational needs (SEN) policies of many

LEAs. Whilst few have denied the importance of notions of 'inclusion' and 'integration', their actions in sustaining (and in some cases increasing) their special school provision have suggested that special schools continue to have a central role in meeting special educational needs. Although the Audit Commission (1992a) reported that the proportion of pupils placed in special schools had fallen by a little over ten per cent in the eight years since the implementation of the 1981 Education Act, this can hardly be seen as a dramatic shift of focus or intent. Even this small fall has not been accompanied by a significant redistribution of resources. According to the data cited by the Commission, the per capita cost of a special school place has risen significantly more than that of a place in an ordinary school. The case for 'rationalisation', a euphemism for special school closure as the Audit Commission's (1992b) handbook revealed, appeared then (and might still appear) to be very strong.

The reason for LEAs' reluctance to redistribute special school funding to follow pupils with SEN was identified by the Audit Commission (1992a). Elected members and LEA officers were unwilling to risk the opprobrium which might occur if they did so. The status quo, it was suggested, was retained because of fears of the consequences of change, however 'rational' this might be. If LEAs couldn't put their own house in order, then the government would have to make them or take powers to do the job itself. The White Paper (DFE, 1992) which preceded the 1993 Education Act was resolute. The Secretary of State was to have the power to direct an LEA or the newly-proposed Funding Agency to rationalise its special schools and at the same time would be able to put forward his own proposals. If LEAs, whose role was gradually being whittled away by successive legislation to leave them with little to organise other than SEN provision, could not administer the treatment, then government would have to do it for them. Somehow, though, the strength of this determination was not translated into the 1993 Act or the Code of Practice. The government, like the LEAs before it, still needed special schools.

The case for restructuring and redefining the role of special schools has long been made. The Warnock Committee (DES, 1978) envisaged less reliance on special schools in meeting children's special educational needs, and around this time we saw a number of writers (e.g. Galloway and Goodwin, 1979; Booth, 1981; Barton and Tomlinson, 1984) who represented the start of a decade of questioning the social function and implicit purpose of special schooling. Put simply, their argument presented special educational needs as defined by the narrow perspectives encountered within the education system. If we change the system in such a way that it accommodates greater numbers of pupils, we can in consequence eliminate the requirement for separate special schools. Logically, the main functions of special schools appeared to be to work towards their own redundancy. While some special school headteachers adopted this stance (e.g. Hall, 1992) it was understandably more common to encounter a strongly-argued case for the preservation of specialist expertise and resources under one roof.

The Audit Commission documents and the White Paper appeared to give practical support to often-repeated cries for a changed system. However, in the wake of the 1993 Education Act have come the Code of Practice on Special Educational Needs (Section 157) and the regulations enabling LEA maintained special schools to become grant maintained (Section 186). The first gives significant emphasis to parental choice; the statementing process obliges the LEA to comply with a parent's preference for any school within the maintained sector – unless it can be demonstrated satisfactorily that it is unsuitable. The final arbiter of such unsuitability will be an Appeals Tribunal whose main stance will almost certainly be legalistic rather than educational. If a parent wants a special school, then the LEA will have to make a place available so long as three conditions apply: appropriateness for the child, compatibility with the interests of other children at the school, and the efficient use of resources. These last two have caused considerable vexation under the 1981 Act, and we have yet, of course, to see how Appeals Tribunals will resolve them. What is clear, however, is that special schools have achieved a new lease of life. To emphasise this, we have only to look at the draft circular on the development of special schools, published in December 1993. Spelling out the general duty of LEAs to promote integration, it concludes (paragraph 15): 'These measures do not, however, detract from the continued need for special schools.' Like the man in the story, it seems that the education system still needs the eggs.

Although the theme of this book centres upon staff development, I have provided this brief summary of external events to emphasise the current position for special schools. They still have an acknowledged place in the education system. They have, with local management of special schools (LMSS) and the requirement for delegated management by April 1996, formula-funded powers of self-determination which are similar to those of mainstream schools. They will soon have the opportunity to apply for grant maintained status, if they see this separation from the LEA bringing them particular advantages. Yet the special school which does not embark – or has not already embarked – upon a process of planned change is placing itself at risk. As we will consider later, the conditions in which maintained special schools are likely to operate in the future will differ markedly from those which they have experienced in the past. Externally imposed reform can be a cause for anxiety and stress; it can also, if harnessed, provide a catalyst for internal change and development. It is the latter which I wish to address.

'Improving' special schools

The notion of staff development as a vehicle for school development is not new. Indeed, special schools have traditionally adopted it with some vigour. Current DFE statistics show that around a third of all staff in maintained special schools and over half of those in non-maintained and independent special schools hold a one-year-equivalent specialist qualification. For a long time, however, it has been acknowledged that change within an organisation is not readily facilitated by training individuals separately (e.g. Georgiades and Phillimore, 1975). Special schools have therefore readily adopted more corporate approaches to change. Classically these have involved staff development days, although internal activities such as those of working parties on implementing the National Curriculum, establishing policies on behaviour management, child protection and so on have also provided a focus for development and change.

Staff development can be, but is not necessarily, a vehicle for organisational change. Attempts to systematise the processes by which changes are accepted and become a permanent part of the organisation have been labelled 'school improvement' (Huberman and Miles, 1984; Fullan 1992; Hopkins and Ainscow, 1993) but in fact owe their origins to the general principles of organisation development (OD) propounded by French and Bell (1978), Fullan, Miles and Taylor (1980) and Burke (1982). In a nutshell, the major characteristics of OD can be summarised thus:

(i) Change is *planned* rather than haphazard and reactive (Huse and Cummings, 1985).

(ii) Change is comprehensive. The entire organisation, or an identifiable unit within it, provides the focus of development (Schmuck and Runkel, 1985).

(iii) The nature of change is defined by members of the organisation and not by any outside parties, and ownership of the results is theirs also (French and Bell, 1984).

(iv) Change is long-range. OD does not involve 'quick-fixes', even if these are what are desired at the start of a project (Albrecht, 1983).

(v) Some form of third party 'change agent' or catalyst is necessary since freedom from the constraints of the organisational culture is seen as an advantage (French and Bell, 1984).

(vi) In OD there is active intervention in the ongoing activities of the organisation. The involvement of the change agent as 'action researcher' in attacking practical problems is seen as central to the process (Luthans, 1989).

For those managing schools in today's climate, these six points may seem all too abstruse and academic. For them, change arrives in a brown envelope. Letters, circulars and regulations from the DFE appear to become increasingly prolific. Edicts and pronouncements on the nature and balance of what is to be taught and how it will be assessed emanate frequently and often unexpectedly from agencies with confusingly changing acronyms. News of impending expectations on the part of central government, which increasingly have direct impact upon them, reaches them through the media. Documents for consultation, their contents with statutory significance, arrive with brief turn-around times for any reading and reply. As I write, eight draft circulars, five sets of draft regulations and a draft code of practice to be laid before Parliament, all of them concerned with special educational needs, are subject to consultation. The contents of each spell significant changes for schools, services and LEA officers alike. Response times are short, and the reflex answer often involves anger or frustration over what is expected of already overstretched systems when no extra resources are made available. It is hardly surprising if planned long-term change, implying as it does a locus of control internal to the organisation, is not seen as an attractive undertaking in an environment of external control and apparent short-termism. For special schools in particular, when their funding lies outside their hands, determined by an LEA's planning of its 'place elements' rather than by parental choice and pupil numbers as it is in mainstream schools, this lack of self-determination may be even more apparent.

Yet it is precisely at such times of uncertainty that long-term reappraisal and planning is most important. The apparent chaos of short-term, context-based changes can best be coped with by an organisation which has developed processes which can incorporate their themes and implications and can adapt altered circumstances to its own advantage. Peters (1987), having examined a wide range of organisations which succeeded or failed in dramatically changing circumstances, has identified three main components for growth and achievement. The first is a *commitment to quality*, defined primarily in terms of *customer requirements*; the second is a dedication to *constant retraining*, acknowledging that new circumstances require fresh knowledge and skills; the third is the encouragement of *self-managing teams* which can respond easily to changing requirements. Internally generated change, it seems, can prepare an organisation for the exigencies of altered demands from outside.

Meeting the future

A whole set of new circumstances is lined up for special schools. I commented at the start of this chapter that we still apparently need them, despite the rhetoric of the past decade which has called into question their purpose as 'segregated' institutions. Until now, however, their function has been to enable the LEA to meet its planning requirements. The LEA, as I have pointed out elsewhere (Bowers, 1991, 1993a) has been the decider of provision and the decider of placement. In a politico-educational system which has placed increasing emphasis upon parental choice, the 1981 Education Act stood out as empowering the LEA rather than the parent to be the arbiter of what was a suitable place of education. The 1993 Act, however, places a duty on an LEA to provide for a child's needs in a school which is not a special school (subject to certain conditions which an Appeals Tribunal will ultimately have to assess). This duty becomes nullified, however, when a parent expresses a preference for a special school; not just any special school, but one which he or she nominates. The single 'purchaser' or customer system which LEA-run special schools have largely enjoyed is about, it seems, to be broken. This is likely, as place elements under LMSS become modified in line with actual numbers, to place maintained special schools on a similar footing to those in the mainstream.

This decentralisation of decision-making and its associated funding has so far had significantly more acute impact upon another area of special educational needs provision. Support services, restricted through the dwindling proportion of the Potential Schools Budget which LEAs have at their disposal, have been forced to reappraise their purposes, ways of working and relationships to schools (Bowers, 1992a, 1992b; Diamond, 1993). In working with these to achieve change, several features have been evident. First, senior managers or service leaders have seen the necessity to introduce new attitudes, approaches and practices but have been aware of an underlying refusal on the part of some service members to accept the need for change. 'If they hear it from you, they'll take more notice,' is a recurring theme. It is this stage of information-giving which can, if conducted in a way which retains an element of safety for the recipients, create an awareness of the need for change. Direct work with these services has sometimes been brief or sporadic: reducing budgets have not encouraged the continuing long-term involvement which OD or 'improvement' projects might ideally demand. However, one way to circumvent the temptation to try a 'quick-fix' activity has involved key personnel attending courses in Cambridge and themselves continuing the intervention process. Within the development of such services, we have identified seven 'I's' which appear to play a crucial role in change.

(i) *Information.* A lecture or presentation, with perhaps a brief involving activity, is used to pass on particular facts about legislative changes, alterations in funding, altered demands from central government, etc. Examples of what has gone on in other areas may be provided. The purpose is to heighten awareness of a modified external environment.

(ii) *Inquiry*. Questioning, probing and challenging characterise this phase. These may be accompanied by an element of denial: 'That couldn't happen here', or 'I can't see our schools doing that'.

(iii) *Irritation*. Annoyance that things have to be done, that change evidently needs to be considered, is common. There aren't enough resources, in terms of time, money or personnel, to do any more than is being done. This can easily be displaced onto the messenger, the manager, or both.

(iv) *Inventiveness*. Correctly handled, from the former phase can come a collaborative approach to problem-solving which leads to exploring new ways of doing things. Humour is often a characteristic of this process, and wild and sometimes satirical ideas can form part of it.

(v) *Inclusion*. Now a way has to be found for any planned changes to be built into what is being done already. Methods and systems may have to be devised to achieve results.

(vi) *Implementation*. Putting the change into practice can take up time and energy. One service, whilst still centrally retained by the LEA, started a system of 'zero-invoicing' schools to develop awareness of the true cost of the service. Not only did they have to create administrative and accounting mechanisms (which could of course still be used at a later stage of devolved funding) but the nature and purpose of the change had both to be understood by members of the service and explained to schools.

(vii) *Incorporation*. Finally, the changed approaches or ways of working become fully integrated with the operation of a particular team or of the organisation as a whole. They are no longer seen as new or different: they are just part of what is done.

Special schools have had more time to come to terms with a new market-orientated environment than have SEN support services. Some schools, or at least their headteachers, have not used that time well, and have relied on what can only be called a divine right to exist because of the 'good work' they are doing. Others have been highly proactive in examining their practice and modifying it appropriately. For the former group, such outside interventions as OFSTED inspections are seen as a threatening intrusion; for the latter, their prospect is seen as an opportunity to examine the relationship between teaching and learning and to ensure that policies are not merely in place but are actively adopted and integrated within practice.

Putting things in place

Because budgets are small, the prospect of the long-term employment of one or more outside interventionists is not realistic. So what happens when a long-term change project is envisaged? In one school for primary-aged children with severe learning difficulties in the north of England, a three-faceted approach has been used. First, I have been involved in establishing systems in the school. A problem which the head identified as 'interdepartmental communication', or the lack of it, was first put to the staff. Most worked principally in one of three areas: the nursery, which included facilities serving the local community, or in the 'upper' or 'lower' age-related groups. After examining the nominated issue, it became apparent that there was confusion over who made decisions in the school, disenchantment with the ways in which decisions were communicated and a general feeling of disempowerment among the staff. As a result, there was a pulling-back into work-related groups which effectively constituted small autonomous structures and which offered their members meaningful identity.

Special schools such as this contain certain staff members, significant both in terms of numbers and influence, who are not teachers. Nursery nurses and other special support assistants all took part in two training days in which we moved from the points above as it became apparent that 'quality' was an over-arching theme which was of significance to all of them. Quality of working life, quality of pupil care, quality of relationships between one another, status differentials between teachers and others, quality of teaching and quality of parent or 'customer' care were all explored. These were big issues, although not unusual in a school of this nature. We approached them by examining the merits of 'quality circles' (Oakland, 1989). This involved not only traditional and apparently logical team structures being cut through; it also entailed looking at new approaches to prioritising, at decision-making which avoided majority voting, and at new structures of leadership which might operate within the circles.

Although the circles were established in those two days, what happened over the next two terms was perhaps more interesting. Some staff members took to them with enthusiasm, whilst others were dismissive or didn't see the time devoted to them as worthwhile. As a problem arose, it became a bit of a joke to say 'I think this needs a quality circle.' Membership of the circles, never closed off, started to rise as it was seen that real issues were being brought to them, that results were being achieved, and that belonging to a circle allowed input to issues that otherwise would not be available. There is insufficient space here to describe in detail the conditions for such circles in special schools, but these are elaborated in Bowers (1992c).

The second part of the process involved senior staff (the by then acting headteacher and the acting deputy head) attending short courses and seminars where they could examine with others the process of change and notions of 'total quality management' (TQM) as a process of continuous improvement. The implications of this for special schools are outlined in a package of special school improvement activities (Bowers, 1992c) published to encourage effective movement into LMSS. In addition, it was necessary for these managers to understand the implications of staff empowerment for their own exercise of leadership: they would have to listen and be responsive to suggestions and be prepared to resource relevant suggestions for change. Finally, staff development activities, effectively 'distance' materials, were prepared to resource the work of the circles and the staff as a whole. For example, as part of the TQM programme in the school it was seen as desirable to reframe interprofessional relationships in terms of the 'services' which one member of staff would provide for others and 'services' which he or she received in turn from them. This, it was felt, would emphasise the interdependence of all staff on one another in meeting children's needs and cut across status barriers. An entire set of materials relating to this and to other aspects of the development of quality systems was generated for the purpose of this third area of intervention and support. Some of this set appears in a recently published handbook (Bowers, 1993b).

While not fitting all of the criteria set out for OD or 'improvement' earlier in this chapter, this staff development project has demonstrated the importance of in-school activity which involves all staff. Policies which previously were paid lip-service but seldom observed or acknowledged have now, having been revised or recreated by those expected to implement them, become embedded in practice. The quality of relationships with parents has been examined and responded to by circles within the school. Particular scrutiny has been paid to the ways in which parent support groups for young children with disabilities can be involved with the activities of the school, and to the ways in which school staff can work in greater collaboration with the various health professionals working with the children and their families.

Conclusion

Maintained special schools will be with us for the foreseeable future. They cannot, however, count on their traditional sponsor and patron, the LEA, as a means of sustenance as they have in the past. The future of local authorities as we know them is by no means certain, but beyond that the elements of preference and choice which have entered the mainstream system will shortly impact on special schools which in the past have relied solely on one customer. This is likely to prove a major vehicle for reform of special education: perhaps larger than anything which we saw arising from the Warnock Report.

The principal resource of any special school is its staff. Unless such schools pay adequate attention to the ways in which all members of staff contribute to the growth and development of the organisation, the market forces which the 1993 Act has introduced to them may see the start of considerable external change for which they are as yet ill-prepared.

References

Albrecht, K. (1983) *Organization Development: A Total Systems Approach to Positive Change in Any Business Organization* (Englewood Cliffs, New Jersey: Prentice-Hall).

Audit Commission/HMI (1992a) *Getting in on the Act* (London: HMSO).

Audit Commission/HMI (1992b) *Getting the Act Together* (London: HMSO).

Barton, L. and Tomlinson, S. (1984) *Special Education and Social Interests* (London: Croom Helm).

Booth, T. (1981) Demystifying integration, in Swann, W. (Ed.) *The Practice of Special Education* (Milton Keynes: Open University Press).

Bowers, T. (1991) Issues in marketing, in Bowers, T. (Ed.) *Schools, Services and Special Educational Needs: Management Issues in the Wake of LMS* (Cambridge: Perspective Press).

Bowers, T. (1992a) 'A question of support', *Special Children*, 54, pp.23-25.

Bowers, T. (1992b) 'Planning for the future', *Special Children*, 61, pp.16-19.

Bowers, T. (1992c) *LMS and Special Schools: Resource and Activity Pack* (Cambridge: Perspective Press).

Bowers, T. (1993a) Funding special education, in Upton, G. and Visser, J. (Eds.) *Special Education in Britain after Warnock* (London: Fulton).

Bowers, T. (1993b) *Special Schools in a Climate of Choice* (Cambridge: Perspective Press).

Burke, W.W. (1982) *Organization Development* (Boston: Little, Brown).

DES (1978) *Special Educational Needs: Report of the Committee of Enquiry into the Education of Handicapped Children and Young People* (London: HMSO).

Diamond, C. (1993) 'A reconsideration of the role of SEN support services: Will they get in on the act?', *Support for Learning*, 8, pp.91-98.

French, W.L. and Bell, C.H. (1978) *Organization Development (2nd edition)* (Englewood Cliffs, New Jersey: Prentice-Hall).

French, W.L. and Bell, C.H. (1984) *Organization Development (3rd edition)* (Englewood Cliffs, New Jersey: Prentice-Hall).

Fullan, M. (1991) *The New Meaning of Educational Change* (London: Cassell).

Fullan, M., Miles, M. and Taylor, G. (1980) 'Organization development in schools: The state of the art', *Review of Educational Research*, 50, pp.121-183.

Galloway, D. and Goodwin, C. (1979) *Educating Slow Learning and Maladjusted Children: segregation or integration?* (London: Longman).

Georgiades, N.J. and Phillimore, N. (1975) The myth of the hero-innovator and alternative strategies for organisational change, in Kiernan, C. and Woodford, F.P. (Eds.) *Behaviour Modification for the Severely Retarded* (Amsterdam: Associated Scientific Press).

Hall, J. (1992) 'Segregation by another name?', *Special Children*, 56, pp.20-23.

Hopkins, D. and Ainscow, M. (1993) 'Making sense of school improvement', *Cambridge Journal of Education*, 23, pp.287-304.

Huberman, A.M. and Miles, M.B. (1984) *Innovation up Close: How School Improvement Works* (New York: Plenum).

Huse, E.F. and Cummings, T.G. (1985) *Organization Development and Change (3rd edition)* (St Paul, Minnesota: West).

Luthans, F. (1989) *Organizational Behavior* (New York: McGraw Hill).

Oakland, J.S. (1989) *Total Quality Management* (Oxford: Butterworth-Heinemann).

Peters, T. (1987) *Thriving on Chaos* (London: Macmillan).

Schmuk, R.A. and Runkel, P.J. (1985) *The Handbook of Organization Development in Schools* (Palo Alto, California: Mayfield).

CHAPTER 14

SHAKESPEARE AND SCHOOLS : Transforming INSET Into Classroom Practice

Rex Gibson

This chapter will describe how an INSET project, 'Shakespeare and Schools', has very directly and positively affected teachers' classroom practice. However, it must necessarily begin with a brief identification of the purpose and nature of INSET. The aim of all INSET must surely be to improve the quality of school pupils' learning. But such a bald generalisation obscures the rich variety of INSET provision. Different elements of INSET have very different time orientations to the achievement of that aim. Some courses set their goal as immediate and direct effect on classroom practice. They have a very legitimate place in any INSET scheme and have for too long endured the inappropriate and pejorative label of 'tips for teachers'. All teachers need, want and are entitled to professional 'tips'. Other courses make no such claim of immediate impact. They have longer-term goals, and are predicated on the assumption that sustained reflection and careful analysis will result in improved practice. These too are self-evidently a necessary part of INSET provision. There is a wealth of evidence that the reflective teacher is an effective teacher, engaged in the long-term project of improving the quality of his or her students' education.

The history of the 'Shakespeare and Schools' project of the University of Cambridge Institute of Education is testimony to how both types of INSET, with short-term and long-term goals, can improve classroom practice. The project shows clearly that INSET is not a 'top-down' activity which imposes on teachers a predetermined programme or set of ideas. Rather, the best INSET is an organic and negotiated process. It arises out of a genuine need or problem, and changes as everyone involved, providers and teachers, jointly address the complexities of principles and practice. This flexible, democratic conception of INSET implies that some outcomes will necessarily be unpredictable. The aim of 'the improvement of quality of practice' accepts that the means of ensuring such improvement are in large part the open subject-matter of any INSET course. To believe otherwise is to assert the 'top-down' view that only INSET providers have 'the answers'. Such a claim is patently nonsense.

The 'Shakespeare and Schools' project illustrates the qualities described in the two paragraphs above. It shows that the project arose from professional needs, and was greatly influenced by the contributions of practising teachers. Further, it confirms the claim that successful INSET has outcomes unforeseen and unplanned at the outset. What follows is an account of the origins, aims, and still-developing procedures and outcomes of the project.

Origins and aims

In the first half of the 1980s, I had been heavily engaged in the Institute's Accountability Project (Elliott, 1981). As that project drew to its close, my mind turned to the next research project I could undertake as part of my Institute responsibilities. I decided to take the advice I had for many years offered to my research students: 'If you are going to spend several years of your life undertaking intensive research, make sure the topic is something in which you have a genuine interest.' Well, I had no doubts about that. Shakespeare had always been my passion (sadly, there is no space here to rehearse the sources, nature and evidence for that burning personal interest). I'd almost completed a book on critical theory (Gibson, 1986) which dealt with the issue of the committed researcher. It attempted to find some accommodation between objectivity and ideology, and was much concerned with the place of 'great literature' in schooling. I'd also recently published a book on structuralism (Gibson, 1984) which arose from the 'structuralism debate' at the University of Cambridge. That often acrimonious exchange of views had sparked off great national interest in the nature of the canon of English literature, particularly the place of Shakespeare (Dollimore and Sinfield, 1985). Both books therefore drew heavily on my interest in literature, literary theory, research methods, and the quality of the school English curriculum.

Shakespeare, then, was at the centre of my personal preoccupations. But personal interest is not enough. INSET and research must be firmly rooted in professional concerns: practical problems in classrooms. Here, INSET work already in place at the Cambridge Institute proved fortunate preparation. Part of my responsibilities at the Institute had always included supervision of the English and drama teachers who came to study for a wide variety of courses. That responsibility brought me into frequent and regular contact with many English and drama advisers and inspectors around the country. It was fertile ground for identifying need. In most of our INSET discussions, the question of Shakespeare and the school canon invariably arose. The question was usually in the form 'what should be the nature of school Shakespeare?' It was time to check that impression more formally. A survey of past and present Institute students, and of inspectors and advisers showed that the teaching of Shakespeare had highest priority for secondary schools. There was near unanimous agreement that Shakespeare should be taught, few doubted its value, but how it should be taught was an area of great professional uncertainty. Any detailed knowledge of successful methods was lacking. School students' experience was typically reported as unsatisfactory, because classroom encounters were dull, uninteresting and demotivating. The all too familiar 'it's boring' echoed through almost every report. There was a pressing need for a sustained and intensive investigation of classroom practice.

Out of this fortunate conjunction of personal interest and professional need, the 'Shakespeare and Schools' project was born. With the help of teachers and advisers (and some theatre professionals and teachers of Shakespeare in higher education), I put together an application for funding to the Leverhulme Trust. It was granted, in full, for a three year period, 1986-89. Since that time, the Cambridge Institute has continued to support the project through its INSET work and my teaching and research responsibilities.

The aim of the project was to improve the quality of pupils' encounters with Shakespeare in all educational settings (schools, tertiary colleges, etc.) for pupils up to 18-19 years of age. Through research linked to an extensive INSET project, good practice was to be identified, recorded and disseminated. The INSET scheme was crucial. The project was fortunate to catch the tail-end of 'pooling', a now defunct iNSET funding scheme which enabled teachers to be seconded for a term's study or research. Each term between seven and sixteen teachers were released from their normal school duties to spend their whole time researching the teaching of Shakespeare in the schools of their own Local Education Authorities. This INSET research scheme was truly national. It brought together teachers from Cornwall to Newcastle, Hereford and Worcester to Havering. These Teacher Associates attended four one-week courses during their term's secondment, at different locations around the country. Each of these Institute-provided courses was carefully structured. The teachers worked in schools, pooled expertise and information, and prepared reports on their own research activities. The tip of that iceberg of teacher-conducted research can be seen in *Secondary School Shakespeare* (Gibson, 1990). For my own part, the Leverhulme funding was especially valuable. The project enabled me to return to school-teaching, to research my own teaching of Shakespeare in junior and secondary school classrooms. That very direct experience was utterly necessary to ensure that I was not a remote University-based researcher, but a schoolteacher familiar with the practical problems of classroom life.

Project outcomes: INSET into practice

The project has resulted in a national network of teachers of Shakespeare, resourced partly through the *Shakespeare and Schools* magazine (Gibson, 1986-94) and UCIE INSET courses. The magazine records many examples of good practice, comprising reports written by teachers, for teachers. The INSET courses have been of many types. They range from whole-term units for MA students, through week-long residential courses at Girton College, to single days on different plays on different age levels, or on Key Stage 3 SATs. The KS3 courses provided a powerful sounding-board for the vehement protest against the wholly inappropriate 1993 SATs. They contributed in some measure towards the rejection of these SATs and their revision in more appropriate form (King, 1993).

It is impossible to overstate the key contribution that the INSET scheme has made to the advancement of knowledge about classroom practice and the identification of successful methods. During the Leverhulme funding period each Teacher Associate had the vital ingredients of time and support to conduct their investigations. Subsequently, the generous support of the Institute enabled the provision of a wide variety of INSET courses at which teachers shared ideas on Shakespeare teaching, evaluated classroom practice, and proposed fruitful extensions to that practice. Not only did the project INSET contribute to the research aim of the project, it also resulted in the establishment of LEA INSET networks which have continued to develop and sustain Shakespeare teaching within LEAs (Cattanach, 1989-93), even in the face of Government attempts to weaken LEA influence.

The research and development work of the 'Shakespeare and Schools' project analysed over two thousand lessons. As described above, teachers on INSET courses undertook that analysis, and identified a number of principles which underpin and resource the active methods which characterise good school Shakespeare practice. 'Good' here means that pupils enjoy the experience, learn from it, and are motivated to further Shakespeare study. The identification of these principles, through research and shared collegial discussion and critique, is striking evidence of the contribution of INSET to professional development. Readers will quickly note that nearly all the principles, which are listed below, characterise good INSET itself.

Learner-centred: active methods acknowledge that the reader actively makes meaning. Students of all ages seek to create meaning from experience. Active methods (which do not treat the learner as passive and spongelike) are not only more enjoyable but promote greater understanding. This principle thus militates against 'top-down' Shakespeare, because it does not attempt to force a single, authoritarian interpretation on students.

Social: active methods are collaborative and participatory. They encourage sharing, negotiation and co-operation. The older tradition of Shakespeare teaching as an individual, isolated experience is unsuitable for most students. Active methods recognise the vital importance of group work and the use of groups of varying size: achieving a suitable balance between individual work, pairs, small groups and whole class activities. The similarity to 'rehearsal methods' of actors is plain.

Physical: active methods are precisely that: physically active to promote imaginative, intellectual and emotional involvement. Quite simply, Shakespeare 'doesn't stop at the Adam's apple.' It involves the whole being of each student and 'suits the action to the word'. In practice that means students sometimes get out of their desks! There is a wealth of evidence to show that such active engagement promotes understanding.

Choice: active methods accord choice and responsibility to students. In all lessons students should have some choice in their work or how to do it. Quite simply, students enjoy having choice and find it a strong motivator. Just as importantly, choice implies differentiation. Students choose activities suitable to their particular needs, interests and abilities. The nature and degree of such choice depends on particular circumstances. Such choice enables all students to enjoy Shakespeare.

Encouraging a wide range of response: dramatic, theatrical, written, discussion, expressive, artistic. This may seem self-evident, but there is an obvious contrast with the traditional demand of written work (often in a particular limited style). Variety of response modes enhances quality.

Involving a wide range of resources: video, film, programmes, photographs, posters, reviews...and some traditional criticism. Again, the principle seems obvious, but the many negative student reports of 'single style' lessons (typically, the teacher explaining every word) was a depressing experience in reports of unsuccessful teaching.

Celebrating imagination and understanding: it is essential to avoid students becoming trapped solely in the discourse of literary criticism. That register or style of discourse is much more suitable to university study of Shakespeare. In sharpest contrast, the aim of school Shakespeare is to enable students *to inhabit the imaginative world of the play.* For most of the INSET teachers, that imaginative enterprise became the most important principle, because it gives priority to expression, spontaneity, and motivation. It recognises that such qualities make important contributions to understanding and insight. It is also utterly 'true' to Shakespeare: a poet-dramatist of supreme imagination.

Exploratory: school Shakespeare should always be somewhat open and unpredictable. That is a necessary consequence of being invited to make personal, imaginative responses to the play. Such exploration implies that for some of the time, the school Shakespeare teacher must be non-judgemental, in order to avoid forcing particular interpretations on students. Every line, speech or scene of a Shakespeare play is an invitation to inference. Those inferences can rarely be tied down to a single, right answer. The contrast with traditional 'right answer' methods is striking, and once again this principle speaks for a prime characteristic of Shakespeare: openness to reinterpretation in every age and culture.

Setting appropriate tasks: task setting is crucial in school Shakespeare. Activities, experiences, assessments, should be appropriate to the needs, aptitudes and abilities of the students in the class. The principle clearly applies to all classroom activity, but the number of 'mismatches' reported were high and were a major cause of student demotivation. Adherence to the principle ensures that a proper balance can be struck between analysis and expression, the cerebral and the creative.

Plurality: forget 'Shakespeare', think of 'Shakespeares'. There isn't *one* interpretation, *one* definitive production, *one* way into a play, *one* method. Instead, there are many. Students should be encouraged to make up their own minds, rather than having to accept a single, dominant interpretation. Shakespeare necessarily demands the acceptance of multiple possibilities and interpretations. Where this principle is not put into practice, it is impossible to achieve the aim of all literature teaching: 'informed personal response'. Plurality denies the arbitrary restrictions imposed by Key Stage 3 SATs (King, 1993), and also ensures that students have open to them the widest possible range of interpretations and approaches, for example both Bradley (1904) and Drakakis (1983).

Enjoyment: above all, remember Shakespeare is to be enjoyed! The 'Shakespeare as medicine' principle (it may be painful but it does you good) is both discredited and discreditable.

These principles, the product of INSET teachers' analysis of successful practice, clearly indicate that there is no 'one way' of teaching Shakespeare. There simply is no single method that works for all. But from all the INSET work and research, a key, necessary ingredient of successful teaching and learning emerged: active methods. Such methods open up the dramatic and imaginative possibilities of Shakespeare's plays. Over and over, the INSET teachers reported that the great majority of students enjoy such methods. The research also established that active methods are within the compass of all teachers, not just those with dramatic training or skills. These approaches, 'research lessons' or 'rehearsal lessons', treat Shakespeare less as a 'text' or 'book' than as a script for dramatic exploration. A script encourages play, it is something to be 'made', not simply 'taken'. It yields to, invites and demands inference and interpretation. Crucially, a script is something that requires readers and performers to bring it to imaginative life through action. The simple formula 'Shakespeare is a script, not simply a book or a text' (now a common element of school Shakespeare), came directly out of the INSET courses provided over the past eight years.

One paradox identified repeatedly in the variety of INSET courses was that of the dialectic between individual and social experience. Shakespeare teaching, like all English teaching, is centrally concerned to evoke 'informed personal response', but not under the same conditions as public examinations making the same claim. Examination Shakespeare is typically solitary and silent. It is individual, literary and cognitive (characteristics absurdly embodied in the ill-fated Key Stage 3 SATs of 1993). In contrast, school Shakespeare (like INSET) as shown in the principles above, is a co-operative and social experience. It is a matter for negotiation in groups of various sizes engaged in self-chosen tasks, concerned as much with process as with any product.

The origin of the unsuccessful school model is clear: in the traditional study of Shakespeare in higher education. There, Shakespeare is treated as a literary text, to be studied word by word, line by line. Each crux is to be clarified rather than exploited and enjoyed. Analysis is privileged over expression rather than being held in appropriate balance. The traditional aim of such courses was to produce literary critics. Even today that narrowly conceived tradition still flourishes in post-18–19 courses. But only one or two students in a hundred go on from school to read Shakespeare in university. And even fewer have any desire to become the pale imitations of literary critics the tradition typically produced. If the 'literary critic' model is inappropriate to the majority of higher education students, it is utterly unsuited to almost all school students in the 1990s. Pseudo-scholarship has no place in school Shakespeare.

That inappropriate tradition was sharply highlighted in the INSET work of the project. This is not the place to rehearse the familiar problems of school Shakespeare (Gibson, 1991). However, one particular factor causing difficulties for students (and teachers) was increasingly identified in research by INSET teachers. That factor was (and is) the nature of the editions of the play used in schools. The 'major' editions (e.g. Arden, Oxford, New Cambridge) enjoy high status in the world of Shakespeare scholarship. That reputation is deserved. They have been written by academics, for academics. They are redolent of scholarship. Commentary, notes and glosses, speak of the world of traditional Shakespeare criticism. But therein lies the rub. Those texts (sic: for that is what scholarship has turned Shakespeare into), have not been written for school students, but for other, quite different audiences. Yet the prestige of such editions is so strong that, in spite of all the very obvious difficulties they pose for students, they are often recommended by some teachers.

In INSET course after INSET course, the problem of 'which edition?' was constantly raised. The 'school editions' which exist are usually little more than watered-down versions of the scholarly editions. They see their task as to explain, to explain again and yet again. The effect on students is numbing. The overwhelming impression students gain is that Shakespeare is a foreign language. It is to be translated, not respected for its inherent power and dramatic and imaginative potential. Opening a Shakespeare play, was, for most students, a daunting and depressing experience. A small section of Shakespeare's language is set in a bewildering, overwhelming context of explanation. The following example from an INSET course illustrates the problem. It is typical of so many others that were identified.

In 'scholarly' editions, explanation is often unintelligible. Opening the Arden *Macbeth*, the student locates (after 65 pages of 'Introduction'), the first scene of the play. What does she find? Four lines of Shakespeare and 52 half lines of explanation. The gloss of the first line ('When shall we three meet again?') reads, enigmatically, '1.) Hanmer's emendation, though generally accepted, is superfluous'. Student response is bafflement, frustration and a sense of failure. Such demotivating information may rivet a tiny number of Shakespeare scholars. It totally subverts the imaginative appeal of the witches' scene for most school students, and confirms their view that Shakespeare is not for them. What, after all, dear reader, does it mean to *you*?

School editions have traditionally taken their cue from the 'scholarly' editions. A school edition of *Macbeth* published as recently as 1988 (claiming to offer 'the clearest possible complete and unabridged text for GCSE students') gives no fewer than eighteen explanations for the twelve lines of Scene 1. The explanations tell students the meaning or significance of 'thunder and lightning', 'witches', 'hurly burly' and 'done'. This is the overkill of overexplanation. Shakespeare's imaginative invitation is reduced to mind-numbing pedantry (Lickindorf, 1988). As one INSET teacher said, 'If you wish to explain hurly burly, you may as well give up. The students may not be able to speak the definition – but they can certainly *show you!*'

The impression conveyed in such editions is that 'Notes' are more important than the script. Students and teachers find themselves bogged down in the inappropriate discourse of literary criticism. They feel excluded, diminished, disvalued. Many INSET courses offered dozens of examples of the unsuitability of such an approach for school students. The courses also identified the paradox that, in spite of all the critical interpretation offered, Shakespeare's script appears to students as fixed, determinate, objective. It is turned into an authoritarian 'text' which rules imaginative responses out of court. Such editions suggest that the students' role is simply to soak up and regurgitate the meanings of others. It is a depressing exercise in suggesting that Shakespeare in schools is about giving 'right answers': those the critics or the examiners prefer.

This close attention to the problem of editions of Shakespeare used in schools was one of the major features of INSET activity. It had previously gone unreported or unremarked in the scant literature on Shakespeare teaching (and had not been a formulated objective of the project). Perhaps this teacher-identified research finding seems obvious and unsurprising. But the real surprise is that it had not been recognised and acted upon long before. INSET had sharply identified the problem – and was to contribute strongly towards its resolution.

I claimed earlier that a criterion of good INSET is that it should have unpredictable outcomes. One outcome, which has been very influential in transforming practice, is the publication of the

Cambridge School Shakespeare series. I have to declare that at the outset of the project, I did not have such a series in mind. I knew we *would* publish materials that could aid teachers to improve practice. But I had no precise idea as to the nature of those publications. It was the daily, regular, repeated reminders by teachers in the classroom and on INSET courses of the unsuitability of classroom editions that sharpened my understanding of the need.

Right from the start of the project I was continually propositioned by publishers to 'sign up' to produce printed materials. Indeed, another unexpected outcome was the regular invitations to lunch 'to discuss possibilities'. I am not claiming prescience in rejecting all those invitations. All I knew was that the time was not ripe. We had to work through the three years of the funded project to accumulate and interpret the evidence, to take detailed soundings of teachers' and students' views and experience, to find methods which were successful in classrooms of all types, with students of all abilities. The INSET activities were central in that endeavour.

It was not until after the end of the funded period of the project, during the period that the 'Shakespeare and Schools' project was incorporated into the Institute's normal INSET and research work, that the decision to launch the *Cambridge School Shakespeare* series was taken. The series grew organically out of the whole INSET and research process. If there was an element of luck, it is only in the sense that luck is where preparation meets opportunity. Throughout the project the staff of Cambridge University Press had taken a strong interest, joining in some of the INSET experiences and developing a dialogue with teachers. The Press is situated next door to the Institute, and a mutual respect and trust, quite unplanned and unenvisioned at the beginning of the project, grew. The Press decided, on the basis of its acquaintance with the INSET and research and development work of the project to launch a brand new School Shakespeare series. It would be based on project principles and would make available successfully classroom-tested activities to all teachers. The first play was published in 1992. By 1994 eighteen plays were available, strikingly different in form from all preceding editions.This radically new series has been strikingly successful. It has been adopted in many schools in Britain and in fifty-five countries overseas (Gibson, 1993). Its wide choice of classroom-tested activities has dramatically improved practice and student motivation.

The opening page of the *Cambridge School Shakespeare Macbeth*, (set opposite Shakespeare's script), illustrates the difference. The project principles listed earlier in this chapter are immediately evident in the form and content of the *Cambridge School Shakespeare* below.

Macbeth

Three Witches vow to meet Macbeth after the battle. Their familiar spirits call to them. As they leave, they chant ominous words, Duncan hopes for a battle-report from a wounded Captain.

---

1 Act it! (in groups of three or more)

The best thing to do with the opening scene is to act it out. It doesn't take long to learn the lines. Present it as dramatically as you can. Prepare sound effects - thunder, rain, battle sounds, cats, toads - and anything else you think you'd hear in such a fearful place. Use your imagination on some of the following to create what you feel is the mood of the opening scene.

How do the Witches enter?

How do they move?

Are they old? young? male? female? (In Shakespeare's time they were played by males.)

Do they like each other? hate each other?

How is each Witch different from the others?

How are they dressed? What are they carrying?

Might they be father, mother and child?

What do they do as they speak?

Electrify your audience!

2 Familiars (in pairs)

Witches were believed to have familiar spirits: demons who helped with their evil work. These familiars were usually animals or birds. The First Witch's familiar is a grey cat ('Greymalkin'). The second Witch has a toad ('Paddock') as her familiar. But the Third Witch does not name her familiar - she says only that she'll come at once ('Anon'). Talk together about what creature the Third Witch's familiar might be. Invent a name and the sound it makes.

Graymalkin/Paddock grey cat/ toad (see 2 above)
Alarum trumpet call to battle
sergeant a soldier who, at the time, could be the equivalent of a captain

fought/'Gainst my captivity rescued me from capture

Because it puts into practice the principles that the INSET and research had so clearly identified, the series has been warmly welcomed by students, teachers and reviewers (Self, 1992). What the success of the new *Cambridge School Shakespeare* series demonstrates is that successful INSET and successful curriculum dissemination and development are integrally and organically linked. The series grew from deep and wide-ranging research into classrooms that identified what students and teachers both wanted and needed. It is in large part due to INSET that a major contribution has been made to the improvement of students' learning.

Afterword

In January 1994 Rex Gibson received the Sam Wanamaker International Shakespeare Globe Award in recognition of 'the most outstanding contribution to the world's knowledge of the works of Shakespeare and his contemporaries'.

References

Bradley, A.C. (1904) *Shakespearean Tragedy* (London: Macmillan) (republished by Penguin, 1991).

Cattanach, R. (1989-93) *Hereford and Worcester Shakespeare* (Worcester: Worcester Teachers' Centre).

Dollimore, J. and Sinfield, A. (1985) *Political Shakespeare* (Manchester: Manchester University Press).

Drakakis, J. (Ed.) (1993) *Shakespearean Tragedy* (Harlow: Longman).

Elliott, J. (1981) *SSRC Cambridge Accountability Project* (Cambridge: Cambridge Institute of Education).

Gibson, R. (1984) *Structuralism and Education* (London: Hodder and Stoughton).

Gibson, R. (1986) *Critical Theory and Education* (London: Hodder and Stoughton).

Gibson, R. (1986-94) *Shakespeare and Schools*, 1-24 (Cambridge: Jaggard and Blount).

Gibson, R. (1990) *Secondary School Shakespeare* (Cambridge: Cambridge Institute of Education).

Gibson, R. (1991) *The Problems of School Shakespeare*, unpublished report.

Gibson, R. (1992+) *Cambridge School Shakespeare* series (Cambridge: Cambridge University Press).

Gibson, R. (1993) 'Szekspir w szkole angielskiej', *Politkya Kultura*, Warsaw, 27.11, p.111.

King, R. (1993) 'Teaching and Examining of Shakespeare in the National Curriculum Key Stage 3', TUSCS Report, *Times Educational Supplement*.

Lickindorf, E. (1988) *Macbeth: Bankside edition* (London: Hodder and Stoughton).

Self, D. (1992) 'The play's the thing', *Times Educational Supplement*, 14 February.

CHAPTER 15

SUPPORTING INTERNATIONAL INNOVATION IN TEACHER EDUCATION

Mel Ainscow

Throughout the world many countries are attempting to improve the quality of education provided for children in their communities. In developing countries the emphasis is on increasing participation levels, whilst in more advanced systems the concern is with raising standards of achievement. Central to all of these developments is the preparation and support of teachers. Consequently there is evidence of increased activity to upgrade the quality of pre- and in-service teacher education internationally (e.g. Levin and Lockheed, 1993).

In this chapter I examine my experience of directing an international project that seeks to support initiatives to improve the quality of teacher education, particularly in developing countries. From my analysis of this particular project I will determine some recommendations as to the types of strategies that need to be adopted if such developments are to be successful.

Clearly the success of any innovation that attempts to work across a range of national contexts requires powerful implementation strategies. Problems created by distance, language and cultural differences, plus difficulties arising as a result of political factors, can magnify the intensity of barriers that occur whenever changes are introduced into educational contexts. By examining a project that seems to have been reasonably successful in overcoming such barriers we can draw some lessons that may well be of value to others involved in international development activities in the field of teacher education. More generally this analysis points to the importance of certain strategies for supporting any educational innovation, however limited the context.

Special Needs in the Classroom

The aim of the UNESCO teacher education project 'Special Needs in the Classroom' is to develop and disseminate a resource pack of ideas and materials that can be used by teacher educators to support teachers in mainstream schools in responding to pupil diversity. In order to develop the pack an international network of teachers, teacher educators and administrators was created. The members of this network read draft materials, made suggestions and, in some cases, put forward materials of their own. Following this period of consultation a pilot version of the pack was trialled in 1990-91 by a team of resource people in eight countries (i.e. Canada, Chile, India, Jordan, Kenya, Malta, Spain and Zimbabwe). The style adopted in these trials bore many of the characteristics of action research as developed by Kurt Lewin, with participants encouraged to work in teams, using 'reflective thought, discussion, decision and action' in order to develop and refine the thinking and practice of the project (Adelman, 1993). Within this broad orientation the resource team collected detailed data about their use of the pilot materials and produced case studies of their work (Ainscow, in press). In addition they kept journals in which they made detailed records of their actions, thoughts and feelings, and their interpretations of the data they collected.

These data indicate that in all the field-testing sites the materials were used as intended and that course leaders worked in ways that were largely consistent with the thinking associated with the project. They also support the view that the content of the materials is appropriate for teachers in each of these national contexts, focussing on issues that they find meaningful and relevant. Furthermore, it seems that the activities and process used are successful in helping teacher educators and, in turn, teachers, to develop their thinking and practice (Ainscow, 1993; and in press).

Through systematic analysis of all these data a series of rationales was developed that could be used to inform the design of the resource pack. Specifically, rationales were developed that could provide specifications for the content of the materials; the approaches to teacher education; and the strategy for dissemination. As a result of these formulations the pack was rewritten to include a manual and associated video programmes. Subsequently it has been introduced to groups in over 30 countries and is now the basis of regional development projects in Africa, Asia, Latin America, the Caribbean and the Middle East and, more specifically, as part of major national initiatives in China, India and Thailand. The pack has been found to be useful in in-service, pre-service and school improvement contexts.

Teacher education

The approaches to teacher education adopted in the UNESCO project are based upon a particular view of how teachers develop their practice. These approaches assume that the development of practice occurs in the main as a 'trial and error' process through which teachers develop their repertoire of responses as a result of what seems to work for them. Their previous experiences as pupils may be very influential here in shaping this development process, plus their observations of other practitioners, including those who lecture them in teacher education contexts. In this way teachers create their own individual theories of teaching that guide their day-to-day practice. These theories are largely unarticulated. They represent the 'tacit knowledge' (Polanyi, 1967) that has been created through a mainly intuitive process of learning from experience.

Often teacher education appears to ignore or even deny the existence of this process of professional development. Rather, the process of becoming a competent teacher is characterised as being about acquiring knowledge about content areas (e.g. maths, science) and foundation subjects (e.g. psychology, sociology), and then transferring this knowledge into ways of working in the classroom. This transfer is seen as being the responsibility of the teacher, with teacher educators seeming to see this as being outside their own area of responsibility.

Michael Huberman (1993) describes this predominant approach to teacher development as 'swimming against the tide'. He argues that it would be more appropriate to recognise the reality of teachers' lives, including the processes through which their practice develops, by adopting approaches that build upon the way they carry out their work in the classroom. In this way teacher education activities can 'swim with the tide'.

Having said that, it would be dangerous to underestimate the problems that occur when attempting to change the thinking and practice of people who work in education. Teachers, and teacher educators, bring to their work strong beliefs about their roles, the nature of their practice, the ways in which children learn, the purposes of schooling and the needs of their students. Generally these beliefs are deeply held and are resistant to changes. Mitchell and Barron (1993) suggest that such beliefs represent a person's construction of social reality, whilst Abelson (1986) argues that if threatened they tend to increase in value. Meanwhile researchers continue to struggle with the problem of how to get people to discard particular beliefs and consider new possibilities for improvements in their practice (e.g. Fullan, 1991). Clearly it is insufficient simply to show that a belief that is held is in some way limiting or unsatisfactory. In order to change, individuals need to be able to identify with others who have alternative beliefs and to feel that they are likely to gain more than they give up (Abelson, 1986). They also need to feel some dissatisfaction with their existing beliefs and perceive the new propositions intelligible, plausible and fruitful. Furthermore in order to bring about change they must be provided with a safe learning environment in which 'they are comfortable in taking the risk of sharing themselves and engaging in public examination of deeply held beliefs and practices' (O'Loughlin, 1992).

Within the UNESCO project we have attempted to work in ways that are consistent with these arguments. Specifically we have tried to develop ways of working that can help teachers to become more confident and skilful in learning from experience. Rather than simply leaving this to chance we believe it is possible to create contexts that enable individuals to recognise the value of this form of learning and to gain greater control of the processes involved. In this respect we have been influenced strongly by Donald Schon (1983, 1987). His emphasis on 'reflection-in-action' as an intuitive means of developing practice seems to be consistent with the argument that teacher development initiatives should swim with the tide. Specifically it recognises the ways in which teachers adapt their plans in the light of changing circumstances and pupil feedback, and, in so doing, experiment with minor alterations in their repertoires of responses.

In emphasising the importance of reflection we are seeking to introduce teacher educators to ways of working that will influence their own practice and, in turn, the practice of the teachers they teach. We are pointing the way towards forms of classroom practice that recognise that the learning experience of each student is unique. In this way we are helping teachers to recognise that a particular lesson is experienced differently by each member of the class in the light of their previous experience, existing knowledge and understanding. This perspective on learning, sometimes referred to as a constructivist view, assumes that people's perceptions, appreciations and beliefs are rooted in worlds of their own making that come to be regarded as reality (Goodman, 1978).

There is a rather obvious weakness in this emphasis on learning from experience through a process of reflection. It may lead to situations where individuals are left alone to make sense of their experience and to draw whatever conclusions they can determine. It is, therefore, potentially a restricted and restricting source of learning. Consequently within the UNESCO project we have placed considerable emphasis on social processes in order to widen the resources available to individuals as they seek to develop their thinking and practice through the process of personal reflection. The aim is to encourage teachers to recognise the value of dialogue with others in order to gain better understanding and to see further possibilities for improvements in practice. In this respect 'others' include colleagues, pupils, parents and, of course, teacher educators. All of these are seen as sources of inspiration and support that can be used to facilitate learning. In addition, they are all seen as offering alternative perspectives that can help individuals to interrogate their experience in ways that may suggest alternative possibilities for development. In the same way information from articles and books provide further resources that can be used to inform and extend the process of learning from experience.

These two ideas, reflection and collaboration, are, therefore, at the heart of the approaches being developed within the UNESCO project. The evidence of our experience of using approaches based upon these ideas in many different countries suggests that they can be influential in encouraging teacher educators and teachers to see improvement as a fundamental area of their work. We have also found that these ways of working can encourage teachers to adopt a more flexible view of difficulties experienced by pupils in their classes, a view that sees such difficulties as sources of feedback on existing classroom arrangements. Indeed, this feedback provides pointers as to how classroom arrangements can be improved in ways that are beneficial to the whole class (Ainscow and Hart, 1992). As a result, schools can be helped to provide teaching that is more effective in responding to the experience and existing knowledge of individual pupils (Ainscow *et al.*, in press).

Supporting innovation

The implementation of these approaches to teacher development is by no means straightforward, particularly in contexts where they are fundamentally different from existing ways of working. In addition our experience has been that teacher educators in some countries are not used to the idea of strategic thinking, nor do they necessarily see the implementation of changes as being part of their responsibility. Consequently greater care has to be taken in establishing a project design that includes arrangements to provide optimal support for those involved over a period of years.

With this in mind, we have found it helpful during the initial stages of such an innovation to work in a small number of contexts in order to establish local models of practice. These can be used later to illustrate what is possible. This strategy is also a means of establishing teams of resource people that have competence and confidence in using the recommended approaches. Subsequently they can be used to lead wider dissemination activities.

The preparation of these teams is a vital factor in the development of an initiative. A model of preparation that we have used in a number of countries seems to be effective (Ainscow, in press; Jangira and Ahuja, 1992). Usually this takes approximately a year to carry out.

Initially participants take part in a two-week introductory workshop/seminar led by a small team of teachers who are experienced in the use of active methods. The first week consists of a workshop that is planned in order to demonstrate a range of approaches that are based upon the overall rationale. Sometimes local school teachers are included as additional participants during these sessions in order that the teacher educators are reminded to bear in mind the day-to-day problems of life in schools. Following this demonstration workshop a short seminar is held to debrief the experience and to explain the rationale that has informed the activities. Video recordings of other similar workshops may also be viewed at this stage.

Participants then work in twos or threes to prepare workshop sessions that they will be asked to lead during the second week.

These practice sessions are followed by feedback from other participants and the leaders of the workshop. Towards the end of the two weeks time is set aside to allow participants to plan strategies for their follow-up implementation activities.

Sometimes this period of initial preparation, involving as it does demonstration, analysis, practice, feedback and forward planning, is spread over a period of weeks. This allows participants to carry out interim practice activities in their own workplaces. This design has been found to be generally more powerful as an introductory strategy (Ainscow, in press; Jangira and Ahuja, 1992).

Follow-up activities are usually characterised as a process of action research. In this way participants are encouraged to work in small, local teams in trying out the approaches, collecting evaluation data and, in doing so, making modifications to fit in with their circumstances. Adaptations, improvisations and new ideas that arise can be used to refine overall thinking and practice within the project. A deadline is set for this follow-up work and the teams are expected to produce a detailed evaluation report within a predetermined protocol (Ainscow, in press). During this period occasional meetings of the various teams are held, when possible, to share ideas, solve problems and maintain the overall impetus. Links are also facilitated between the work of the teams through the publication of occasional newsletters reporting on developments in each context.

Some recommendations

Our experience of setting up initiatives based upon the UNESCO pack in a range of countries indicates that those involved have to be prepared to anticipate and meet difficulties that are likely to occur. This experience confirms the existence of what others have described as 'turbulence' (Huberman, 1992), 'destabilisation' (Hopkins and Ainscow, 1993), or the 'implementation dip' (Fullan, 1991), as being an inevitable feature of attempts to innovate in educational contexts. The nature of this phenomenon varies from place to place, but in general it seems to be as a result of the reactions of individuals within a system to ideas and approaches that disrupt the status quo of their day-to-day lives.

In the light of these likely difficulties it is vital to create a strong infrastructure of teamwork so that individuals can support one another in dealing with the inevitable pressures of leading the

process of change. It is also important that the innovation is con-
ceptualised in ways that allow flexibility for it to accommodate the
circumstances in particular contexts.

From our experience in this particular UNESCO project five
main strategies seem to be powerful in encouraging the implementation of innovations. These are as follows:

(i) *The use of adaptable materials.* The rationale of the project
has led to the preparation of teacher education materials that are
intended to encourage reflection and collaboration.
Consequently the materials are designed in such a way as to
include short pieces of text that will stimulate course participants to draw on their own experience and knowledge. In this
way course sessions focus on agendas related to workplace concerns and address problems faced by teachers in their
classrooms. Of course it is also vital that the content of the
materials is based upon well-developed principles and a cohesive rationale.

(ii) *Preparation of personnel.* An important key to successful
implementation is the careful preparation of those personnel
who will be asked to adopt co-ordinating responsibilities. Within
the UNESCO project small teams of co-ordinators are created in
particular settings (e.g. in a college or a school). They are introduced to the thinking and practice of the project through
demonstrations, explanations of theory, practice and feedback,
following the advice of Joyce *et al.,* (1991). Members of the teams
then collaborate in the process of implementation in their workplace, using the notion of peer coaching within which partners
assist one another to experiment with new approaches.

(iii) *Delegation of decision-making.* In order that local circumstances and needs can be accommodated it is helpful for planning
decisions to be made by those near to 'the action'. Consequently
within the project co-ordinators are asked to take responsibility for
formulating their own action plans. In this way appropriate adaptations are made to the materials and, at the same time, co-ordinators
develop a commitment to the success of *their* initiative. Loyalty
amongst members of the team adds further to this sense of responsibility for what occurs. We have found that using the idea of action
research is a powerful means of encouraging these developments.

(iv) *Opportunities for personal development.* Within the project it is recognised that success is often dependent upon the actions of particular individuals. As a result, individuals are invited and encouraged to see their involvement in project activities as a means of developing their own careers. In addition to the recognition they may receive for taking a lead in a significant innovation, they may be offered other opportunities that provide further incentives. For example, they may be invited to contribute to publications or to travel to other districts as resource people assisting in the development of new initiatives.

(v) *Support at all levels.* Involvement in innovatory projects can, at times, be stressful, particularly during the early days when there is a strong possibility of turbulence. Consequently the implementation strategy must place particular emphasis on the establishment of a support system for key individuals. Of course the creation of teams of co-ordinators is an important factor here but we have found it helpful to encourage people to think strategically about other possible sources of support. It is particularly critical to ensure the goodwill of important individuals and agencies within the community so that, at the very least, their active opposition is prevented. The establishment of networks of communication, both formal and informal, are important means of encouraging a feeling of involvement in project activities.

Some final reflections

At the outset of the UNESCO project that forms the basis of the ideas presented in the chapter, a number of colleagues suggested that the idea of one resource pack that could be used in many countries was impossible. Their judgements were that contextual and cultural factors would make the content of such a pack unusable in many countries. In some senses, of course, these colleagues are correct. If we were to develop a pack requiring the rigid acceptance of specific content it would likely only be relevant in a limited range of contexts. This is why our approach has been to emphasise process rather than content. The content offered in the resource pack is, therefore, used to stimulate the creation of appropriate responses to specific situations rather than to encourage the adoption of ready-made prescriptions imported from elsewhere.

This is arguably the most significant outcome of the research associated with the project. What we have learned is that improvements in teacher education are most likely to occur when groups of people collaborate together to explore their experiences and understandings. This so often seems to inspire creativity and innovation.

To those readers wishing to develop innovatory projects in education, therefore, the important message is that people matter most. Your best strategy is to create networks of colleagues who are then encouraged to collaborate in making the innovation succeed. They may draw on ideas and even materials from elsewhere, but the basis of improvement is their own combined efforts. In my view this message applies to national, district and school-based initiatives.

For my own part I have found that collaborating with colleagues in many countries within the UNESCO project has had a considerable impact upon my thinking and practice. Working in unfamiliar contexts has led me to see new possibilities for my work with teachers and schools in this country. This being the case I believe that the ideas for supporting innovation in teacher education outlined in this chapter, relevant as they seem to be for countries as diverse as Canada and India, have an important contribution to make to the development of the work of the Cambridge Institute of Education and the teachers and schools who work with us.

References

Abelson, R.P. (1986) 'Beliefs are like possessions', *Journal for the Theory of Social Behaviour*, **16**(3), pp.223-250.

Adelman, C. (1993) 'Kurt Lewin and the origins of action research', *Educational Action Research*, **1**(1), pp.7-24.

Ainscow, M. (1993) Teacher education as a strategy for developing inclusive schools, in Slee, R. (Ed.) *Is There a Desk with My Name On It? The Politics of Integration* (London: Falmer Press).

Ainscow, M. (in press) *Special Needs in the Classroom: A Teacher Education Guide*, (London: Jessica Kingsley/UNESCO).

Ainscow, M., Jangira, N.K. and Ahuja, A. (in press) Responding to Special Needs through teacher development, in Zinkin, P. and McConachie, H. (Eds.) *Disabled Children and Developing Countries* (London: MacKeith Press).

Ainscow, M. and Hart, S. (1992) 'Moving practice forward', *Support for Learning*, **7**(3), pp.115-20.

Fullan, M.G. (1991) *The New Meaning of Educational Change* (London: Cassell).

Goodman, N. (1978) *Ways of World Making* (Indianapolis: Hackett).

Hopkins, D. and Ainscow, M. (1993) 'Making sense of school improvement: an interim account of the 'Improving the Quality of Education for All' project', *Cambridge Journal of Education*, **23**(3), pp.287-304.

232

Huberman, M. (1992) Critical Introduction, in Fullan, M.G. *Successful School Improvement* (Milton Keynes: Open University Press).

Huberman, M. (1993) The model of the independent artisan in teachers' professional relations, in Little, J.W. and McLaughlin, M.W. (Eds.) *Teachers' Work: Individuals, Colleagues and Contexts* (New York: Teachers' College Press).

Jangira, N.K. and Ahuja, A. (1992) *Effective Teacher Training: Co-operative Learning Based Approach* (New Delhi: National Publishing House).

Joyce, B., Murphy, C., Showers, B. and Murphy, J. (1991) School renewal as cultural change, in Ainscow, M. (Ed.) *Effective Schools for All* (London: Fulton/Baltimore: Brookes).

Levin, H.M. and Lockheed, M.E. (Eds.) (1993) *Effective Schools in Developing Countries* (London: Falmer Press).

Mitchell, J. and Barron, J. (1993) *An early childhood professional development programme in New Zealand*: paper presented at the Third European Conference on the Quality of Early Childhood Education, Kriopigi, Greece, 1-3 September.

O'Loughlin, M.O. (1992) 'Engaging teachers in emancipatory knowledge construction', *Journal of Teacher Education*, **43**(5), pp.336-46.

Polanyi, M. (1967) *The Tacit Dimension* (New York: Doubleday).

Schon, D.A. (1983) *The Reflective Practitioner* (New York: Basic Books).

Schon, D.A. (1987) *Educating the Reflective Practitioner* (San Francisco: Jossey-Bass).

CHAPTER 16

DEVELOPING TEACHERS DEVELOPING SCHOOLS

Howard Bradley, Colin Conner and Geoff Southworth

In the introductory chapter we identified five interrelated themes which run through the experiences of school and individual development portrayed in this book. They are:

(i)   the relationship between INSET and change and the factors which influence it;
(ii) the appropriateness of the concepts of training and education to professional development and school improvement;
(iii) the quest for quality and the debate about effectiveness or efficiency;
(iv) the development of reflective practitioners and their roles in schools;
(v)   professional development in the context of lifelong learning.

In this chapter we shall examine these themes one by one, ending by bringing together the issues in a series of points for consideration by three different constituencies; schools, providers of INSET and policy makers.

INSET and change

Throughout the various development experiences described in the earlier chapters there is an underlying assumption that the relationship between in-service activities and change, in a teacher or in a school, is problematic. Over the past twenty years there have been more negative research conclusions than positive. For example, we know now that INSET does not necessarily change teachers; that individual teachers, or even groups of teachers, find it hard to change schools and that schools find it hard to change without bringing about change in their teachers. There is in this situation the potential for a 'Bermuda triangle' in which INSET effort repeatedly disappears without trace. If we are to avoid such waste it is important to recognise the contextual factors which maximise the likelihood of INSET effecting change and to manage these factors actively.

Contextual factors

One of the most significant contextual factors emerging in our studies is the extent to which individual and institutional needs are each recognised as important. If, in addition, teachers play an active part in establishing the priorities which emerge from the two types of need, the chance of INSET leading to change is enhanced.

Another major contextual factor is the extent to which the staff as a whole feels it has control over the way in which the school moves forward. Schools confidently setting about their own development are characterised by a belief in individual development and by a sense of common purpose. Schools struggling with the concept of change often present themselves as inundated with directives from outside, moving like flotsam at the whim of each passing current. There are common organisational features of schools which feel they have control. The leadership style is usually delegatory, though active in ensuring things happen; there are many people taking leadership initiatives and people are given the space to work in their own way. They have support, within the school and from the LEA, but the support is facilitating rather than directive.

Sometimes change in schools fails to get off the ground because the proposal runs counter to the staff's beliefs, experience or practice. This is a third contextual factor. It is in these conditions that short INSET fails, because changing attitudes is a longer-term process. For this reason the IQEA project described in chapter 9 makes its fundamental precept that organisational conditions must be addressed alongside the introduction of an innovation.

Our final contextual factor might simply be described as another aspect of staff experience, but it is sufficiently important to consider separately. It is the question of the staff's past experience of change - when they took an initiative was it supported and encouraged, were their efforts welcomed, was it integrated into the school's practice? There is little doubt that one of the best indicators of likely success in bringing about change is the school's previous record of innovation.

Methodology

If contextual factors are well-managed in the school, we are able to concentrate on the second major opportunity for optimising the relationship between INSET and change. This is the choice of the INSET methodology to suit the particular circumstance. Although the examples in this book demonstrate that there are many approaches to INSET and that flexibility, adaptability and choice are vitally important in the design and implementation of in-service activities, there are nevertheless some lessons which are common.

The first lesson is that INSET activities succeed if they are learner-centred, when the learner sees the task as appropriate, finds the activities enjoyable and also finds them underpinned by an element of exploration and problem-solving. Successful INSET activities are also almost always social and collaborative in nature. The second lesson is that INSET activities work well when they are focussed on a school need which the learners know is relevant. Typically the learner has experienced preparation within the school before the activities take place, recognises the commitment of senior staff to it and is confident that follow-up support will be given priority. Almost always, the learner has an expectation that the outcome of the work will be a change in the school's practice. Finally, in many of our examples, the INSET activity is embedded in a widely-embracing strategy for development which includes researching and learning from the teacher's everyday experience, together with shared planning and teaching which challenges perceptions. Staff in the school demonstrate that they value ideas and have a commitment to evaluation as an essential tool for development.

Education and training

In this book contributors have explicitly and implicitly advanced the case for in-service education rather than training. This emphasis reflects a belief that education is more appropriate than training for both professional development and school improvement. So saying, we need to acknowledge that there is a place for training activities. They can be beneficial when improvements in specific skills and competencies are sought, or for awareness-raising when large numbers of teachers need to learn about some new initiative. However, such activities generally deal only with relatively surface matters; when deeper concerns need to be addressed training is usually less appropriate. Training can also create dependency. If teachers begin to feel that they are always in need of retraining to keep abreast of innovations and that they can only learn about these matters from external agents and providers, they may well wait to be told what to do instead of attempting to find their own solutions. Training, therefore, is of limited value and can be severely limiting on teachers' development. Education, by contrast, is a more appropriate concept because it is consistent with adult learning as well as with what we now know about successful school improvement.

The professional development of teachers is a form of adult learning and providers of INSET need to recognise that adults learn in a variety of styles. Short training sessions can rarely cater for this variety of learning styles amongst the participants and are ineffective because they are ill-suited to many members of the audience. In addition, they are often ill-suited to the changes envisaged. Many of the changes teachers are being asked to consider, either by their colleagues in school or by external agents, require them to alter or modify their thinking and understanding as well as their practice. In turn, these modifications may mean that teachers' educational beliefs need to be re-evaluated. Such changes in understanding and belief are deep changes and all our experience demonstrates that these take time to occur and require a supportive environment. Teachers are often anxious in their own teaching to establish a productive learning environment for their pupils. Exactly the same kind of environment needs to be established for teachers' learning.

If teacher development is to lead to school improvement three things need to be recognised. First, we must accept that school improvement is a long journey. There are no quick-fix solutions to developing schools. Training sessions, of course, can play a part in the improvement of schools. Yet the process of improving schools is a long-term one where the staff learn their way forward. Second, the conditions in the school are vital to the degree to which the organisation makes progress. School improvement is a collaborative activity. Staff need to work together and to learn with and from one another. Learning your way forward is a social activity and dependent upon the social dynamic of the staff group. External agents can play a part, as we have seen in some of the chapters here, but the contribution of outsiders is contingent upon the school's organisational culture and the capacity of the staff to deal with ideas and challenges. However, learning and improving do not have to wait for a positive social dynamic, rather the process of learning can simultaneously facilitate the development of a collaborative school culture. Nevertheless, it is also likely that for cultural development to occur staff development activities need to be seen as part and parcel of a larger educative enterprise rather than as a series of one-off training events. Third, only when the culture is conducive to collaborative growth and the organisational arrangements in the school foster professional learning will the school become a learning organisation. Such organisations are highly developed, mature institutions where staff are constantly learning and growing. Simply by being a member of staff in such a school a teacher has a far higher chance of developing than in other schools. One of our goals should be to create schools which are learning organisations, that is, they are communities in which adults and pupils alike are learners.

Efficiency, effectiveness and quality

Recent debate about the in-service education of teachers, reflected in the contributions to this book, makes a distinction between in-service education which is *efficient* and that which is *effective*.

The radical programme of reform that was initiated by the Education Reform Act of 1988 and other legislation which has followed, has required teachers to implement new programmes very rapidly. This has created a demand for INSET to be efficient, when efficiency is measured in terms of handling large numbers at minimum cost. The support offered has often been in the form of short training experiences dealing with large amounts of information, often in large groups and most certainly over a very short timescale. The responsibility for implementing the ideas presented lay with the school and there is evidence to suggest that schools often received very mixed messages from such initiatives (Conner and James, 1991).

There is some evidence to suggest that on occasions short INSET provides an effective experience, as is reflected in the OFSTED review of the management and provision of in-service training funded by GEST (OFSTED, 1993). Nevertheless, OFSTED remarks on the limited impact on the school, even when the training was judged to be good. We conclude that short INSET can be, and often is, efficient, but it is not often effective. In his chapter, Bradley indicates that it is possible to offer efficient INSET when dealing with national initiatives and large numbers of teachers, and to make it effective, provided considerable thought is given to the organisation and structure of the experience and to relating it to the existing context of the school. Where large amounts of information or the widespread introduction of new skills and competencies are concerned, efficiency is an important consideration. The major question, however, is whether efficient INSET is also effective.

When we ask questions about the effectiveness of in-service experiences we go beyond concern for the cost of the enterprise or the efficiency of its delivery and address more fundamental issues related to changes in thinking, values and beliefs of the participating teachers and to the effects of their experiences on the learning opportunities provided for children. We are concerned with issues of quality, a dominant theme in the process of school inspection. As Fielding suggests in chapter 2, 'quality has to be more than the capacity to deliver'.

The writers in this book are strongly committed to INSET that is both efficient and effective, but emphasise that effectiveness takes time to achieve, that it is as much an emotional experience as it is a cognitive one and that it relies on collaboration and support for it to be successful. In-service activities which are dominated by the delivery model place teachers in the role of passive recipients, technicians receiving the delivered wisdom and implementing someone else's reforms, rather than treating them as capable and thinking professionals. Effective in-service education leads to teacher development but also to action in schools, provided that within schools there is an expectation that in-service experiences will be used for the benefit of others.

Reflective practitioners

A dominant theme among the contributors is the need for reflective practitioners. The value of reflective practice has been promoted since the 1930s when Dewey advanced the case for reflective teaching. In essence Dewey was making a distinction between routine action and reflective action. Routine action, being guided by tradition, habit and authority, is relatively static and thus unresponsive to change and development. Reflective action is concerned with engaging in critical review of one's practice. It involves focussing on the puzzles and dilemmas one encounters in classrooms and around the school (see Pollard and Tann, 1993). Moreover, such analysis fosters a reflective approach to one's work and therefore enables individuals to be more responsive to change and development. Reflective teachers are constantly learning and adapting their practice.

Reflection can be conducted in isolation. Teachers can appraise their work on their own. However, since school improvement is a collaborative activity, we need to consider how reflective teachers can make a contribution to the growth of the school as well as to the pupils they teach. As several of the chapters here show, schools need to attend to the opportunities they provide for teachers to interact, collaborate and share their insights about their practice. A key question is how do schools enhance and capitalise on the skills of those colleagues who are, or are becoming, reflective teachers? In the light of our experience there are two main issues to address.

First, staff development policies need to build upon those processes which sustain reflective teachers. Staff development policies should not be wholly centred upon national initiatives or obsessed with dealing with the latest demands from outside the school. These demands are undoubtedly important, but schools need to avoid being overly reactive. Rather, a school's policy for staff development needs to concentrate on developing its staff so that they feel willing and competent to contribute constructively to change and derive satisfaction from doing so. It should ensure there are many opportunities for staff to reflect upon their present practice and to take the lead in moving the school forward.

Second, it follows from much of the above that reflective practice needs to be collaborative. Teachers and headteachers need plenty of opportunity to discuss their teaching and work. However, such discussion also needs to lead to decisions to try out new approaches or ideas in the school or the classroom. Reflection should refine perception and understanding and these, in turn, should lead to a resolution to try a new or different strategy. In other words, from reflection should flow action. Reflective practitioners are thinkers and doers. And from the new action should come further reflection, analysis and evaluation.

Continuing professional development

In his review of in-service education and training, Williams (1991) commented:

> The whole conception of the continuing professional development of teachers, perceived as the preparation of teachers for lifelong education, would appear to be a romantic one. It appears to have a rainbow's end quality – eminently attractive and desirable but unachievable....While acknowledging that there are strong forces operating against any conception of the continuing professional development of teachers, it is important to continue to argue the case and develop the necessary infrastructure to accommodate such a conception.

The contributions included in this book provide illustrations of the infrastructure to which Williams alludes. They identify a wide range of activities which have engaged teachers in learning, for their own benefit as well as for the school. Evidence is offered of the extent to which the teachers who have participated in the activities described have enjoyed and benefited from the engagement with educational ideas. In a period of dramatic change, we have argued that in-service education is more important than ever before and that the opportunity to learn with and from others and to apply that learning for the benefit of the school is a necessity. It is experiences of this kind that allows teachers and schools to face the future with confidence, to turn initiatives to their advantage and to link them with the current conditions and needs of the school.

A major message which emerges, therefore, is that a climate needs to be developed in the school in which learning is of fundamental importance, where the focus is on what staff can learn from the children, what we can learn from each other and what the school can do to develop as a 'learning system' (Schon, 1971). The in-service education of teachers is the key to this learning.

We have already stressed the importance of a staff development policy which motivates the staff and makes them feel valued in their job. To put this into practice schools need a practical staff development plan, which includes the commitment of resources and widespread discussion of priorities. School needs are identified in school development plans and as a result of OFSTED inspections. Individual needs are identified in teacher appraisal. There cannot, however, be separate action plans for these three. They must be brought together into a series of priorities accepted by the whole staff. It goes without saying that prioritising may be hotly argued when resources are short. It is essential to consider during the prioritisation process how the skills gained by individuals or groups will be used for the benefit of the whole school.

If this infrastructure is built up in the school, teachers will have little difficulty in recognising how their own continuing professional development will contribute to the growth of the school. Equally the school and the individual will benefit from the consideration, not of isolated INSET experiences, but of a planned development for each individual.

What have we learned?

(i) Lessons for schools

We highlight three significant lessons for schools. First, there is an overwhelming message in the experiences of INSET we have described that the climate must be encouraging if development is to take place. What is under debate is how to create a climate in which teachers enjoy and value change, seeing it as an expression of their own professional skills.

The second lesson suggested by the examples in this book is that there will always be the need, no matter how sophisticated the school, to work on developing the organisation alongside introducing innovations. There is considerable evidence that it is better to see INSET as embedded within, and integrally part of, the development than it is to see it as a preliminary to the action or indeed as a separate discrete thread in the life of the school.

The third lesson for schools is that they need to set out to develop systematically a cadre of reflective practitioners and to evolve ways of using their skills for the development of the school. At the same time schools need to consider how to maintain and enhance those skills still further.

(ii) Lessons for providers of INSET

There are three lessons for INSET providers. The first lesson that arises from the chapters in this book is that INSET is something that is done with teachers, not done to them. In the many forms it takes in our examples, some points are common. There is a need for planning and negotiation, for the partners to know their roles and to know each other's expectations. In many of the examples the INSET is embedded in a much wider process, centred upon the school and its needs as well as the individuals and their needs. The second lesson is that successful INSET work is collaborative between school and provider. It is interactive between provider and learner and between learner and school. It builds upon the teacher's prior knowledge and experience. It is also very often formative, in that in the process of INSET the goals may be modified.

It goes without saying that INSET must be full of variety and full of activity. It may need saying that it should pay attention to the affective needs of teachers as well as the cognitive aspects of their work. We have stressed that INSET is part of adult learning. The third lesson for providers is that good INSET should be relevant to the needs of adult learners and should use methods which are appropriate to adult learning. Equally its outcomes must be relevant to the needs of the school.

(iii) Lessons for policy makers

The justification for government funding for continuing professional development is that it brings about improvements in teaching and learning in schools. As OFSTED (1993) showed, GEST-funding and pressures following the Education Reform Act led to much of INSET being very short activities. The quality is often high. The survey found that every contribution by HE lecturers was good or very good. However, the report says involvement in staff development of that kind does not lead necessarily to change in practice. It also says that schools' own training days are of variable quality and that INSET is not embedded in a coherent training programme for the teacher and the school. The impact on other colleagues is limited.

The first lesson for policy makers is therefore that to bring about change in practice across a school needs more than short 'how to do it' activities. These do not help teachers to solve their own problems but instead bypass the problem, promoting a solution which may or may not be appropriate to that teacher or school. The next time that there is a problem they have to seek INSET again. Dependency on outside help is increased.

Through the work in the 1970s of Booth (1975) and the Impact and Take-up Project (Schools Council, 1980) we know that impact is greatest when the innovation is close to the teacher's present position and least when it requires substantial changes of practice, attitude or philosophy. Too many projects have suffered either rejection or copying without understanding. This is the danger in GEST.

Successful change needs more substantial INSET. It requires several people in the school who understand the issues involved in bringing about change and are capable of leading their colleagues in it. School-based INSET can be valuable and useful but to be more effective it relies on the existence of something more than can be produced by school-based INSET alone.

The second lesson for policy makers is that current policies are not strengthening professional development. Glickman and Dale's scrutiny of LEATGS (1990) noted that LEATGS was not fulfilling its promise of promoting the professional development of teachers. GEST has not repaired that gap and schools are still relying very much on the experience gained in the period when longer, deeper study was more accessible. That stock is running down.

HE's longer courses provide that expertise and are in forms that relate very closely to national priorities. Paragraph 40 of the OFSTED report says:

> '...much of the written work relates very closely to a specific curriculum or management issue in the writers' school; there is a strong overlap between national priority areas for training and the topics which students elect to study in depth. Reading and intellectual analysis are generally intended to lead to the solution of practical problems and many students talked of the impact on their department or school of the work they had been doing'.

244

Bradley and Howard (1991) and others have shown that when teachers with this expertise are placed in positions of leadership, changes happen. We need more of them, not just in senior management but in middle management, where innovation often gets bogged down, and ideally throughout the school.

This brings us back to the title of our book 'Developing Teachers Developing Schools'. Our examples have shown that INSET activities take many different forms. There are, however, common features which underlie this diversity and give unity to it. The first feature is that school development and teacher development are regarded as shared activities, performed in partnership and with jointly agreed goals. The second feature is the belief that in order to bring about innovation we must work simultaneously on the innovation and on the school's organisation. The final feature is the growing understanding that the most effective way to help schools develop is through helping their teachers to develop. Developing teachers produce developing schools.

References

Booth, M. (1975) 'The impact of science teaching projects in secondary education', *Education in Science*, 63.

Bradley, H.W. and Howard, J. (1991) 'Where are they now? – the impact of long courses on teachers' careers and development', *British Journal of In-service Education*, **18**(3).

Conner, C. and James, M. (1991) *Bedfordshire Assessment Training 1991: an independent evaluation* (Cambridge: Cambridge Institute of Education).

Glickman, B.D. and Dale, H.C. (1990) *A Scrutiny of Education Support Grants and the Local Education Authority Training Grants Scheme* (London: DES).

OFSTED (1993) *The Management and Provision of In-service Training funded by the Grant for Education Support and Training (GEST)* (London: DFE).

Pollard, A. and Tann, S. (1993) *Reflective Teaching in the Primary School* (London: Cassell).

Schon, D.A. (1971) *Beyond the Stable State* (New York: Norton).

Schools Council Impact and Take-up Project (1980) *A Second Interim Report to the Schools Council* (London: Schools Council).

Williams, M. (1991) *In-service Education and Training: policy and practice* (London: Cassell).

INDEX

246